MAKE YOUR WAY

Being Intentional about Your Unique Vocational Design

Spencer J. Bauer

*with **Dr. Jeanie Nishime***

Being Intentional about Your Unique Vocational Design
www.MakeYourWayResources.com

Copyright © 2012 Spencer J. Bauer
All rights reserved.

ISBN: 0615682359
ISBN-13: 9780615682358

Contents

Preface v

Part I: Today's Employment Environment 1
   Chapter 1:   A Biblical View of Work 5
   Chapter 2:   Career Planning Is for Everyone 9

Part II : The Network Advantage 13
   Chapter 3:   The Importance of Networking 15
   Chapter 4:   Networking Techniques 35
   Chapter 5:   Social Media as an Enabler 57
   Chapter 6:   Networking Resources 67

Part III: Career Development Planning 71
   Chapter 7:   Know Your Design 73
   Chapter 8:   Career Development Planning 85

Part IV: Job-Capture Coaching 95
   Chapter 9:   Effective Job Searching 97
   Chapter 10:   Build Your Resume 111
   Chapter 11:   Tailor Your Resume 133
   Chapter 12:   Confident Interviewing 169
   Chapter 13:   Win-Win Negotiating 203
   Chapter 14:   Job-Capture Resources 211

Part V: Goal Getting 217
   Chapter 15:   What Goal Getting Is Not 221
   Chapter 16:   How Our Brains Work 227
   Chapter 17:   Biblical Importance of Self-Image 239

Chapter 18:	A New Language		247
Chapter 19:	Renew Statements		255

Afterword 283
Acknowledgments 291
Appendix A: Sample Career Plan 293
Appendix B: Sample Job Requisition 299
Appendix C: Sample Cover Memo 301
Appendix D: Resume Format Samples 303
Works Cited 311
About the Authors 315
Make Your Way Resources: www.MakeYourWay
    Resources.com 317

Preface

I didn't see it then, but it turned out that getting fired from Apple was the best thing that could have ever happened to me. The heaviness of being successful was replaced by the lightness of being a beginner again, less sure about everything. It freed me to enter one of the most creative periods of my life. [...] Sometimes life hits you in the head with a brick. Don't lose faith. I'm convinced that the only thing that kept me going was that I loved what I did.

—*Steve Jobs, 2005*
commencement address at Stanford University

Getting Hit in the Head with a Brick

During the summer of 2010, I met with our church's executive pastor to get his response to, and hopefully his approval for, the idea of my hosting a weekly men's career small group at the church. I knew of five men who were unemployed or about to be. I suspected other men might be *under*-employed (working in a job that doesn't align with one's strengths) or just stagnated in a job that was not allowing them to develop new skills. In any case, I felt I could help mentor these men, teach them resume-writing and job-searching techniques, and offer words of encouragement. Optimistically, I thought a handful of men just might show up, and even a few would make it worthwhile for me.

This notion of starting a career group actually had been conceived a month earlier while I was attending one of our men's early Monday morning church prayer meetings. That morning we prayed with one of the men who had recently retired from active military service and was transitioning into the private sector. He had a job interview scheduled for later that morning. We also prayed for other men who were unemployed. With my years of business experience, I felt I could really help these men *capture* rewarding employment—if I weren't so busy with my own job.

My job had become very demanding, as the company was positioning itself to be sold (divested from its holding company), which in turn was imposing some very challenging *stretch* revenue goals on the division's leadership. I had been in the aerospace industry for years. Work in this industry inherently includes continuously hiring and *right sizing* throughout the changing program phases, cycling from early development to production to system sustainment activities. Through the staffing process of writing job requisitions, reviewing hundreds and hundreds of resumes, interviewing candidates, negotiating salaries, and working closely with the Human Resource personnel and recruiters from external hiring firms, I had learned what things work best for candidates and what things don't work so well.

I thought to myself, *If only I had a little extra time …* I knew that I could help focus these men's efforts and get their skill sets matched with jobs that would develop them and prepare them for even more opportunities in their futures. Helplessly, I realized that coaching takes time, and extra time was something I had very little of—after taking care of my family, business, and life.

That same morning, I did something unusual. Instead of rushing off to the office for another ten- or twelve-hour day, I decided to slow down and smell the roses so to speak. I took a walk by the beach to collect my thoughts and plan the week's activities. Unintentionally I began reflecting on my career and where it was going with my current employer.

My thoughts were interrupted as I came upon a familiar spot that my wife and I often passed on our walks. She would instantly recognize this spot as one of our *together* places. I wanted to share the moment with her, so I took a photo of the walking trail scene with my smartphone to send to her along with the text message, "Wish you were here." I dismissed my earlier career thoughts for a later time and proceeded back home to get ready for work and start my weekly routine.

After arriving at work later than usual, I was preoccupied with getting to the tasks of the day when my newly appointed boss (as a result of a recent reorganization for right sizing), who had unexpectedly arrived in town on Sunday night, suddenly entered my office. With a great sense of urgency, he said we needed to meet with the human resources manager immediately. He then told me that I was not going to like what he had to say.

At the meeting, I was told that my services were no longer needed and that this had nothing to do with my performance but rather was a financial necessity. The company was being put up for sale, which meant the overhead costs had to be reduced to show a higher forecasted profit ratio against revenue. I was presented with a handsome severance package and asked to sign an agreement letter indicating I accepted the terms of the termination, which included my full cooperation and compliance with a host of competition-related restrictions spelled out within the severance package. What's more, I only had till the close of business to pack up my personal effects. I was also told that access to my computer accounts would be revoked shortly. What a shock! It was like getting hit in the head with a brick!

Before I had time to recoil, the HR manager informed me that others in my staff would also be let go that same day. Ouch! I didn't have a chance to prepare them beforehand, and I felt terrible. And most peculiarly, my new boss presumptuously requested that I accompany him to a 3:00 p.m. meeting. He requested that I endorse the "way ahead" for the organization now that I (and others) had been let go.

I agreed to sign the severance package, but I declined to attend the meeting or to endorse his plan. Endorsing something I had no knowledge of would have been totally disingenuous. The HR department manager agreed with my refusal. All the while I quietly contemplated how I was going to tell my wife. I could say, "Yikes, #@%$^&#!" or maybe, "Honey, I was canned today! By the way, how was your day?"

Stunned, I could only agonize about how ironic this day had become. Just that morning, I wanted to somehow, in some way help the unemployed men I knew; now I was unemployed. Just that morning I was thinking about my career and what the future held with my current employer; now I was no longer employed by that company. As I retraced the events of the morning, my darkness was interrupted by the pleasantness of the walking trail and thoughts of my wife; but the relief lasted only for a moment as I slipped deeply into the dismal reality of the consequences of unemployment. Embarrassed, betrayed, and resentful for having been *thrown under the bus*, I was bombarded with feelings of total failure, along with other emotions.

A New Outreach—*Make Your Way*

Fast forward—back to the meeting with the executive pastor where I had proposed getting together with a few men I felt could benefit from some career coaching. After listening to my ideas and being keenly aware of my new availability, the pastor's face lit up. He responded with a resounding, "Absolutely! We need something like this in the church." Then he went on to say that based on his many one-on-one counseling sessions, this was exactly the training so many in the congregation needed.

His idea was to offer this training to the whole congregation. My initial response was that we should keep career coaching to a small and intimate group so I could avoid overextending myself with additional time commitments. After all, I was busy—very busy: busy establishing my nascent consulting business, busy volunteering with several professional organizations to stay connected within the industry, and busy frantically looking for a full-time position in the aerospace industry during a downturned economy. To avoid an awkward impasse, I cordially recommended that we present this idea for a career program to the senior pastor. My primary objective was to manage expectations along with a sanity check for the executive pastor from the senior pastor in the hope of containing this idea to a small weekly group meeting.

A week later, I met again with the executive pastor, but this time the senior pastor attended as well. To my delight (and later chagrin), the senior pastor also lit up with excitement about my idea and followed with an empathic proclamation that this needed to be an outreach that went beyond our church. He declared that this needed to be our church's outreach to our community at large. My pastors were very much attuned to the far-reaching consequences of the economic recession that had started in 2007. In addition to the high unemployment rate, overall job satisfaction was on the decline for many who were employed. Therefore, my short-lived idea of forming a small men's group expanded into developing a seminar series, which in turn led to the writing and publishing of this book. Alas! Welcome aboard my journey.

My pastors' deeper appreciation of the current need for career development planning provided a sense of urgency for me to make this happen quickly. They also understood the power of having Christian laypeople lead this outreach for several reasons. The first reason is that a layperson who is working day-to-day in the secular workplace can serve as an example or role model for correcting the prevailing, but erroneous, secular viewpoint that work is just a necessary evil that a person needs to endure. Second, a layperson at the management level can provide workers at all levels with a broader industry perspective on achieving success on the job. Finally, although both of the pastors had been successful businessmen prior to entering full-time ministry, their separation from the secular workforce put them at a disadvantage for mentoring people who might presumptuously perceive that clergymen are somehow out of touch with the current pressures of the economic recession and resultant work environment. Thus a lay person outreach was birthed ... to go into all the world.

I began to meet weekly with the pastors to work out the seminar syllabus and to review the course content. As we moved forward, it was suggested that we seek the help of Dr. Jeanie Nishime as a co-developer and co-presenter for the seminars. Jeanie was then the vice president of student and community advancement at a nearby college. Dr. Nishime would bring a wealth of career counseling expertise encompassing high school, college, and continuing adult educational needs. Her role as an executive would also provide an upper level management perspective on successful mentoring, interviewing, hiring, and staffing at all levels within the public educational system. She was also closely in touch with industry's needed job skills as the vice president of community advancement, where she developed training programs for the private sector.

What I haven't told you about Jeanie is that she just happens to be my wife. She and I had already been discussing the need for this undertaking. Thus, having already been inoculated to the idea, she graciously agreed to embrace this new mission as a partner with me. Jeanie and I spent our off-work time researching, interviewing, and passing ideas back and forth. We managed to develop five new just-in-time presentations over the next ten weeks.

This book compiles the material from three of those presentations addressing today's career development needs in the Christian community. This biblically based perspective is presented to better equip the members of the church body to *Make Your Way* through ever-changing and sometimes-turbulent career challenges. The overall objective of the three topics—"The Network Advantage," "Job-Capture Coaching," and "Goal Getting"—is to lay a solid foundation for your individual life-long career planning. Practical tools are provided to help you successfully align your passions with your strengths so you can achieve your God-given potential. Faithfully multiplying your talents through a disciplined career development plan will allow you to "Enter into the joy of your master" and receive the scriptural accolade of "Well done, good and faithful servant" (Matt. 25:21, 23).

My objective when I embarked upon writing this book was to bless and enlighten employees at all levels (after all, we all serve someone) to the *joy* of developing their own vocational success. My hope is that we can quickly get beyond the short-sighted, struthious beliefs that I have repeatedly heard in statements such as, "I don't need to career plan; I have a job." This belief is analogous to the head-in-the-sand, stereotypical beliefs pastors sometimes deal with in statements like, "Pastor, I don't need a Savior. I'm a good person." We will see while reviewing today's dynamic employment environment that our security should not be in just having a job today or being a good employee (or person) but in having a career development plan for tomorrow.

As we proceed through this book, we will discover new concepts and techniques for refining your career plans and goals, concluding with how to successfully accomplish those goals. The last chapters concerning *goal getting* will provide the "stickiness" needed to incorporate the networking and job-capture concepts you will have been introduced to. Incorporating those concepts into your career will have a profound impact on your ability to develop your God-centric self-image in alignment with your unique design and vocational calling.

Background to Steve Jobs' 2005 Commencement Address at Stanford University

In 1985, Apple's board of directors decided that Steve Jobs was too volatile to be Apple's CEO and went with John Scully. Previously both Steve and John had served as co-CEOs. In response, Steve turned in his resignation; that is to say, he was fired. Jobs moved on and eventually founded NeXT. As fate would have it, NeXT was later purchased by Apple, thus allowing Jobs to reconnect with his former company. On September 16, 1997, Steve Jobs was back at Apple as the interim CEO, cleverly dubbed the iCEO. Apple's stock price in September 1997 was under $5 per share (adjusted for dividends and splits). By the year 2000, Jobs was officially Apple's CEO. Under his leadership, the company's stock climbed to over $400 per share before he died in October 2011. In 2010, *The Harvard Business Review* ranked Steve Jobs as the number-one

CEO on their list of "The 50 Best-Performing CEOs in the World." Well done!

Make Your Way

Make Your Way is dedicated to those courageous individuals who seek to achieve the joy of their calling: "You were faithful with a few things, I will put you in charge of many things; enter into the joy of your master" (Matt. 25:21). Just how faithful we are is within our control. We must be intentional about our vocations to be successful. As I encourage you in this book to be intentional, I too am on an intentional journey. My passion is to help equip and enable you to achieve your calling. I am humbled by the responsibility that has been given to me, and I am truly honored to be afforded such an opportunity to be faithful. Thank you for joining with me as we begin to *Make Your Way*.

Part 1

Today's Employment Environment

> Nothing changes but the changes.
> —*Yogi Berra*

At a recent seminar, the question was asked, "On average, how many career changes should a person expect to make in a lifetime?" The answer was, "We can only answer with certainty that it will be a lot more than your parents' generation experienced." The US Bureau of Labor Statistics (USBLS) does not collect specific career-change data from employers or employees, but it does provide an estimate with a caveat that their estimate is derived from other related metrics. Those metrics indicate that, on average, we can expect *at least* seven significant career-type changes per person. However, the USBLS does publish statistical data for the number of employer changes per person (versus career field changes). Astonishingly, between the ages of eighteen and thirty-eight, the average American has ten employer changes! In essence, that averages out to a job change every other year for people during those years. With that many job changes, personal career planning now becomes not merely a consideration but rather an absolutely essential element for successfully navigating today's dynamic employment environment.

Tenure data is collected by the US Department of Labor (USDoL) for wage and salary workers from every employer. Employers are required by law to report data regarding new hires and employees let go. Surprisingly the median tenure—meaning there are as many employees with greater as with lesser seniority within that particular industry sector—peaks at only 5.9 years. This peak is for the more stable manufacturing sector, where workers are often unionized and generally older than workers of the other sectors that were tracked. The remaining sectors, all having shorter tenures, are listed in descending order: transportation and utilities, 5.1 years; information, 4.7 years; wholesale and retail, 3.2 years; professional and business services, 3.1 years; and leisure and hospitality 2.1 years. No wonder we see so many new faces when we are greeted by the staff at our favorite restaurants.

The higher unemployment rates that are being generated by the downturned economy has only exasperated the impact of short tenures as people struggle to maintain their lifestyles and find new jobs. Nonetheless even before the country's employment rate plummeted in late 2007, the dynamic nature of the workforce was having a widespread impact; it was just easier to find a new job and flow with the changes then. Today, however, the gap between when an employee is let go from a job and the time of re-employment is much greater. This is an obvious result of the tightened job market.

Fortunately, despite the downturn in the economy, there is good news. Due to the dynamic nature of the job market, there are always new opportunities for those who are prepared. As you *Make Your Way*, a solid career-development plan will get you focused on your desired career path. It will also help us avoid the pitfalls from *uninspired drift* as we float along in a volatile sea of changes—changes that are often outside our control that result from: unpredictable market forces, changes in the political landscape, global economic pressures on another continent—and the list goes on.

No matter how well-intentioned a private corporation or public institution is about providing job security, there simply is no guarantee for any of us, as is evidenced by the USDoL statistics. Earl Nightingale, author and motivational speaker, admonishes, "The biggest mistake that you can make is to believe that you are working for somebody else. Job Security is gone. The driving force of a career must come from the individual. Remember: Jobs are owned by the company, you own your career!" Even if you happen to be fortunate enough to have an employment contract, you are only *secure* for the length of the contract. These contracts are typically no more than a few years—not the length of a career.

Therefore, now is the time to accept your role as the CEO of *YourName*, Inc. This means you will become the CEO of your career. CEOs do not check agendas or check to see if things are getting done—no, not at all. CEOs make the agendas, figure out what to do next, and determine how to do it. The very good news is that being the CEO of your career is easier today than it has ever been in the past. We will be discussing your support staff (a.k.a., network) and the many available resources available to you as the CEO of *YourName*, Inc. Go ahead! Fill in your own name and add "Inc." Say it out loud a few times (e.g., *Spencer Bauer*, Inc.). Sounds good, doesn't it?

Serendipitously, by being not merely reactionary to your employer and to market forces but rather by intentionally changing jobs (and organizations, institutions, or companies) to accomplish your career goals, you will continually create a realignment of your skills toward a better fit. You will also be prepared for greater responsibilities with each new job. This will allow you real growth in the short-term, which in turn will prepare you for taking positive steps in the future.

Research has found that as employees remain with a company (or public agency) longer, moving up the ladder through seniority and tenure, there is generally a reverse correlation of their skill set matching their current job duties. As the fit gets worse, employees are less satisfied and thus less motivated in their work. We have all seen employees who are hanging onto a job just to get vested for the retirement plan benefits but who are all the while unsatisfied in doing their daily work. On the flip side, those employees who have career development plans and are willing to step out and risk being hired by a new company are selected for their next positions because they are, in fact, a good fit for that new position. Thus being a good fit allows them to be challenged in new ways, develop a broader skill set, meet new people, and find even more new opportunities. And they can do all this while they are enjoying a sense of job satisfaction and ownership of their career progression.

However, to effectively advance your career requires a well thought out career development plan. Otherwise, job changes are nothing more than reactionary or the insipid drifting of a ship without a rudder. Your career challenge is to: intentionally take ownership of your journey; know you strengths and weaknesses; follow your passions; and be your own self-appointed career CEO!

CHAPTER 1

A Biblical View of Work

As a result of inadequate knowledge about career planning and the harsh reality of today's higher unemployment rate, an increasingly cynical perspective of work is now permeating our culture. I could not help but notice several of the book titles that jumped out at me as I browsed the aisles of a popular franchise bookstore—titles such as: *I Hate My Boss, The Best-Ever Anxiety Management Techniques, How to Survive the Office When You Hate Everyone You Work With, How to Lead Your Boss,* and last but not least, *Nice Girls Don't End Up in the Corner Office.* Keep in mind that these titles were in the business management self-help section. I had to wonder, "Why is there even a demand for all these cynically titled books that are lining the shelves? And moreover, just how prevalent is this negative viewpoint of work? Are we only working so we can retire someday?"

Starting with the book of Genesis, Scripture gives us a very different and encouraging view of work. We could say it begins with a description of God's own work—that of creating: "In the beginning God created the heavens and the earth" (Gen.1:1). Furthermore, in verse 31 we read, "God saw all that He had made, and behold, it was very good." And after His creation, we read in Genesis 2:2, "And He rested on the seventh day from all His work." Not only did God work, but regarding mankind we also read, "You make him to rule over the works of your hands. You have put all things under his feet" (Ps. 8:4–8).

We have to conclude that our Creator works, and being made in His image, we have been created to work as well. After God created, we read in Genesis 2:15, "Then the Lord God took the man and put him into the Garden of Eden to cultivate it and keep it." We must remember that man (Adam) worked in the garden before the fall. Of course, we know that after the fall (Gen. 3), man's labor became more difficult. But we were created to work from the beginning!

The New Testament further states, "Do your work heartily, as for the Lord rather than for men" (Col. 3:23). Interestingly, the *Oxford English Dictionary* defines the word vocation as: "a strong feeling of suitability for a particular career or occupation; a calling." Jesus teaches us about the rewards of work in the parable of the talents. He tells about a servant who was given a certain amount of money to work with, and this man doubled his talents. He was met with the following greeting from his boss: "His master said to him, 'Well done, good and faithful servant. You were faithful with a few things, I will put you in charge of many things; enter into the joy of your master'" (Matt. 25:21).

Contrast this parable of the good and faithful servant entering into the joy of reward with an incident that made national news in 2010. It involved a JetBlue flight attendant who blew up at Kennedy International Airport in New York. This flight attendant was so upset with his work that he cussed out the passengers, took two beers from the galley, and exited the aircraft through an emergency exit. He was later arrested. The attendant's lack of self-control actually brought him fame and a short-lived nationwide Twitter following. However, even more disappointing than this crew member's inappropriate conduct was the public's acceptance of such immature behavior.

One witness to the event, Mr. Phil Catelinet, is quoted in the account published by the *NY Daily News* (3 September, 2010), "I wish we could all quit our jobs like that." Who exactly is the "we" Phil was referring to? Can we infer that his quote would also include condoning such actions by other employees (e.g., the pilots) of JetBlue? Of course not! I suspect Mr. Catelinet's comment was a sympathetic impulsive reaction from the frustration many of us may have experienced with our jobs from time to time. Over the years, this reaction has become established in our popular culture by the cliché, "You can take this job and shove it."

The eager willingness to justify someone's rebellion against his life's vocation, employer, and customers is truly troubling. The story of the JetBlue flight attendant is just one crazy example of something that went very wrong. However, polls taken shortly after this event showed just how pervasive this anti-job sentiment is in our culture.

> Poll says 52 percent of flying Americans had followed the case "very closely" or "moderately closely" with 25% believing Slater's actions were justified and 32% believing they were unjustified.
>
> —<u>Angus Reid Global Monitor</u>, *August 25, 2010*

As time goes by, the intensity of such an emotional reaction to an event like this subsides as the cognitive, or thinking, part of the brain finally takes over. How distressing it was for this flight attendant to respond in that manner and have all his years of work and effort culminate in such unprofessional, dysfunctional, and unsafe behavior. And this distressing behavior did not just affect him. Consider how unpleasant his actions were for the passengers who were subjected to his dishonorable behavior. Those passengers were his customers—the very people paying a portion of his salary; those passengers were us!

Moving beyond the media's sensationalizing of that extremely disconcerting incident, let's begin to reflect on how rewarding and wonderful our work can truly be. Consider this passage for a moment: "For we are His workmanship, created in Christ Jesus for good works, which God prepared beforehand so that we would walk in them" (Eph. 2:10). So then, as His workmanship, let's find out more about how to walk in those good works that were prepared for us beforehand.

CHAPTER 2

Career Planning Is for Everyone

> Failure to plan is planning to fail.
> —*Author unknown*

The Bureau of Labor Statistics (BLS) publishes a report three times a year. The report is entitled, "Current Employment Statistics and Job Openings and Labor Turnover Survey." As depicted on the BLS graph located on the next page, the nation's total employment (dashed line) had decreased from roughly 138 million jobs in December 2007 to 129 million jobs by April 2010 (right vertical axis x 1,000). However, what is noteworthy from this graph is the sheer number of hires (solid line) and separations (dotted line) reported (left vertical axis x 1,000) for each period (bottom horizontal axis with four-month periods), regardless of whether the total employment was up or down.

Before the start of the recession in December 2007, new hires outpaced separations. This resulted in greater overall net employment for those periods. A typical period pre-2007 may have had 5.3 million new hires and 5.2 million separations, resulting in a net increase in total employment. Conversely, in August 2009, there were roughly 4.1 million new hires, with a corresponding 4.2 million separations, resulting in a net decrease in total employment for that period.

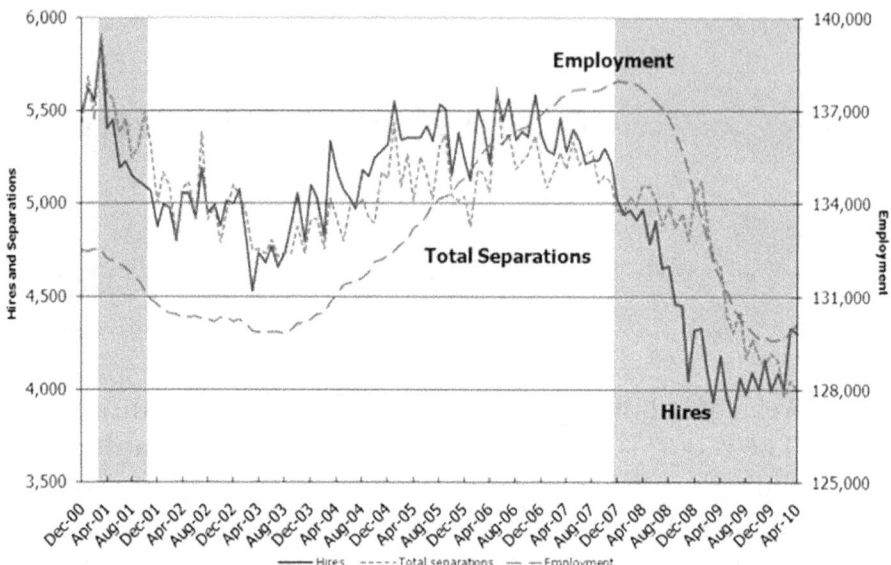

Bureau of Labor Statistics (BLS)
Hires, total separations, and employment seasonally adjusted, in thousands

We can see from this graph that the overall labor market has been a very volatile environment regardless of whether total employment is increasing or decreasing. And it continues to be volatile today. As an analogy, visualize a very large jar of jellybeans having a wide open top, with millions of beans constantly going in and millions of beans going out. The content of the jar is always in a state of flux. It is a similar situation with jobs in the labor market.

For the prepared job seeker (the person actively developing his or her career and seeking new opportunities), this continual flux in the labor market serves as the engine for generating new jobs and career opportunities. On the other hand, this job flux also eliminates existing positions. Therefore, it behooves us all to proactively plan and manage our careers in light of the dynamic nature of the labor market.

Yes, we hear national news media reporting that one hundred thousand jobs were lost in a particular period, but keep in mind that is only the net, just as in the above example with 4.2 million jobs created and 4.3 million jobs lost during that reporting period. Consider for a moment that you only need to land one of the 4.2 million new jobs—the one job that will be a good fit for your current skill set and that will provide advancement opportunities in step with your career path. In essence, the labor market dynamics can be beneficial if one is prepared to take advantage of the changes. In reality, a changing employment environment should be preferred (even embraced) over a stagnant, flat job market, since the changes constantly produce new opportunities for your career growth as you *Make Your Way* along your career path. But you must prepare yourself to take advantage of these many opportunities.

Interestingly, the number of employees hired or separated for a given period is roughly 3 to 4 percent of the total employment for that period (9 to 12 percent annually), regardless of whether the total employment had a net gain or a net loss for that given period. Given the fact that change is here to stay, let's embrace it!

To summarize, millions of jobs are constantly being created while millions of jobs are continually disappearing; the net result being reported as a gain or loss is a relatively small percentage of the overall employment activity. You as the job seeker are only concerned about the one "good fit" job in the huge mix of opportunities. Let the labor department chew on the statistics and trends; all you have to do is explore the many opportunities that are available to you now and in the future as you *Make Your Way*.

Understanding that a dynamic labor market is constantly producing new hiring opportunities provides real hope in a time when we are bombarded with negative economic news about the high rate of unemployment. The following chapters will present the tools and resources you need to tap into the upside of new jobs that are being created every period—that is, your opportunities. Although our initial impetus for presenting seminars on career development and networking was to help those who were out of work due to a recession, the application of career development planning is lifelong and beneficial for any stage of your career.

With the thousands and thousands of new hires and separations reported each period, it becomes clear that career development planning is for everyone. The labor market is not a stable market and hasn't been for some time. By taking ownership of your career, you can direct your journey toward your destination. By tapping into the thousands of new opportunities reported every period, you will be able to capture the next better-fitting position that aligns with your career planning.

However, if you are simply reacting and re-reacting to external forces within the job market and do not proactively manage your career development, you will miss many opportunities. These missed opportunities will not be available to you later if you happen to be let go by your employer. The negative consequences of missed opportunities for the displaced and unprepared employee are compounded by inevitably settling for poorer-fitting jobs due to financial pressures to get back to work. It is all too easy to fall back into the cycle of not being all you can be—and thus not being satisfied with your work.

On the other hand, by being intentional and proactively managing your career path (your calling), you will be prepared for and blessed with new opportunities—new opportunities that will be a good fit. Therefore, whether you are a graduating student just preparing to enter the workforce, a seasoned employee, or an under-employed, unemployed, self-employed, or semi-retired person, career planning is for you.

As we continue through the next sections on "The Network Advantage," "Career Planning," and "Job-Capture Coaching," be mindful of the fact that I too am *Making My Way* toward my career goals as I write this book. I encourage you in this pursuit of excellence. I understand your struggles. I have felt some of the pains and disappointments you may have experienced or will be experiencing, but I also know of the great joy that will come from your effort. It is a journey and an adventure that you will be happy to have taken control of. You are definitely not on your own; I'll provide many resources that will help you *Make Your Way* along the various steps of your unique and exciting career adventure.

Part II

The Network Advantage

An indispensable message repeatedly preached on Sunday mornings in churches everywhere is the fact that we all have a crucial need for a Savior. Essentially, it is not what you know but who you know. *Who you know* refers to the reality of a personal relationship with God the Father through His Son Jesus Christ. We know the fullness of salvation as we build a real and meaningful relationship with God. Networking is nothing more than building relationships; that is to say, it is all about who you know.

The word networking is defined by www.dictionary.com as: "a supportive system of sharing information and services among individuals and groups having a common interest." We gain access to others through our network of contacts. Neuroscientists discovered that the very design of our brains makes us social creatures with a wonderful ability to link brain to brain for the purpose of developing intimacy in our relationships (Goleman, Daniel, 2006 *Social Intelligence*). Therefore, by our very design, networking and building relationships are natural processes that are absolutely essential for our well-being.

In this section, you will learn techniques to boost your networking skills. These skills will help you to build long-term relationships and be prepared to be intentional about helping others. Whether you consider yourself an extroverted socialite or an introverted wallflower, you already have a network. Learning how to grow and leverage your network to help others will be the key to your career success. Having a core understanding of networking principles will help our more-introverted friends be at ease when mingling face to face in social situations. At the same time, this understanding will help our extroverted socialites to become better listeners. Let us move on and explore the paradox of "helps" for effective networking.

CHAPTER 3

Importance of Networking

The California Employment Development Department (EDD) gathers statistics that continually reinforce the fact that over 75 percent of new hires credit their success in getting their jobs to proper networking. However, this 75 percent success rate is not from spamming Internet job sites with hundreds of electronic resumes but by effectively networking through established relationships to obtain critical information and vital referrals. Today's job market is not only dynamic, as validated by the Labor Department metrics discussed previously, but the job descriptions and requirements also continue to be more complicated than in past decades. The complexity and diversity of today's job requirements exasperates recruiters' task of matching hiring managers' needs with the available skill sets found in the labor market. Networking provides the means to make those needed connections in this increasingly complex and diversified employment environment.

My children have had a difficult time in the past explaining to their friends exactly what Dad does for a living. Gone are the days of having only highly descriptive occupation titles such as brick layer, doctor, butcher, or baker. For my children's sake, I had to craft a pithy, easy-to-understand statement for them so they could grasp my vocation well enough to explain it to their young peers.

Likewise, for the sake of your adult peers, a well thought out, informative, interesting, and concise statement describing what you do needs to be carefully crafted and ready on the tip of your tongue. This what-you-do statement is often referred to as an elevator speech, as if you only have a few minutes to get your message to the captive audience during a brief elevator ride between floors. We will discuss more about the content and importance of an effective elevator speech for networking in later sections. Suffice it to say, effectively communicating what you do for a living is more challenging today than it was in past generations. This reality makes effective networking all the more important.

To meet the hiring needs of some of the more specialized industry sectors, a growing number of professional organizations—and nonprofit organizations—are sponsoring job fairs for the sole purpose of connecting workers with employers who need specific skill sets. Industry supports and invests in these activities because of the difficulty in finding the specialized skills that are needed today. Interestingly, industry has been proactively investing in the inoculation of students—even elementary-age children—to meet their future needs. A few examples of the many industry-sponsored programs are: Math Moves You, MIND Institute programs, Math Blaster, etc.

Of particular concern for the high-tech industries are the current and anticipated shortfalls in the workforce for the Science, Technology, Engineering, and Mathematics (STEM) skills, due in part to the fact that baby boomers are retiring. Industry is making investments now to encourage students to pursue the difficult-to-fill jobs of the future. Suffice it to say, some industries are experiencing difficulty finding workers with the required skill sets today. The more technological breakthroughs we enjoy, the tighter the job requirements become for many of the resulting jobs. The sheer volatility of the job market and the increasing complexity of job requirements mandate the need for connections through networking to help you *Make Your Way*.

Connections form the support system for our common interests. However, before you can leverage your network to connect with job opportunities and those key decision makers, you must first build it. Therefore, in preparation for understanding effective job capture, let's learn more about the fundamentals of networking.

Go into All the World

Several reliable sources estimate the number of Christians worldwide today to be over two billion. How did the gospel message get to two billion people? Contemplating just how to go about getting a message "to all the world" presents us with a formidable undertaking, even with today's mass media communications and global satellite coverage. Nevertheless, it is an undertaking that is at least cognitively feasible by leveraging today's communication technologies.

Consider, however, two thousand years ago. How did the Christian message initially get circulated around the world? Recall that after His resurrection, Jesus commanded the remaining eleven disciples, "Go into all the world and preach the gospel to all creation" (Mark 16:15). But there were only eleven disciples at this point, and they were using only word of mouth—without the help of Facebook, tweets, blogs, Internet, TV, radio, or even the telegraph! How did just eleven men get the word out?

Well, we know that the disciples met with the Pharisee Saul, who later became the apostle Paul, in Damascus (Acts 9:19). The apostle Paul's epistles mention the following people by name: Timothy, Euodia, Syntyche, Clement, Epaphroditus, Epaphras, Silvanus, Eunice, Lois, Onesiphonus, Luke, Mark, Tychicus, Carpus, Prisca, Aquila, Erastus, Trophimus, Eubulus, Pudens, Linus, Claudia, Artemas, Tychicus, Zenas, Apolios, Philemon, Archippus, Onesimus, Epaphras, Aristarchus, Demas, and Peter. I would be the first to admit having difficulty correctly pronouncing some of these names, but from this list, I am convinced Paul had a fairly extensive and active network. The eleven disciples connected with Paul, who connected with a host of others, and so it goes. Networking is nothing new; it is proven, and it is effective.

Paul built his network in the same way we would build our network today—around relationships and giving to others. "Each of us is to please his neighbor for his good, to his edification" (Rom. 15:2). Jesus tells us in John 15:17, "This I command you, that you love one another." Furthermore in the gospel of Mark, Jesus said,

"Go into all the world and preach the gospel to all creation … These signs will accompany those who believe … lay hands on the sick and they will recover" (Mark 16:15–18). The disciples were instructed to preach. They were also told that signs would accompany those who believe. Consider for a moment the bond that was built between those who were believers in the gospel and those who were sick and then recovered. Building relationships by helping others is powerful networking! It is so powerful as to "go into all the world."

Intrinsic to networking is a tacit acknowledgment that we are somehow—to one degree or another—dependent on each other. As Americans, we often encounter a contradictory cultural message of self-sufficiency. The epitome is that of America's bigger-than-life movie superstars like John Wayne and other self-made typecast actors. Acceptance of this paradigm is ingrained into us, as if it were the very fiber of our modern American culture. With all due respect to John Wayne's legacy as an accomplished actor, Hollywood isn't the real world; and well, after all, Mr. Wayne was simply acting.

Ironically, our founding fathers quickly acknowledged their dependency and very survival solely on God's providence, not their self-sufficiency or their own strength. Colonial Governor William Bradford's 1623 *Thanksgiving Proclamation* stated:

Inasmuch as the great Father has given us this year an abundant harvest of Indian corn, wheat, peas, beans, squashes, and garden vegetables, and has made the forests to abound with game and the sea with fish and clams, and inasmuch as He has protected us from the ravages of the savages, has spared us from pestilence and disease, has granted us freedom to worship God according to the dictates of our own conscience. Now I, your magistrate, do proclaim that all ye Pilgrims, with your wives and ye little ones, do gather at ye meeting house, on ye hill, between the hours of 9 and 12 in the day time, on Thursday, November 29th, of the year of our Lord one thousand six hundred and twenty-three and the third year since ye Pilgrims landed on ye Pilgrim Rock, there to listen to ye pastor and render thanksgiving to ye Almighty God for all His blessings.

In 1776, 153 years later, Thomas Jefferson, (the third US president and drafter and signer of the Declaration of Independence) penned, "God who gave us life gave us liberty. And can the liberties of a nation be thought secure when we have removed their only firm basis, a conviction in the minds of the people that these liberties are of the Gift of God?" And in 1790, Benjamin Franklin (signer of the Declaration of Independence and United States Constitution) wrote, "Here is my Creed. I believe in one God, the Creator of the Universe. That He governs it by His Providence. That He ought to be worshipped. That the most acceptable service we render to Him is in doing good to His other children. That the soul of man is immortal, and will be treated with justice in another life respecting its conduct in this." From these writings, we can see our nation was established with a very different mindset than that of the self-made hero that Hollywood portrays today.

Members of One Body

When we consider giving, Hebrews 13:16 reminds us, "And do not neglect doing good and sharing, for with such sacrifices God is pleased." Interestingly, the writer of Hebrews acknowledges that doing good requires sacrifices. I believe today, the more onerous sacrifice for many of us may be the sacrifice of our time. Many of us have so little unaccounted-for time (or margin) in our daily schedules that just to fit a *doing good* thing into our day requires giving up some other activity. It becomes a tradeoff; we give up or trade away one activity so we can have the time or resources to help someone else through some other activity. Likewise, building an effective network takes time, not only for a trusted relationship to mature but also for giving of yourself and your time to those relationships. The apostle Paul instructs us, "Do nothing from selfishness or empty conceit, but with humility of mind regard one another as more important than yourselves; do not merely look out for your own personal interests, but also for the interest of others" (Phil. 2:3–4).

Interestingly, I recently came across several studies showing that volunteering (helping others) has a health benefit. One such study by Professor Morris Okun, professor of psychology at Arizona State University, looked at older adults with functional limitation and found, "As functional limitation increases, the risk of dying increases, but not among those who volunteered." Professor Okun went on to say, "By helping other people, you are actually helping yourself" (*Science Daily* Nov 3, 2010). One can only imagine the inferences of this finding toward having a network of relationships grounded on helping others.

Misconceptions Concerning Networking

Furthermore, by using a biblical basis as our reference for networking, we can avoid many of the misconceptions associated with the term *networking*. Let's briefly look at some of those networking misconceptions.

The first misconception is that networking consists of collecting business cards and shaking as many hands as possible at every event. This misconception became evident to me when it was played out early in my career. The office manager asked several of us to photocopy all the business cards we had collected at a business conference. His intent was to forward the photocopy sheets of business cards to his boss, thus justifying the event's overhead business expense with the "networking" benefit from attending the conference. The superficial logic follows that the more business cards one collects, the more people one has met, which implies some measure of one's networking effectiveness.

However, networking for the purpose of building longer-term relationships isn't about the sheer number of people we meet. Rather, it is what we learn about the people we meet so we can understand their needs and develop relationships with them. This requires us to spend more time with an individual than a simple *meet and greet* handshake and exchange of business cards. By the

Importance of Networking

way, whenever you meet a new contact, jot down notes on the back of his or her business card after your conversation. The notes will help refresh your memory when you later follow up with that contact.

As an aside referring back to the office manager photocopying business cards, notes on the back side of the business cards would have revealed more about the effectiveness of networking than the sheer number of cards. Moreover, an even better measure of networking effectiveness would have been the actions taken to follow up with the contacts. We will discuss more about follow up and its importance for building relationships in later chapters.

Another networking misconception was provided to me by a well-intended recommendation from a church council member. His recommendation at a council meeting was to develop a network listing of the church members, their occupations, and contact information to be used by the congregation for making referrals. In these examples, neither the referral list nor the collection of business cards is of much value without your personal understanding (and trust) of how these contacts can help others in your network.

I once received a referral from a well-intentioned acquaintance that I naively accepted—a referral that didn't work out so well. I needed the interior of my house painted. Due to the inexperience of the referred painter, a latex-based paint was applied over the existing oil-based paint. Needless to say, the latex didn't adhere very well to the oil paint, and it eventually required many hours of labor to remove the latex and start over with primers. It turned out that this painter was a good friend of the referring person but not a professional painter. He was moonlighting for some extra income. Never, never risk losing your credibility by making an uninformed referral.

The lesson learned is that we have to know how our contacts can provide a valuable service to others before we can provide a blanket referral—even if the contact is on the church's published referral list. By the way, this rookie painter was a great office manager and could offer exceptional organizations skills to any number of employers; he just didn't know enough about painting to be moonlighting solo.

Finally, by far the most obnoxious networking misconception is that we network to get something from others. Or in other words, "What's in it for me?" The overly eager real estate agent epitomizes this negative stereotype by always opening conversations with, "Hello, are you in the market for buying or selling your home?" "Buying or selling?" "Nice meeting you—buying or selling?" People are not attracted to self-serving charlatans who may not have their best interest at heart. But people are drawn to developing relationships with those who are truly interested in them and not in their real estate or other assets. Effective networking is building long-term relationships by helping others through a support system with a common interest or interests.

Networking definitely is not limited to just matching jobs requirements with skill sets. Since we are by nature social beings, the same networking principles and techniques we will be learning for career success are perfectly applicable and necessary for all the other areas of life that naturally incorporate networking. However, in this section we will be focusing primarily on the networking advantages and examples relative to your vocational pursuits—both the tactical (immediate) job capture and lifelong career development planning.

Networking = Information (Past, Present, and Future)

Networking gives us access to lots of information. But more importantly, it is information that is relevant to our situation based on someone else's personal experiences, complete with real life-tested results and consequences. I highly recommend a book by Daniel Gilbert titled *Stumbling on Happiness*. For me, a key takeaway from this book was the importance networking can play to overcome our limitations. (By the way, Daniel Gilbert's book is not about networking per se.) What the author explains so well is that our ability to forecast what will actually make us happy in the long term is not very accurate without incorporating the perspective of others. We need the help of others to get an accurate picture of how things will be when we finally arrive at where they have already been. We inherently produce a skewed starting point for forecasting our happiness if it is based solely on our remembrances of the past and our perception of the present.

We in fact remember and store past events that more closely resemble an emotional executive summary of those events than a fact-by-fact playback video recording. Consequently, we don't remember movies, books, our childhood, past holidays, etc., verbatim. We merely remember key points and leave information gaps between those points. This is a good thing since not every point is significant or worth our attention when we mentally review a story line. But not only do we not remember movies line-by-line—we actually add our own lines to fill in the blanks when we recall it later. Therefore, if we are asked about something occurring in the gaps, we creatively make sense of our recollection with a logical fill in for those gaps.

Research studies (Buckhout, Figueroa, Hoff) have shown that deliberate suggestions of what might have happened in a story can actually cause our brains to fill in the missing gaps by re-creating the story based on those suggestions. Misremembering could be used as the descriptive term for this process. Naturally, our very creative brains never actually inform us of this filling in of the blanks with an alert cautioning us, "Warning: Oh by the way, I'm making this part up because I didn't record every detail." Therefore, being totally unaware of our misremembering, we are confident we are remembering accurately even if we are not. That is why being a juror is a difficult duty; the jury has to listen to different accounts of the same incident with witnesses who at best have imperfect recollections of what happened. Or just possibly, a witness might have an implicit bias motivating his or her misremembering toward a particular outcome—all the while maintaining a very convincing demeanor to the jurors.

Not only are our past recollections less than accurate, but we also tend to overemphasize the present circumstances when we are considering what the future will be like. In his book, Gilbert presents a wonderful discourse as to the reasons why we rely on our present circumstances too much to accurately predict the future. I reflected on his findings as I tried to make sense of one set of events that took place after the 2008 national elections.

If you remember, the honorable Pennsylvania senator, Arlen Specter, made the audacious and contentious party switch from Republican to Democrat. He justified this to his constituents, who had reelected him to the Senate as a Republican in 2004, as the only way he could get reelected in the upcoming 2010 election, with the Democratic party now controlling the political climate of the day with the momentum of President Obama's, "Yes we can" campaign. Had he waited a few months longer and remained loyal to his party (and constituents), he may have noticed the political winds were already beginning to shift. Unfortunately for Senator Specter, the Democratic voters were not overly impressed with his newfound allegiance to their party, and he was soundly defeated in the Pennsylvania Democratic Primary in early 2010 to a lesser-known challenger.

Ironically in the 2010 mid-term elections, the Democrats, using President Obama's own words, "Took a shellacking," primarily because of the country's dissatisfaction with the economy. The dissatisfaction was directed at the incumbent Democratic-controlled Congress, with Congress's overall *likely voter approval* rating sinking to the lowest in decades. This is a classic example of Senator Specter relying too heavily on the present circumstances in 2008 to predict the future for 2010. This political *faux pas* was a result of a senior lawmaker being blinded by the then-present situation and not being attuned to the imminent shift by the voters toward the Republican Party for the next election. In less than two years, the Tea Party contingent of the Republican Party emerged, rapidly gaining significant national support. The result was that the Republicans picked up several Senate seats and took control of the House of Representatives from the Democrats in November of 2010.

Throughout his book, Daniel Gilbert utilizes many studies and examples to explain why we naturally lock on to our current experiences and then proceed to forecast the future, assuming the future will be very similar to what we are now experiencing. He tells of science fiction films made back in the sixties and how they so inaccurately portrayed life in the twenty-first century (i.e., today). The films assumed we would have super-large IBM 360+++ "Big Blue" mega-computers.

I cracked up laughing as I listened to this section of his book while power walking with my ear buds connected to a standard thirty-two-gigabyte iPhone in my pocket. This same pocket-sized "mega-computer" was also providing me with news feeds and directions to the closest coffee shop based on my GPS-derived current position, all while I was texting my kids about dinner plans. What I had in my pocket far exceeded any capability envisioned in the 1960 mega-size computer era. Nobody forecasted that we would be controlled by our smartphones and that a twenty-four-satellite GPS constellation would be sending timing signals for geo-locating us anywhere in the world. Nor did the early sci-fi film producers predict today's diverse workforce, and particularly absent were women in leadership roles.

We have to be very careful not to rely too much on our current conditions for predicting future conditions, or we may end up like Senator Specter, who made a gross miscalculation by prematurely changing political parties, resulting in the elimination of many of his future opportunities. On the other hand, through networking with key individuals who have *been there, done that*, we can learn from their experiences and acquire a much more accurate assessment of what lies ahead for a given vocational role. It may be very different from what you would expect from your current frame of reference.

Daniel Gilbert also explicitly explains how we change our outlooks of the future when we actually arrive in the future. One of the ways this happens is by our own self-protection mechanism or "emotional immunizations." Emotional immunizations can take many forms. I remember saying things that revealed my own self-inoculation with words such as, "Well the kids are better off now that we are divorced." Really? So how exactly does the same family income that was already tight and causing strife now somehow provide for two separate dwellings without impacting the well-being of the children? On and on we can rationalize, without fully acknowledging the brokenness of the children, as a way to protect ourselves emotionally. Sometimes it just takes time before we can accept the obvious.

This inoculation period is a natural way to emotionally protect ourselves from something that is too painful at the moment. I have limited my divorce scenario example and its consequences to only the financial repercussions, not to be shallow, but for the expediency of making a point and also out of deep empathy and consideration for those who may be in need of a measure of emotional immunization from a not-too-distant divorce. The bottom line is, we can unknowingly protect ourselves (our emotions and esteem) from the reality of an excruciatingly painful situation, which may be very necessary for a time, in order to move forward past the present difficulty.

Gilbert's book also provides detailed studies of victims who have been successfully cured of their diseases and how these victims have a surprisingly different attitude toward their experiences than one would expect. They often make statements like, "Experiencing this disease has totally changed my life; through it all, I have learned to appreciate the joy of life …" Yet, to outsiders, this doesn't seem to make sense. Are these victims serious? Wouldn't we expect victims to be bitter, asking "Why me?" type questions. Could any good come out of so much pain and suffering? The thought of going through an ordeal such as cancer treatment and not feeling worse off is perplexing.

My friend Nina is such a person. She experienced some infrequent internal bleeding that continued to get more frequent and more severe over the course of nine months before she sought medical treatment. Being recently retired, she no longer carried medical insurance coverage, and unfortunately, during this same period, her husband ended up out of work with no medical coverage for the family. Out of financial and physical fear, she denied that there was a serious problem, kept it to herself, and prayed that it would go away.

Over time the bleeding got progressively worse, making her so weak that her friends could not allow her to delay medical attention any longer. They convinced her she needed help and needed help now! The doctor she saw diagnosed her with a life-threatening tumor and immediately admitted her to a hospital for emergency surgery. The tumor was successfully removed. However, three of her fifteen lymph nodes tested positive for cancer, so radiation treatments followed. To assist her recovery, she was placed in an induced coma. Some complications included fluid in her lungs, the inability to breathe on her own, and for a time afterward, she could not speak because her vocal cords were damaged by the breathing mechanisms.

That was four years ago, and she recently told me that now a day doesn't go by that she is not truly thankful. She takes time out of her day to slow down just enough to enjoy and appreciate the life she has. Her message is to encourage everyone not to wait or delay seeking medical attention with this disease because it only gets worse and makes it more difficult for the doctors to help you. The big lesson for her was to accept the help of all those caring people who had been reaching out to her. There is more trying to tough it out all on her own but rather accepting the help of others with genuine humility. She went on to say that she recognizes that we are social beings (not islands) and that the relationships we develop here on earth help us grow a closer relationship with God in heaven. This is not to say that she wasn't a wonderful, engaging, and loving person before; she just didn't allow others to help her. "Oh boy," I heard her say, "I wish I could have learned that lesson some other way than having to go through all that suffering, but now I want to help others to avoid the same mistakes. And I am so thankful."

We can learn a lot from other people—people who make up our network, people we care about, and in turn those that care about us. After all, our past recollections have gaps. As we learned, these gaps are filled in without us being cognitively aware of this less-than-accurate process, resulting in us unknowingly accepting inaccurate representations of past events. We tend to overemphasize the staying power of our present state, and this only exasperates our ability to forecast accurately. And when we do finally get to the future, we change how we feel about it—in unpredictable ways. Therefore we, on our own, are not the best forecasters of what will make us happy.

Likewise with our career development planning, we poorly predict which jobs and career fields will actually make us happy. We tend to forget or mitigate aspects of past jobs we didn't like; we forecast the future by relying too much on the current employment conditions; and we neglect to account for our changing perspective when we enter a new role. Therefore, as CEO of your career, it is essential for you to network and connect with the people in the field you are pursuing. Learn from the people who have already experienced all the aspects of your anticipated career field. These people can provide you with a more accurate picture just by their having *been there, done that*. This will help you to predict your happiness in that career field much better than you can predict it on your own. Proverbs 15:22 tells us, "Without consultation, plans are frustrated, but with many counselors they succeed." Your network provides the available expertise and information for you to be an effective CEO of your career.

Speaking of happiness, is being happy different than having the joy mentioned earlier in Matthew 25? The *Online Etymology Dictionary* provides the distinction, the etymology of the word *happy*: "lucky, favored by fortune, prosperous," of events, "turning out well," from *hap* (noun) "chance, fortune." Incidentally *hap* (verb) means to "happen." (When we consider happiness, it is always associated with events and external circumstances, whereas joy is inwardly focused, not being dependent upon our external circumstances.

The apostle James tells us, "Consider it all joy, my brethren, when you encounter various trials" (James 1:3). Although encountering "various trials" may rob us of our happiness, we can still consider it all joy as we overcome those trials. The apostle Paul encourages us, "You also became imitators of us and of the Lord, having received the word in much tribulation with the joy of the Holy Spirit" (1 Thess. 1:5–7). In another passage he states, "That in a great ordeal of affliction their abundance of joy and their deep poverty overflowed in the wealth of their liberality" (2 Cor. 8:1–3). Likewise, we should not be surprised by career trials as we faithfully pursue "entering into the joy."

Personally, even though I was not happy with my external circumstances when I was terminated from my job, my faith allowed me to not lose hope and to keep my inward joy. What does it mean to be an overcomer? Nothing, unless we have something to overcome. All great athletes, businessmen, chefs, politicians—you name it—have had to overcome many somethings to be as successful as they are. We can rejoice in the trials, knowing we are called according to His purposes. "And we know that God causes all things to work together for good to those who love God, to those who are called according to *His* purpose" (Rom. 8:28). The trials of our career journey will challenge us at times, but we can faithfully press forward with joy.

Networking Equals Opportunities

In addition to providing accurate career development planning information, networking in fact provides the best job opportunity prospects. Job placement companies and recruiters tell us that over 50 percent of today's jobs are not posted on job boards or external company career sites but are filled internally by employee referrals. Companies have discovered that their own employees can often provide qualified job candidates more quickly and less expensively than the more familiar external search methods. This is true for several reasons.

First, employees know where to find other companies' employees who have matching skills in their industry. They may either know contemporaries from attending classes with them, meeting them at technical shows, participating in professional organizations, or having previously worked with them at other companies.

Second, by knowing where to find the talent, company employees can quickly make high-quality candidate referrals that benefit the organization by saving valuable time and money.

And third, the employees performing the work for the company are better equipped to know the job duties, required skills, and the organizational culture for successfully matching the capabilities of a known candidate. The employee's inside job knowledge provides an advantage over a recruiter who is relying on a one-page written job requisition.

Furthermore, employees have a vested interest in getting a good fit for the accomplishment of their projects and for the success of their organizations. The company's HR department recruiters are also constrained by other broader concerns, such as diversity hiring goals, avoiding the perception of unfair hiring practices, keeping salaries equitable, labor and benefit costs, etc. All of these are very important to the HR department; however, employees' focus is just on finding a great coworker to get the job done!

Apply this to your own career advancement. Being connected to employees within the companies you someday may want to work for will enable you to learn about positions that will be opening up—even before they are posted on job sites. This occurs by staying in touch and anticipating when these companies might need someone with your skills. New needs could develop as a result of a new contract award, a new federal grant, a recent company acquisition, a new branch office opening, etc. Hopefully you will hear about leads well before the job is ever formally posted. Utilizing social media sites is an effective way to connect with inside contacts and the hiring manager.

For jobs that are already posted, one technique is to connect with your acquaintances in that company and ask them for a few minutes of their time. A brief conversation with an insider regarding your skills and capabilities for a specific position will provide you with information to help you decide whether to pursue that opportunity or let it pass and wait for a better fit. People are generally happy to talk about their company. After all, they chose to work there, so they will naturally want to tell others about the good choice they made. Of course, be sure to find out if there is a finder's fee associated with the positions you are considering. A finder's fee of $500 up to $5,000 is not unusual for key positions.

If you decide to pursue the opportunity, ask your insider contact to refer you through the company's employee referral program. Your network connection just has to provide your well-crafted resume (based on the insider information for this position) to the hiring manager and/or human resources department, and then your contact will become eligible for the finder's fee. That's a pretty good deal for everyone: you become prepared to better present your abilities toward the needs of the hiring manager; the hiring manager has a better chance of getting a good fit; and your insider contact gets the finder's fee! To ensure that the hiring manager actually gets a chance to look at your resume, request that your inside contact physically hand deliver your cover memo and resume directly to the hiring manager in addition to making the formal submittal through the employee referral system. We will be discussing other techniques for getting your resume package through the HR gatekeepers and to the hiring manager (the decision maker) in the next section.

As effective as networking is for finding a good fit during the tactical job capture, even more important is the strategic advantage of vocational networking to accomplish the progressive steps of your career development plan. You can avoid pitfalls and gain insight from the "lessons learned" by those who have already traveled that road. Career planning combines your God-given talents with your passions for developing a plan with intentional milestones (and sometimes inch-stones) for your journey toward achieving lifelong career success. How to develop a plan and accomplish that journey is the crux of this book. Networking is an essential enabler.

During our seminar series, I show two very different pictures of freeway traffic, metaphorically providing a visual hyperbole of the art of the possible. One picture shows a bird's-eye view of Los Angeles traffic gridlock extending miles into the distance. With this view in focus, I then relate a true story of a woman I knew who worked as a cashier at the Ralphs supermarket chain in the Greater Los Angeles area. Although there are numerous Ralphs supermarkets near where she lives, she just happened to get hired years ago at a Ralphs store that is twenty-two miles from where she currently resides. I mapped out the route between where she lives and where she works, and guess what I found? MapQuest indicated that there are 150+ Ralphs supermarkets between these two points.

So now comes the imagination part. Let's imagine the Ralphs chain has a computer database sorting program that can link all of their employees who are performing similar jobs to stores located closest to their homes. While we are in the state of imagining, let's go even one step farther. Imagine that the state of California had a similar program that could match people with similar job skills to companies that have similar positions. Administrative assistants, accounts receivable clerks, retail salespeople, schoolteachers, investment brokers, etc., all matched to closer work locations with similar positions with similar employers.

Now imagine a very different picture of an uncongested freeway that is sparsely populated, with many fewer vehicles. This whole picture equates to employees spending much less wasted time commuting to work. Metaphorically, effective networking can be thought of as a support system that reduces the gridlock in your career path, allowing you free access to new opportunities. Hold on to those two images—one image of career gridlock and the other image of a wide-open highway of opportunities for advancement as we continue to learn more about networking.

Networking is the means for reaching out and connecting with others as you *Make Your Way* toward your planned career goals. You will be amazed at the relationships that will develop. "For the body is not one member by many" (1 Cor. 12:14).

CHAPTER 4

Networking Techniques

The term *networking* can be misconstrued as a pseudonym for the online social media applications that have developed over the past decade, as if networking were a new phenomenon. However, as I have previously pointed out, the practice of people networking has truly been around for a long, long time. People today who are considered the social networking "super connectors" were in the past referred to as those very popular folks who knew everyone, and the contacts that today are digitally stored on Microsoft Outlook in the past were arranged in Rolodex files. (For the younger readers, a Rolodex held small paper cards that were attached to a vertical rotating cylinder.)

The concept of networking—connecting people to people—has frequently been illustrated as an iconic "wiring" schematic depicting a physical intranet with hardwired connections from computer to computer (e.g., pre-wi-fi). However, such an iconic depiction can speciously suggest that networking is less about direct contact with people and more about virtual connectivity. Regardless of the worldwide appeal of virtual networking and the plethora of excellent publications dedicated to social media networking, nothing is as effective as actually meeting people face to face for building a network of trusted relationships. Social media is a network enabler, not a substitution for meeting people. Yet for some of us, the thought of intentionally attending an event for the purpose of meeting new people is met with a degree of apprehension or maybe even outright fear. This chapter will introduce methods and techniques to alleviate those fears that perhaps may be preventing you from enjoying the benefits of reaching out to others in a social setting.

As family members or part of the church body, we are already familiar with and somewhat practiced at networking. Just the variety of dishes at a family gathering or at a Sunday-afternoon potluck provides a vivid representation of the extended connections of the many contributing people. Yet as wonderful as Aunt Millie's double-chocolate-supreme-triple-layer-cake is, effective career networking needs to be focused on your career-development goals. Determining with whom you will need to talk and where you could meet these kinds of people is imperative. Asking yourself questions such as, "Who do I know who can introduce me to other key people?" and "Where should I be spending my time networking?" is part of the ongoing process of building and refining your network. Therefore, a disciplined, focused networking approach is essential for accomplishing the various aspects of your career objectives. With such a focus, you will also discover common threads among your other network contacts that tie in with your career pursuits.

Rules-of-Engagement (ROE) for Networking

As we begin discussing the networking rules of engagement (the boundaries that we can operate within), I cannot overemphasize the importance of just *showing up*. I remember a classic case when showing up opened new business opportunities for me that were totally unanticipated, even though I had already been coordinating specific business meetings for this event.

Two of our visiting senior vice presidents serendipitously sat down at an open-seating luncheon with representatives of a company that had capabilities very complementary to ours. The ensuing discussions revealed the potential advantages of us working together to strengthen our offerings for a future near-term competitive procurement. After the luncheon, one of the senior vice presidents exclaimed how amazing it was that we were able to connect with the right decision makers at just the right time for that upcoming business opportunity. I smiled and said, "We were just following the first rule of business development: *show up.*" We all had a good laugh and were pretty excited about getting back to the home office to start the teaming discussions. Hence, whether it is networking or business development, the rule is the same: *show up*! You will never know what could have happened if you do not show up.

Just *showing up* sounds easy enough, but sometimes it can be a struggle. Building relationships takes time, and that time often has to be traded for some other activity. Therefore, the amount of time spent networking has to play into your overall life-balance choices to make the best use your finite available time. Prioritizing your networking activities is essential. What's more, the dynamics of life are always changing, and what may have been a good balance earlier in the fall of the year could be off balance as the busy holiday season approaches. Networking with the intention of building long-term relationships requires pacing yourself as if you were running a marathon and not a short sprint.

Let me give a real-life example of my struggle to just *show up* for an awards banquet to honor our local military customers. Several weeks before this banquet, the president of one of the professional organizations supporting the awards program by sponsoring several scholarships asked me if I could attend in her stead. As an advocate for attending network opportunities and for promoting our organization, I did not hesitate to accept the invitation when she initially asked me.

The black-tie event was on a Friday evening. The work week leading up to the event happened to be very tiring for a number of reasons, and as Friday approached, I wasn't nearly as enthusiastic about spending an evening going solo and all dressed up in a tux. I was going solo because my wife had been out of town all week and was scheduled to arrive at the airport while I would be at the dinner. Feeling a bit haggard, I began questioning my decision to attend. As a result of my reflective self-assessment, I realized I needed an attitude adjustment and I needed it soon. This event was certainly a good thing, and as the representative of a professional organization that was sponsoring several of the scholarships, I needed to genuinely embrace the opportunity and show our sincere appreciation to the recipients.

On that Friday, I decided I would leave work a little early so I could get home to take a twenty-minute rejuvenating combat nap, and allow enough time to unhurriedly get dressed—and most importantly to put on a happy face. To my dismay, on Friday afternoon a crisis hit at work and landed me at another facility to work out the issues. It became apparent that my rejuvenating combat nap was now out of the question because I barely would have enough time to change my clothes. To make matters worse, as I rushed to leave work, I received a call from the military protocol office stating that they must have misplaced my bio (summary resume), and they requested that I resend it ASAP since I would be seated at one of the head tables.

Okay, so it was back to the home office to locate the bio on my hard drive and e-mail it, and—oh yes—I was now going to be late. Yikes! At that moment, I was thinking I'd just rather not be going at all. I wistfully thought I'd rather be spending a relaxing evening at home unwinding with my soon-to-be-arriving wife. But to make a long story short, I went.

Surprisingly, I had three chance encounters that proved to be very beneficial that evening. The first of these was that I reconnected with a colonel I had met some months earlier and found out he was retiring very soon and was considering employment in the aerospace industry. This information later led to offering him a key position in our company. At the second encounter, I was introduced to one of our previous customers who wanted to reestablish our contract with new funding and needed to speak with someone in our management chain to work out the details. As a result, a meeting did take place the following week. The third encounter was a brief exchange with one of our government customers, leading to a formal follow-up meeting with a focused presentation discussing our company's solution to an unmet need of theirs.

Remember, this was a social gathering and not a selling meeting. By actively listening to others, you can lock on to ways to help them. After the reception, I dined with a very charming host and had a fun evening discussing an interesting range of topics and contrasting perspectives. It was a very enjoyable event, especially considering I had been mentally whining a few hours earlier in the day. The point is, we all struggle at times with our commitments and schedules, but networking is worth the effort you put into it. Now, back to the rules of engagement.

Back to the Rules of Engagement
When you are showing up, do show up early. This not only gives you a chance to meet more people, but it also gives you a chance to meet the host or the event sponsors. By meeting the host, you now have a common connection with everyone else who is invited to the gathering. The host can introduce you to the other guests and can provide invaluable information about the interests of those guests. At a business or philanthropy function, getting there early allows you to meet the sponsors and organizers of the event. If there is something you can help with, like registration, greeting, or handing out brochures, you are now situated in a wonderful position of not just attending but of being a contributing member of the event—and people will want to know who you are. Networking made easy!

However, before attending business networking events, prepare yourself by doing a little research so you will be a more effective networker. Even just a little time spent researching can go a long way. Find out the companies, organizations, and customers who will be represented, along with any news releases, company announcements, new product lines, etc. Company websites and Securities and Exchange Commission summary reports (you can Google: SEC 10k) are rich sources of information that let you know where a company is heading, what its interests are, and how you might be of help. Conference organizers will often publish the conference's corporate sponsors, a list of registered attendees, the speakers' biographies, and agenda topics. Preparing yourself with that information beforehand will allow you to focus your networking to your specific interest areas.

Google people you are interested in, and don't forget to review their LinkedIn profiles. Typically you will not have a chance to talk to everyone, so setting a priority list and looking for opportunities to connect with your priorities will give you the greatest benefit from your time and investment. Remember, challenge yourself to meet as many guests as is practicable but not as many as possible. It may be possible to meet everyone, but by merely meeting everyone, you probably will not be very effective in getting to know anyone. You want to get to know your targeted contacts so you can know how to offer to help them. For example, you need to ask these kinds of questions: What do they do? What are their passions? What do they need? There are many other relevant questions.

Keep in mind that getting to know people and learning what their interests are demands that you can't be preoccupied with your own self-interests, and neither should you be stuffing your mouth with conversation-inhibiting foods. As delightful as it may be to fill up on those wonderful coconut-breaded jumbo shrimp, along with a chilled glass of chardonnay, you won't be able to mingle very well. This is true for every event, whether pizza and Pepsi or caviar and champagne are served. Just the art of juggling food and getting something into your mouth without spilling any of it on a nearby guest is challenging.

Taking a popular line found on networking blogs, "Either come to eat or come to network; you can't do both." My recommendation is to never arrive hungry. Sure, enjoy what the host has prepared but only very scantily. The problem is that everyone has learned from their mothers to never approach a pet that is eating, and for good reason! Well guess what? We apply that training to all animals that are eating, including people. So naturally, you can't expect people to be attracted to you with your canine teeth chomping and your hands occupied with a plate, napkin, and drink. It cries, "Leave me alone!"

Being prepared also means developing and having your opening brand statement ready. This is just a short, crisp, and interesting opener describing who you are and what you do. As an example, "Hello my name is John Smith. I work at the community college teaching astronomy." This crisp, to the point opening line generates an interesting set of talking points that can flow nicely into a conversation about the college, astronomy, public funding for schools, the sciences, a nephew attending the college, etc.

Keep in mind that good brand statements take some effort on your part to craft well. People often tend to be too general with their statements, and this doesn't help the other person lock on to anything about them. Or at the other extreme, they deep dive into too much detail, which turns people off in a social setting, especially those who are not familiar with specific industry or job jargon. By having a good opening statement, you graciously allow the other person the opportunity to quickly understand enough about you to engage in a fluid conversation. Help others help you with networking!

Also be sure to have business cards readily at hand for the event. When you are representing your company, you will typically use the company cards. However, your brand transcends any particular company, so it may behoove you to have your own personal cards printed for the times when it is more appropriate to be representing yourself (e.g., professional organization sponsored events, employment interviews, etc.). Today, it is very easy to design and order business cards online for as little as twenty dollars for 250 cards.

As a consultant, I use different business cards depending on which company I am representing or the job I will be performing. I have a different look for the motivational speaking card I use for my business versus a company-issued business card I use as their representative. Don't be overly creative; keep your brand simple and specific, with just enough information for someone to easily contact you. Include your name, e-mail address, phone numbers, and LinkedIn URL, with a font large enough for people over forty years of age to read without glasses. Furthermore, keep the backside of your cards blank for your new acquaintance's note taking. Of course, along with your business cards, always have a pen available. Shortly after your conversations, jot notes on the backside of their cards for your personalized follow-up call. People will be impressed with the specific details you remember about them later. Taking just a few quick notes on the back of their business card will later trigger your memory to those important specifics about them.

A conference event's key speakers are the attractors that draw attendance. Those same speakers will be inundated with handshakes and will receive a plethora of business cards by the end of the event. The attendees (not the speakers) are typically the connections you will want to add to your network first; you most likely will have more opportunities to help them and what's more, meet other people through them. A quick, somewhat formal exchange with the key speakers is all that can be expected, so after the introduction, provide an interesting reason why you should meet with them after this busy event. Then simply let them know you will be calling their office next week to set up a meeting. Yes, now you have the opportunity to meet privately without the distractions and schedule constraints of the busy conference environment.

For career networking, in addition to your introductory brand statement, have your elevator speech primed and ready for responding to any potential employment opportunity. This is a short, well-rehearsed speech that intrigues a hearer in a short time span, such as an elevator ride (thirty to sixty seconds). Your elevator speech should roll off your tongue effortlessly. Have it carefully thought out, well-rehearsed, but preferably not memorized so it is easily adaptable to any audience. Different circumstances and listeners will require you to modify and adjust your elevator speech based on what you believe they need from the conversation. Keep it interesting, vividly expressing what you are passionate about while absolutely avoiding any unfamiliar job jargon or acronyms. Leave the listener wanting to learn more.

As an example, suppose you are in the lobby of a hotel waiting for the shuttle bus to the airport (and it could arrive any minute) and you happen to recognize an industry colleague you have not yet officially met. This is a great opportunity to simply acknowledge each other with a smile and then exchange introductions. This leads to some form of the question: "What do you do?" You respond effortlessly to this casual encounter with your well-rehearsed elevator speech: "Well, you know many companies today have had to cut back on their overhead expenses and no longer have full-time business development staffs. I work as a business development consultant for them—helping these companies capture new business opportunities to increase their revenue and profits."

This speech provides more information than an introductory brand statement, but it is not so long that it would exceed someone's attention span (or the opportunity's span), and again, it contains no jargon. For the situation in this example, the elevator speech should be just long enough to capture your colleague's interest for a follow-up meeting while allowing time to exchange business cards and still catch the shuttle bus to the airport. With the business card in hand, you are ready to follow up with a phone call or e-mail to set up the next meeting—a meeting you can be fully prepared for with information based on his or her personal or company websites about his or her business needs. Your new acquaintance now knows that you consult for business and that you could help his or her business increase its revenue and profit. What's not to love?

In addition to your elevator speech, have some good stories in mind to make an impression while utilizing them to immediately establish who you are. Being prepared and having done your homework allows networking to be much more relaxed and effective. Stories that are memorable and stories that convey your passions are the best; they will make you stand out so people will remember you. Also be sure to brush up on current events just for fun talk. You will need some newsworthy talking points at times just to keep the conversation fresh.

One caution regarding current events: be careful not to come across as negatively as the mainstream media often does. Your attitude is contagious; you want people to feel an upbeat, good feeling about your conversation with them. Therefore, bringing up the latest celebrity divorce debacle may not be the best topic to have associated with your brand, nor would any of the other sad tabloid stories, such as celebrity drug rehab, arrests, or extramarital affairs, be advisable. Tsunamis, fires, and earthquakes can dominate the news at times, but again, look for topics that lift people up and make them feel good about talking to you. Likewise, before throwing out some cleverly worded political barbs, know your audience. Keep the conversation light and fun, listen to their stories, and tie in your own personal stories with theirs.

Having some good, open-ended questions in mind can go a long way toward successfully engaging others into a meaningful conversation. Asking, "So what do you like best about what you do?" gets people talking about all kinds of things they like to do. Often these things are outside of work activities that are interesting and fun to hear about. You'll be told about things like skiing, surfing, vacationing with the grandchildren, and other enjoyable activities that you can then connect to with your own experiences.

At a business event, you might try asking, "How did you get started in the advertising industry?" and seeing where that takes the conversation. Or, "What were some of the challenges you faced with …?" Asking, "How did you first meet the hostess?" allows you to learn more about the background of the person you have just been introduced to. Getting people's thoughts away from their work and having them talk about themselves and others important to them is interesting, and it builds the personal side of the relationships. Another great lead-in question is, "What do you like to do best in your spare time?" By the way, this question will also reveal if the person is a workaholic by his or her lack of outside activities. As the conversation flows, do not be afraid to ask, "Who do you know who could help me with …?" kind of questions, remembering that people generally feel good about helping others, and offering advice and referrals is an easy way for them to help you.

Build Your Network before You Need It

The networking examples we have discussed are focused on building relationships and helping others. Whether helping with philanthropic activities such as supporting the military awards program or volunteering to help with registration at a luncheon, we should be constantly seeking ways to give to others as we build trusted relationships. "Giving people" are attractive people; others want to get to know them. Conversely, self-centered people drive others away. We should think of networking as a way of giving to others. This mindset of networking is analogous to planting seeds and cultivating a garden over the long term. It is very different from hunting for our next meal, which is analogous to the quick kill for selfishly taking what we want for ourselves.

Consider the following example of how an informal potluck social gathering can connect people so they can help each other. Imagine that your teenage daughter is looking for some extra spending money. At the same time, an expecting couple, whom your family has been getting to know socially over the past few months, happens to mention to you how anxious they are to find a trustworthy babysitter for their soon-to-arrive baby. Bingo—by attending this potluck, a connection is made between the expectant couple's babysitting needs and your daughter's ability to help. However, without having already built a level of trust beforehand, this win-win solution would not have materialized. After all, without knowing the parents and a little about their teenage daughter, this match almost certainly would not have happened; the expectant parents are not going to trust their bundle of joy to a stranger. Establishing trusted relationships for effective networking takes time. There is no shortcut for understanding the needs and capabilities of each other.

This is no different when making connections and building relationships for your career-building goals. Cultivating relationships through networking helps produce career opportunities for you. The stronger the network, the greater number of opportunities you will discover. As you develop and refine your career plan, your network will be the mechanism to help you reach your planned goals.

An essential relationship for your career network is a mentor. Mentors are those people who can provide career insight you won't have for years to come, and mentors also can provide you with a significant set of connections. If your career field has an established mentoring program, either sponsored by your employer or a professional organization, sign up. If such a program is not available, you can start your own by first determining who are the successful people in your career field and who of your contacts may know them.

Most people who love what they do are happy to talk with you about their work. Therefore, one great way to meet new people in your vocation, and to learn about them and what they do, is by requesting a short twenty-minute informational interview with them. This is a very powerful first step in building a potential key relationship as you research your career field. The following chapters dealing with job capture will address the informational interview in detail. But for now, start thinking of the three people you should have in your network and possible ways to connect with them.

Overcoming Networking Fears

Some of you might be thinking, *Okay I get it that you have to show up and prepare beforehand to be effective at networking. But if the truth be known, I am not an extrovert by nature, and I certainly am not someone who enjoys making small talk with strangers. How do I connect with new people and build relationships when I am more comfortable in less socially demanding environments? How do I smile and put on that cool composure and friendly body language so people will want to meet me?*

Surprisingly, the easiest answer to those questions is simply to do what you already know. Actors are pros at having the correct facial expression and demeanor to charm and hold their audience captive for hours. Most of us, however, do not have that talent or the years of training needed to perfect those stage performance skills. Your best option is to do what you already know how to do.

You already know how to comfortably greet an old friend. Practice meeting new acquaintances as if you are meeting a very close friend whom you have not seen for some time. Would meeting your old friend be difficult for you? Of course not! Your body language will signal friendliness, and your facial expressions will be warmly received. Just by bringing the old friend sentiment into your thoughts, you create a welcoming manner for meeting people and avoid a multitude of awkward and clumsy nervous behaviors. So relax and expect to meet your good old buddy from years past. Imagine how you would feel, and then naturally react with your smile, handshake, eye contact, attention, etc. Being at ease allows you to be yourself as you meet new acquaintances. Once the introduction and the initial conversation begin, you can forget about your old buddy, take a relaxing breath, and enjoy the conversation with your new contact.

In business, networking events are often sponsored by a non-profit professional organization. By volunteering to serve in such an organization, you instantly become its representative. This creates a natural opportunity to welcome guests at the event as a way of introduction. The ice is easily broken, and the conversation begins to flow. You may even be given a name tag with your title! Wow! Now it is even easier for people to meet you. Better yet, volunteer to be the host. Have you ever seen a host who wasn't active? Being a host requires you to be engaged with your guests as an ordinary responsibility of that role. There is no time for staring at your watch (or your shoes); gone are the times of wondering if this social will ever end.

The structured social networking events I mentioned earlier are by no means superior to everyday, casual networking opportunities. I couldn't help noticing a rather peculiar work ethic when viewing photos taken of a local church's community outreach project. One of the photos was of over twenty volunteers who were dressed in work garb. They had been given the task of digging, weeding, and building planting boxes at a public elementary school. The planting boxes would help the school children learn about planting seeds and growing crops.

The project turned out to be a big success, with appreciation letters received from the school's principal, teachers, and students. Interestingly, of the twenty volunteers shown in the photo, four had shovels and were digging the soil to prepare for the laying of the planting box frames. The camera caught the others standing in the background, basically just talking, when the lens focused on them. In addition to building planting boxes, relationships were being built among the volunteers. This is a wonderful example of networking by building relationships between and among the volunteers of the school and the church through a local community project.

The relationships among the school group of volunteers and the relationships among the church group of volunteers were enhanced by working on the common goal of finishing a gardening project. Working together for a common goal can develop stronger bonds for a congregation in one afternoon than scores of Sunday-morning hellos and greetings in the church foyer. Likewise, the school volunteers participating in the project didn't often get a chance to work hand in hand with other teachers or administrative employees. The demands of attending to hundreds of students during a busy school day didn't allow for that kind of camaraderie.

It is also interesting to note the significance of the dissimilar backgrounds but complementary interests of the church and school volunteers. These newly formed relationships are weaker in the sense of mutual interest, beliefs, values, etc., but surprisingly provide stronger building opportunities for networking. The paradox of weaker connections generating a stronger network is caused by the greater number of links the weaker connected contacts will provide to each other.

The church volunteers already have a level of familiarity with each other and thus many common connectors. Likewise, the school volunteers have common friends and colleagues through attendance at conferences, union meetings, etc. Therefore, by reaching out to one new acquaintance in a totally different field (weak link) you open many new opportunities (strong network) for connecting. The weak connection has many new contacts for you to meet. Both groups have the common bond of supporting the community and will benefit from the support of each other's network. The support can include recommendations for pediatricians, restaurants, tutors, local political propositions, dentists, etc. Connecting a church member with a school employee allows both to link their networks together, thus expanding their contacts with few duplicated connections. Very powerful!

Networking Basics

Remember, a warm introduction is always better than a cold one. What *warm* refers to is the friendliness and commonality of the introduction. Asking someone else to introduce you to his or her acquaintance (contact) is definitely preferred over simply approaching a potential contact as a complete stranger (cold introduction). It is certainly okay to be bold in the absence of someone to help you, but there is no reason to do it alone when there is help at hand. Don't forget about your host, who you met earlier in the evening (say, helping to put out napkins?) as a person who can help you connect. Find out any mutual interests or common acquaintances before the actual introduction so you can be prepared to get off to a smooth start following the warm opening.

By doing your part to initiate a warm introduction, you will make it easier to get started building a relationship. The strength of the relationship depends in part on knowing the person's skills, abilities, and passions. Those attributes can be learned by active listening. Keep in mind that normal speech is paced at around 125 words per minute, while we can listen at a rate of 500 words per minute. This gives you, as the listener, time to actively listen to and really understand your new acquaintance.

Actually around 80 percent of communication consists of nonverbal micro-expressions, vocal inflections, and body language, with only 20 percent being oral communications. By actively listening and picking up nonverbal communications, you will naturally be better equipped to empathize with the needs of others. This allows you to help others by offering a needed contact, a well-placed referral, or some bit of needed information that lifts the relationship to the next level. Quoting Ivan Misner, PhD, cofounder of Business Networking International (BNI), "It is not called net-sit or net-eat, it's called net-work." The preparation, practice, and follow-up efforts that go into networking are intentional and focused work. And like all work, great rewards come from doing your work with excellence.

Mingling

I generally consider myself someone who is easily approachable, with a friendly demeanor; however, I had to take a few lessons from my son, Michael. One weekend when Michael was just a toddler, I took him to the neighborhood market I had visited many times by myself, usually on the way home from work for any last-minute items needed for dinner. Young Michael also visited the market often but always with his mother.

It turned out that everyone knew Michael, but they had never connected that I was his father. On this visit, the butcher was the first to notice Michael and me together. He stopped restocking the meat section to introduce himself to me and immediately engaged with Michael in what was obviously a familiar routine of joking together. The butcher and I chatted about Michael along with that day's meat bargains and what cuts were going to be on sale the next week. But Michael's popularity didn't end with the butcher.

The store manager approached us to introduce himself to me and then entered into some very silly toddler talk with Michael. The manager was excited about receiving a very nice shipment of Port wine just in from Spain and wanted our family to have a bottle for the holidays. He said it would be at Mary's checkout and she would know not to charge us.

Wow, I was thinking, *how does Michael know these folks?* I was hoping he would know who Mary was when we went to pick up the Port at the checkout. And guess what? He did know Mary! She was happy to see Michael, and he was happy to see her. I remember thinking, like any father, that my son was a very special toddler and those folks at the grocery store must really have a thing for toddlers.

Years later, when Michael was a senior in high school, I noticed that some things had never really changed. We were walking on a narrow sidewalk in a beach city known for its college party atmosphere. My wife and I were walking behind Michael and his friend on a narrow sidewalk. Approaching us were two attractive college-aged women who were scantily clothed in beach attire. I was anticipating the awkwardness of us all maneuvering to allow the young ladies enough room on the sidewalk to get by us. As they approached us, one of the girls put on a big smile and said to Michael, "Hey, give me a high five." I must have looked a little taken aback by the friendliness of these college girls since they were older than Michael and complete strangers. Apparently to put me at ease, one of girls said, "Hey, and your dad too. High five, sir." My reflection at the time was that my son had always been a natural people magnet. He didn't appear to have lost any of it as he had grown up, as many other examples came to mind from that incident.

One last example was when I recently spoke with his high school cross-country coach about a conflict between Michael's academic schedule and his ability to make the practice schedule. The coach just said, "Tell Michael to make whatever practices he can, and we will try to have him compete at whatever level he attains."

The coach went on to say, "I want Michael on the team because he is very good for the team's morale. He motivates others and is just fun to have on the team."

I realized that many of us could do a better job of seizing the moment and connecting with people by learning from watching Michael in everyday situations. Michael naturally draws people to him, and he is always willing to help out anyone. I personally do not have the same natural ability to connect instantly with everyone, but there are simple techniques I have discovered that anyone can learn to help them be at ease in social situations. These techniques are the next topic for discussion.

Many books have been written about mingling techniques. One book I recommend is titled, *How to Talk to Anyone: 92 Tricks for Big Success in Relationships* by Leil Lowndes. What I like about this particular book is the short, practical techniques that are easy to adapt to your networking situations. She refers to these techniques as tricks but not in the pejorative sense. It is a fun and easy read. I'd even recommend listening to it in the audio version while driving or exercising.

To whet your appetite, Leil Lowndes' trick #49, titled, "How to Make 'em Think We (Instead of You vs. Me)," I found to be very clever. The author describes four levels of relationships that are characterized by our communications. The first level is clichés. This includes clichés and trivial conversation topics, such as the weather, which you might discuss with a stranger you just met. The second is the facts level; this can be used with an existing acquaintance. Again the topic could be as trivial as the weather, but now facts, like the number of inches of rain for the year, are included.

The third level is feelings. Friends share their feeling with statements like, "I really like these sunny days; they remind me of growing up when I would go swimming in the river." And finally, the fourth level is characterized by we statements. These generate a higher level of intimacy than is found in level three. The forth level is about we and us rather than I and me. The fourth-level statements can have the same topic of weather but with we, such as, "If this rain continues any longer, we are going to end up with trench foot." It is now personal between them; this is how close friends talk.

To enhance your networking relationships, move to level four with a premature use of we in your statement. As an example, "If this sunny weather holds up, we are going to have a great day of golf." Please note, if you are at a well-attended networking event that includes a shotgun golf tournament (meaning the players are distributed in foursomes at each of the eighteen holes for a simultaneous group tee off), it is highly unlikely you will actually be randomly paired up with the person you are currently mingling with. However, by saying, "*We* are going to have a great time golfing," you have prematurely taken the relationship to level four. By jump starting your new acquaintances to the fourth level with we statements, you develop intimate and meaningful relationships more quickly. There is nothing more discouraging than showing up at the same conferences year after year, only to factually compare this year's weather against last year's weather with your level-two acquaintances. Help yourself build more intimate and meaningful relationships more quickly. Get to level four prematurely!

After each of these techniques, Lowndes includes a summary box. Trick #84 follows with, "The most guarded safe haven respected by big winners is the dinner table. Breaking bread together is a time when they bring up no unpleasant matters. While eating, they know it's okay to brainstorm and discuss the positive side of the business: their dreams, their desires, and their designs. They can freely associate and come up with new ideas. But no tough business."

I'll let the reader explore the other ninety tricks Leil writes about in her book. What is really fun is to purposely try out a few of her tricks at events and observe how others respond to them. The ones that work for you will stick as you develop your repertoire of networking techniques. Eventually you will become a networking pro.

When Is Networking - Just Not Appropriate?

This is a bit of a trick question. Let me preface it by saying that whenever we place networking in the perspective of building long-term relationships through helping others, networking is *always* appropriate. We must be socially sensitive and aware of our circumstances to network appropriately. For example, attending your local chamber of commerce holiday mixer is a very different situation for networking than attending your uncle's funeral. But in either case, you can look for opportunities to help those around you.

You may be thinking, *For heaven's sake, networking at a funeral?* Absolutely! People think about different things and reflect on life when confronted with the death of a loved one and by the realization of the sheer brevity of our time here on earth. The thought of a living trust may have been prompted by the funeral situation, which could lead someone to share with you that he has been meaning to get a living trust established for some time but has always been just too busy to get to it—but now he is going to be putting a higher priority on it. After thoughtfully suggesting that you know of an excellent living trust and estate-planning professional, offering to send him the referral's contact info next week would be very appropriate. This simple gesture shows your concern for the other person's need; it is that simple. In that particular situation, you may have just helped someone with a special need that would have gone unspoken and unmet in a different setting.

Therefore, networking is always appropriate, whether at a funeral, holiday party, or business event. Just be sure to network in a way that honors the event and is in the context of helping others.

Our guiding principle as to the how to and when to should always align with a back-to-the-basics approach of building long-term relationships by offering genuine help to others. With that frame of mind and serving attitude, you should do quite well.

Have you ever wondered why corporations sponsor events? After all, the money they spend sponsoring conferences, seminars, and social events comes right off the top (i.e., their profit line). There are many reasons why these investments make good business sense. The advertisement aspect is one, but many of these events do not have any direct selling of merchandise or displaying of their products. What these events do offer is an opportunity to meet people, brand your company, and gain ideas. Companies will spend large amounts of money to sponsor dinner events just for an opportunity to network with many colleagues, customers, and peers at the receptions before and after the actual dinner. Building relationships takes an investment of their time and resources. Successful businesses understand the benefits of effective networking, and so should you.

CHAPTER 5

Social Media as an Enabler

Developing meaningful relationships (a.k.a., your network) does indeed take an investment of your time and energy. Fortunately, today we have many social media applications to help us network more effectively and much more efficiently than ever before. Alexander Graham Bell's invention the telephone in 1870 helped people to communicate much more efficiently than ever before, in turn facilitating the nurturing and building of relationships. I remember a time long ago (pre-cellular phones) when the Mother's Day holiday weekend phone calls would overwhelm Ma Bell's land-line capability, forcing callers to hang up and redial many times until getting through to dear ol' Mom. Relationships matter—especially the one with your mother! Today communicating through social media provides an even greater leap of efficiency for the nurturing and building of relationships, with applications and functionality that Mr. Bell could never have imagined.

Popular sites such as LinkedIn, Facebook, and others connect you not only to your contacts (level-one contacts) but also to your contacts' contacts (level-two contacts), which is very powerful. The linking doesn't stop there but continues to the third, fourth, and deeper levels, depending on the application (and membership level). You also have opportunities to join forums and groups with others who share a common interest. These groups and forums in turn link their members' contacts directly to you. All of this exponentially increases your contacts.

Getting started with social media online sites is easy enough. Typically there is no charge or monthly fee for the basic membership, which is quite adequate for most of us. The real question is which of the social media sites are best for which purpose and ultimately best for your circumstances. Also consider, "How do I make the best use of my limited time on these sites?" We'll use the term Return-On-Investment (ROI) to address the issue of assessing the value of a particular social media site for our situation and the corresponding time commitment needed to get the desired results.

I know of teenagers and retired people who are consumed (and happily consumed) with Facebook and Twitter, keeping busily connected for hours. What is the return on their investment? They probably have a very high ROI or they would not be investing that much of their time doing so. It also may be absolutely wonderful for Grandma to reconnect with people she hasn't corresponded with for years, but those same social networking activities won't get you where you need to go with your career. We have to evaluate how much time we want to invest and assess which applications will provide us a reasonable return. Once again, we see that taking control of your career includes another C-level role— Chief Information Officer (CIO). We're adding to your CEO role, so let's think about what it means to be your own CIO. Oh by the way, a big congratulations on your new assignment. It is yours to own!

Despite the many advantages of social media networking, I have heard disconcerting responses from people who resist getting on board. Usually their resistance has to do with fears of identity theft or the invasion of their personal life. The truth is that your information most probably is already out there without your consent and without your control of the content or the users of that information! Social media sites allow you to control what you want others to see. You are your own career CIO for your brand and for what you want people to know about you. You control who has access to what content.

Jason Alba, author of *I'm on LinkedIn—Now What???*, correctly instructs us regarding social media sites, "Everything has to be 'On Brand and On Purpose.'" You are in control of your brand and also in control of what others can learn about you through what you post. By being intentional about your social media messages, you not only protect your image, but more importantly, you also promote what you want others to discover about you and ultimately what others will think about you (a.k.a., your brand). Effectively employing social media sites is not about protecting your identity but rather about utilizing a powerful enabler for being found—and found with an image you control.

As a professional, you would not want to post the photos of your college spring break party bashes, off-color jokes, hobbies, political affiliations, or anything else that doesn't support your professional brand. Now if you happen to be a professional political lobbyist in Washington DC, then political affiliations would not only be appropriate but absolutely necessary. The same is true regarding religious affiliations if you happen to be working in a religious organization. However, the same religious affiliations would be inappropriate for a different career field, such as the admissions director at a public college.

The litmus test is whether the materials posted are "On Brand and On Purpose." Anything not "On Brand and On Purpose" is at best a distraction from what you want others to learn about you and at worst a negative tainting, which often tends to be very sticky. As an example of this stickiness, suppose you are branding yourself as a reliable executive assistant and you proudly display a family photo with your four darling preschool children. That image could send the unintended message of job absenteeism and tardiness due to daycare hours, ill children, mandatory school functions, etc. Therefore, a posting that is not "On Brand and On Purpose" has the potential to stick if it is perceived adversely, thus preventing any further serious hiring consideration. Federal and state discrimination labor laws prohibit employers from asking certain categories of questions to prevent unfair discrimination. There is no good reason to offer prohibited information that could work against you; therefore, keep your postings "On Brand and On Purpose."

Building your network through electronic social media is based on the same foundational networking principles discussed earlier—that of developing long-term relationships by helping others. Astoundingly, there are many new ways to help people through social media by simply sharing needed information. And there are so many sites available to easily find and connect with others that share your common interests. Summarizing just a few of the more popular social media sites will get us started. Recognizing today's dynamic growth and popularity of social media doesn't lend itself to publishing static summaries. Hopefully as you continue to learn more about social media, you will develop a thirst for exploring more ways to control the content posted about you and to make your brand easily known to others. Maintaining a disciplined "On Brand and On Purpose" mindset regarding social media will alleviate any worries about identity theft or the invasion of your privacy. The cliché, "A good offense is the best defense" is true for what you want others to find out about you online.

LinkedIn

The first thing you want from a social media application for your career is to find contacts and to get found. I can't think of a better site than LinkedIn for those purposes. LinkedIn's tagline is, "Relationships Matter," and that is what LinkedIn is all about. Simply set up a free account and you can get started. With LinkedIn, it is easy to search for contacts and invite them to join your personal network. One LinkedIn function I really like for job searchers is the "companies" feature. By clicking on the companies search tab, you can begin to follow companies you are interested in. I would recommend following three to five companies you would want to work for someday. LinkedIn provides the names of other LinkedIn users within those companies, along with their profile information. This allows you to reach out and connect with insiders of the companies you are interested in.

LinkedIn users are categorized by levels. Level 1 contacts are those users that are already connected with you. Level 2 are those LinkedIn users who are connected to someone with whom you are connected, and level 3 are members connected to someone in your level-2 contacts, etc. LinkedIn also allows you to sort by location, industry, past company affiliations, and schools. For an upgrade, there are additional filters. All of this sorting allows you to find people who you may already know or people who have a common interest with you. This then allows you to invite them to connect with you through LinkedIn. The invitation consists of a brief message relaying who you are and why you would like to connect with them. It is that easy!

LinkedIn exceeded 100 million members worldwide in March of 2011. At that time, CEO Jeff Weiner said LinkedIn was adding approximately 1 million new members every week, with each member having a unique story to share. That same year the company went public with an Initial Public Offering (IPO) price of $45 per share, giving LinkedIn a market value of $4.3 billion. Amazingly, on the first day of trading on the New York Stock Exchange, the price per share doubled! You can tap into this billion-dollar resource by becoming a member without paying a dime; that's a pretty good deal!

In addition to finding company contacts, LinkedIn has a tab for new hires. New hires are wonderful network contacts to have as a job seeker. They understand what you are trying to do and are likely to be empathetic with your situation. Simply inviting them to your network with a short invite such as, "Congratulations, I see you recently were hired by XYZ company. XYZ is a great company that I would like to work for someday as well. I would appreciate finding out more about the company and how you found your position. I am a (fill in the job title) and would very much like to add you to my personal network." This is easy enough, and chances are this new hire would love to discuss his or her recent career achievement with you.

The companies tab also has posted chats by these employees and even lists the total number of employees using LinkedIn as potential contacts for you. People naturally want to talk about their companies and jobs; LinkedIn provides the venue. After all, people's companies are where they chose to work forty or more hours a week, so why would they not want to brag on their company and share information with you?

The real strength of electronic social media networking is its ability to grow your contacts exponentially. Take, for example, connecting to others through the group function. LinkedIn makes it easy for members to form groups to discuss topics of interests. Many of the LinkedIn groups are open, meaning anyone can join. There are also closed groups with membership controlled by the originator. Generally the closed groups are very easy to join. Simply stating your interest in the group usually qualifies you for membership. Bear in mind, closed groups are not closed to be snobbish but rather to facilitate a more focused discussion between members toward their common interests.

As important as it is to find others to connect with, the huge benefit of LinkedIn is for others to find you. Your profile page is where you can brand yourself with taglines, a summary of your skills and accomplishments, links to your resume and other published materials, professional accomplishments, schools attended, groups you are a member of, and a host of applications—all so others can find you. Additional applications allow you to post MS PowerPoint presentations, YouTube videos, and lists of books you are interested in. It allows you to do polling (incidentally, by setting up a poll you not only gain insight but you also brand yourself as an expert in that area), set up links to blogs, and the list goes on.

Remember that you want to be found. Recruiters pay for subscription upgrades that allow them to mine data for specific skills and experience. One of the easiest ways you can help recruiters help you is by having a specific tagline and summary. It is much easier for a recruiter to find you if you have a tagline such as "IT Architect, ABC Enterprise Information System, fifteen years" versus a generic "IT professional." The more descriptive and focused your tagline is, the easier it is for someone to find you and visit your profile.

Consider for a moment searching Craigslist for a used car. If you know what you are looking for, a descriptive title will catch your eye, whereas a more general title tends to get lost in the heap of ads. Recruiters are looking for specifics, so your tagline should be specific to attract their attention. Spreading your net too broadly with a general tagline will work against you. Once your specific tagline attracts a recruiter to your profile, then a good summary telling an interesting story about your passions and your capabilities will keep him or her digging for more information about you.

Your LinkedIn summary should also be sprinkled with enough searchable words to get electronic hits directly from your profile. The searchable words for the IT architecture candidate could be words such as: ANSI/IEEE Standard 1471-2000, certifications, enterprise, Service-Oriented Modeling Framework (SOMF), Open Distributed Processing (ODP), etc. We will return to the topic of searchable keywords and how to find more of those descriptors in a later section on resume building. On that note, you will find many of the techniques presented in part IV on job capture to be helpful for developing and enhancing your LinkedIn profile.

LinkedIn is the place to be found and to find others. Just Google someone, and chances are his or her LinkedIn profile will be on the top of the list. Increase the search engine's ranking of your LinkedIn profile by adding more links on your profile, such as links to websites, blogs, and even to your resume via a free service called Emurse. Emurse will notify you by e-mail whenever your posted resume is visited, along with information regarding who visited it.

Only a quick synopsis of LinkedIn functions has been provided in this chapter. Suffice it to say, LinkedIn is for being found. The advantage is that it allows you to control the content of your profile so you can effectively establish your brand—while still providing privacy settings and guidelines. I mentioned Jason Alba's book, *I'm on LinkedIn—Now what???* earlier. Although LinkedIn is very intuitive, I highly recommend reviewing his books and DVDs on how to take full advantage of this very powerful social media networking tool.

JibberJobber

Before leaving author and network expert, Jason Alba, let me tell you about a resource he developed. Jason is the founder of JibberJobber.com. This site allows you to organize all your contacts and job-capture activities online with a tool that provides all the functions you wish a Microsoft Excel spreadsheet could do for you. As Jason personalizes the story of his difficult job search, including the frustrations he (and everyone searching for work) experienced, he was prompted to develop the "personal relationship manager" to help other job seekers during this process. Quoting from the JibberJobber website:

> As the months passed, and as Jason learned the importance of networking, he incorporated a major networking piece into JibberJobber. This has shifted its focus from a tool just to be used during one job search into a tool to be used to manage job transitions during your entire career. So what is JibberJobber? Is it a job search tool? Is it a networking tool? It is more like a personal relationship manager that allows you to do everything you need to do to manage a job search and optimize your network relationships—for the duration of your career!

Facebook and Twitter

Both Facebook and Twitter are wonderful sites for communicating with instant connectivity to your established contacts. Although LinkedIn has its own e-mail, getting to the e-mail functions requires you to actually log on to the LinkedIn site. However, LinkedIn does allow incoming messages to be routed and read to another designated e-mail address of your choice. But with LinkedIn, it is still e-mail, whereas Facebook and Twitter provide instant message connectivity.

The big caution still applies: remember to keep all you networking communications "On Brand and On Purpose." One way to do this is to establish a separate Facebook or Twitter account for your professional contacts, thus keeping your personal and professional networks separated by using different user names. Separate accounts make it possible to keep yourself "On Brand and On Purpose" for both your personal and professional networks, as each has a different purpose. However, that is not to say anything goes on the personal network. Be intentional about what you post because it is often not possible to undo what has been released to the public.

CHAPTER 6

Networking Resources

Thus far we have just begun to explore the powerful discipline of networking. I refer to networking as a discipline—a lifelong practice that develops relationships over time. Just as crash diets don't achieve long-term weight loss results, networking surges don't achieve long-term relationship results. My encouragement to the reader is to continue practicing what you have already learned while searching beyond this book to embrace the plethora of networking resources that will enhance your career development and lifelong vocational journey. Therefore, to facilitate your career journey, I have included a resources chapter within the various parts of this book rather than simply listing all the resources as an appendix.

By having resources explained and integrated throughout the book, the reader is allowed an opportunity for immediate engagement, thus accelerating one's understanding of what is possible. Applying the biblically based principles discussed in this book will provide the critical thinking framework to correctly capture and apply the golden nuggets contained in the countless secular networking resource materials available. After all, the unregulated Internet is a free-for-all forum of opinions, some of which may be in error, incomplete, or just not biblically sound in doctrine. Therefore, we must test everything discovered on the Internet with our scriptural understanding of relationships.

The following websites have an enormous amount of information. I highly recommend searching more than one site to pick up the recurring themes. The usual secular justification for investing your time, emotions, and energy into networking and helping others is the beneficial results ascribed from the law of reciprocity, which basically states that eventually good things will be returned to you.

As Christians, however, we are commanded to love one another, and God desires obedience, not sacrifice. He will provide for us. Matthew 6:33 tells us, "But seek first His kingdom and His righteousness, and all these things will be added to you." While our motivations may differ from the secular world, the same law (the truths) applies to all of us. Just as gravity affects us all the same, regardless of our level of understanding of the physics behind the gravitational forces exerted upon objects relative to their mass and inversely to their distance from each other, likewise networking truths (relationship building by helping others) affect us all, despite our frame of reference.

Below are some excellent networking resources:

Keith Ferrazzi: http://www.ferrazzigreenlight.com/Keith
Business Networking International: http://www.bni.com/
South Bay Professional Association:
http://www.torrance.com/sbpa/
Fellowship of Companies for Christ International (FCCI):
http://www.fcci-online.org
Man in the Mirror: http://www.maninthemirror.org

Surfing through these sites will reinforce what you already know about building relationships and also will stimulate you to move to a higher level of involvement in relationship building. To further expand your knowledge, I recommend the following books. All of these are easy to read, and they will definitely get you thinking.

- *Never Eat Alone*, K. Ferrazzi
- *How to talk to anyone*, L. Lowndes
- *Masters of Networking*, I. Misner

Networking Resources

Social media sites such as LinkedIn and the numerous other professional network sites are very popular and offer a lot of opportunities for us to reach out to others. As is the case with most of these network sites, LinkedIn (basic account) is free, with options for expanded capabilities for super users like recruiters or business-to-business users. Facebook and MySpace are also very popular but tend to contain far too much personal information, thus making it difficult to control the brand you want others to find. These social sites can inadvertently reveal more personal information than you may want to reveal and far more than is required by law for you to voluntarily provide to current or prospective employers. If you have some very fun, and let's say even wild and crazy, friends on either Facebook or MySpace, remember information about those relationships becomes public and you now may be unknowingly branding yourself with a less desirable professional image.

Keep it professional, "On Brand and On Purpose." Once something is posted on an Internet site, there is no getting it back. Will Rogers once said, "Lettin' the cat outta the bag is a whole lot easier'n puttin' it back." Will's quote is certainly applicable today, especially when it comes to Internet postings. Populating your profile on LinkedIn to establish your career brand is a much safer and more controllable method of leveraging social networking for job search purposes.

JibberJobber was designed to help you organize and stay on top of your job-capture activities. Another helpful site is Warm Caller Center. Check it out. This allows you to warm up those sometimes necessary cold calls. More on job-searching techniques using social networking will be provided in later chapters.

Some quick links to get started:

- imonlinkedinnowwhat.com
- jibberjobber.com
- warmcallcenter.com

As with many things that are very good, too much of a good thing is not always good. Just as dysfunctional obsessions with physical exercise or weight loss can take a good and healthy practice to an unhealthy extreme, excessive time spent networking can result in a condition that is off balance with what God's overall plan is for your life. So set appropriate limits for your social media commitments, just as you would any other activity. As you find yourself engaging in more and more networking activities, consider making a "do-not-do" list. Everyone has lists of things to do, but as successful people become more successful, they learn to prioritize and purposefully not do certain things to maintain a balanced life.

Finally my encouragement to you is to be aware of the amount of time you are spending with social media. Assess the return on investment (your limited time versus benefits), and then manage it appropriately for your life situation. Consider scheduling time for social media like you would any other meeting or your lunch break, all of which have set time limits.

It may appear a little ironic that after writing pages about social medial and encouraging you to make use of it that I end with a caution to not overdo it and to keep your life in balance. Remember, social media is only an enabler for your networking and relationship building. Relationships remain what are important. Therefore, nurture those relationships with the people around you, and have margin in your schedule to be available to help others when they have needs.

Part III:

Career Development Planning

> The future is something which
> everyone reaches at the rate of sixty
> minutes an hour, whatever he does, whoever he is.
>
> —C. S. Lewis

Career development planning addresses the importance of assessing your personal strengths, passions, and weaknesses in light of achieving career success. Understanding and incorporating your unique design into to your career-development planning will allow you to leverage your strengths and passions while mitigating the impact of any weaknesses as you move forward. Planning is an ongoing iterative process that focuses your thinking and energy toward goals as you *Make Your Way*.

As you proceed along your path, you will gain more knowledge and insight for refining your plans. In this part of the book, we will discuss how to get started and the considerations for establishing near- and far-term planning objectives. The next chapter deals with discovering our unique design, which is foundational for career-development planning.

CHAPTER 7

Know Your Design

A recent inquiry on the very popular job board, Monster.com, resulted in 450 new jobs posted for that particular Saturday in the state of California. By changing the search criteria to include new job postings for the last two days in California, Monster.com indicated 2,045 jobs. Further expanding the search for the last three days produced over 5,000 new job postings! And Monster.com is only one of hundreds of job boards. The thought of searching through thousands of job requisitions can be daunting unless you have a plan to fine-tune your search.

Proper career planning will enable you to have a focused search as you work to match your skill set and your passions to specific opportunities. Career planning is a lifelong pursuit that takes into account many factors. The motivational series *Winning at Work and Home* by Robert Lewis presents a particularly revealing summary of the "employment energy" spent by age group. As we age, we are naturally motivated by different drivers.

For employees in their twenties, employment energy is primarily spent on just surviving. This age group typically dominates the entry-level positions. Such positions require these younger people to work hard just to maintain self-sufficiency. Nevertheless, making it on their own is their motivation; they want to be out from under their parents' roofs if at all possible.

When examining the thirty- to forty-year-old age group, we find they spend their employment energy toward achieving success. They are motivated toward getting firmly established in their industry and to accomplish as much as they can. Next the forty- to fifty-year-old age group is looking for significance. They are concerned with significance in their work and the impact their work has made on their field or society at large. They think more about what their legacy might be and less about salary. The final group, the fifty- to sixty-year-old age group, is interested in sustainability. This group is motivated to sustain themselves in their final vocation; they would even consider continuing to work in their craft without compensation.

Having an awareness of these career phases will help establish the longer-range career planning vectors, which in turn will fashion the planning details for accomplishing a meaningful vocational journey throughout life. The planning process is iterative and flows with internal and external drivers. Let us first consider one of those internal drivers: our design. Knowing the unique aspects of your design and understanding how to incorporate your strengths into career planning will ensure that you are on the right track for achieving success.

At the onset of the this assessment process, let me step on a few toes by dispelling a pervasive myth propagated by education professionals manifesting itself in some form of, "Graduating class of 2012, each one of you can now accomplish whatever you set your mind to. The world is yours … blah, blah, blah." Yes, education is very important for growth and expanding your career opportunities, but your unique design may be calling you for something quite different from what you set your mind to.

A quick case in point is the story of a successful engineer at the senior management level. He told me he had gotten into his particular engineering discipline of configuration management only after struggling to be a design engineer after graduating from college. His boss candidly explained to him during his annual appraisal that although he was very good at reviewing Interface Control Drawing (ICD) details and resolving anomalies within design packages, he showed little aptitude or creativity for actually designing anything on his own.

Ouch! This frank assessment was painful for this young, aspiring design engineer to hear at the time, but he later realized that it was a blessing to get such an honest assessment of his abilities early in his career. He was able to steer his career toward another engineering function—configuration management—where he had a much better fit that provided him daily job satisfaction and ultimately long-term career success.

Remember, he didn't gain that awareness at the university, since he never considered doing anything other than design engineering until he found himself struggling in the role of a design engineer. Also of note, his acceptance of such a discouraging appraisal truly demonstrated a high level of emotional intelligence on his part. He could have chosen to ignore the obvious and instead waste years of his career trying to develop a weakness area (designing) while neglecting opportunities to excel in his strength area. This "better fit" provided him years of rewarding work as he advanced in the configuration management discipline with a sense of fulfillment and accomplishment for doing excellent work. His story now starts off with, "I always wanted to be a hot-shot design engineer, but …"

The message is clear in Psalm 139:13–14: You are "fearfully and wonderfully made." God created you for a purpose. It is critical to discover your unique design and build on your strengths.

Interestingly, if you think of some very successful people, you probably are also aware of some weaknesses these successful people have had. Consider the talented Michael Jackson, the eloquent President Bill Clinton, the gifted Tiger Woods, the intelligent Albert Einstein, or the very entertaining Jay Leno. By reading their biographies (or the current tabloids), we realize they all have their weaknesses, but they became very successful by leveraging their strengths. Spending your time and energy trying to develop your weak areas at the expense of not exercising your strengths makes for a very dull, vanilla world—a world void of greatness and genius.

That is not to say that we can ignore a fatal weakness (those weaknesses that would either prevent or limit our success). An example of a fatal weakness that should not have been ignored might be that of a gifted chef who proceeds to open an upscale restaurant without the business training to manage the cash flow and ends up bankrupt after six months. Another might be the county treasurer who lacks the presentation skills to adequately convey to the elected county supervisors the convoluted financial risk within their proposed budget approach. The chef doesn't need to be a CPA nor does the treasurer need to be a motivational speaker, but each needs a minimal proficiency level in the areas required for the job. The chef who becomes restaurant owner has to understand at least the basics of running a business, and the treasurer has to be able to present the budget information to the decision makers in a coherent way.

Jay Leno happens to be dyslexic, but his "coding-decoding" skills only have to be good enough to interpret those well-placed cue cards as he magnificently works the audience into laughter as the host of *The Tonight Show*. Leno's show has consistently maintained its status as the number one rated late night show with Jay as the host. That is using your strengths for greatness while not letting your weakness be fatal.

Therefore, if *setting your mind to do* it and successfully accomplishing all the necessary prerequisites, education, and training for a position are not a guarantee for a good fit on the job, how do we discover where we will fit? Realistically for many, it is unlikely honest feedback will be given early in their careers. Our young design engineer is probably the exception rather than the norm. Actually, honest assessments are not as forthcoming today as they were in past generations. Today private and public organizations can easily get entangled in lawsuits and messy grievances for the mere perception of unfair or discriminatory employment practices. As a result, annual assessments tend to be less contentious and thus less meaningful and helpful to the employees who are hoping to understand their strengths and weaknesses.

After all, employers can take advantage of the dynamic job market with frequent downsizing and various types of "re-organizing for efficiencies" changes to let people go without all the effort spent (due process) of a formally documented HR department termination process, such as the dreaded Performance Improvement Plan (PIP). It sounds a bit cynical, but the truth is those employees who are contributing less to the organization are the first ones to get layoff notices. Not surprisingly, the layoff notices never include a final employee appraisal with recommendations for improvements for the next job. No, mum's the word when companies let employees go: "We're sorry, your services are no longer required. We wish you well. Thank you."

Fortunately, there are many excellent resources to help you attain an accurate assessment of your strengths. Incidentally, by enrolling in just one class at most community colleges, you will gain access to free vocational assessments and career counseling as a student. Nonetheless, to get us started straight away, I highly recommend the *Servants By Design Inventory* assessment. One very critical aspect of any assessment is the repeatability of the results. In the four years after I first took the *Servants By Design Inventory*, I had experienced life changes in many areas, including: the company I worked for, my job responsibilities, marital status, and my overall financial situation. Amazingly, when I retook the inventory for the second time, one might have concluded that I had wasted my money because the results were absolutely consistent with the previous test results; there were no significant changes whatsoever. Of course my investment of thirty-five dollars was well worth the peace of mind I received from having my *design* revalidated after experiencing so many life changes. The consistency of the test results transcends external conditions, which is a very important attribute for ensuring dependable self-assessment in the dynamic employment environment of today.

Furthermore, what is really beneficial is the clear presentation and understandability of the results. Although your individual report can be fourteen or fifteen pages in length, the depictions and categorizations are easily understood. I've taken other personality and vocational assessments during my career that often required a trained or certified facilitator for interpreting what the results mean and how they might be incorporated into your work environment. The value of self-assessment information derived from multifarious systems is often diminished shortly after the initial session of training. This is simply because it is too difficult for the layman to retain what was taught and to become proficient putting the knowledge into practice.

As an example, I have participated in several company-sponsored off-site events that included personality assessments, along with work-related scenario exercises for assessing one's personality type. This information then translates into recommended techniques to help you more effectively interact with the various categories of individuals at your work. Trying to remember exactly what it means for you to be categorized as an INTJ type for effectively interacting with someone you assessed as most probably a ENFP (or maybe a ESTP) is tough stuff. Yikes! Can I really process all those letter codes and still let the person know I need a report done by Tuesday? As fascinating as it was to spend a day out of the office participating in these exercises, the interest ended when the off-site event ended.

Fortunately, The *Servants by Design*© Inventory presents very useful assessment information without the level of complexity requiring an in-house interpreter. I have found the results to be easily applied to career-development planning. The excerpt below is a direct cut-and-paste of the introductory paragraphs of the report that was prepared for me. I've included it to spark your interest so you will initiate your own *Servants By Design* profile.

The *Servants by Design* inventory and profile report have been adapted, in part, from the Process Communication Model© developed by Dr. Taibi Kahler in the 1970s. Since its inception, this model, and adaptations of it, have been successfully used in industry, schools, correctional work, mentoring programs, clinical settings, marital seminars, vocational guidance, and even as part of the selection process for NASA astronauts. It was chosen by NASA because of its accuracy in assessing compatibility between members of a team and because of the model's unique ability to predict how people are likely to react under stress. Over the past three decades, tens of thousands of individuals around the globe have been introduced to the *Process Communications Model* and profited from the insights and self-awareness it has fostered.

Dr. Kahler's original work was translated by Dr. Robert S. Maris for Living Hope Press, L.L.C. into *Your Great Design,* an adaptation reflecting a biblical and Christian worldview. The *Servants by Design* Profile—Your *Unique Design Edition* is a special application of the original model along with additional materials developed by Dr. Robert Maris and Dr. Jerry Richardson. These tools were designed specifically, and have been used successfully for several years, to help individuals in churches discover, learn to appreciate, and develop their God-given gifts and find appropriate missions or works of service in which to utilize all that has been designed into them.

The *Servants by Design—Your Unique Design Edition* Profile report contains these ten key features:

Personality Structure – your unique six-floor condominium	**Abilities** – the specific activities that best fit your design
Personality Strengths – the core assets of your design	**Setting** – the environment which best supports your design
Viewpoint – the perspective from which you view life	**Relationships** – leadership and supervision preferences
Motivators – the needs and wants that energize you	**Life Tips** – for connecting to others and motivating yourself
Subject Matter – the resources you enjoy working with most	**Potential Pitfalls** – ways you may react negatively to stress

Taking this assessment and understanding your design relative to the ten key factors of this report is a tremendous help in guiding your search for your next position and for your long-term career development planning. I specifically remember one incident where this information *jumped out* to help me in making a career decision. My work setting was changing due to a re-organization that had some detrimental and unintended consequences, which in turn generated a very chaotic and frustrating work environment for me. By recognizing my preferred work setting as being, "best unleashes my gifting will be one that will include: clear job descriptions and goals, an efficient schedule, clearly defined roles and responsibilities, and an appreciation for your hard work and clear thinking …" I understood just how difficult it would be for me to effectively contribute to the success of the organization in this newly created, unstructured environment. My difficulty working in this environment would eventually have drained my energy and enthusiasm, along with any creativity toward my work. By understanding the situation relative to my strengths and limitations (in this case understanding more about my limitations than strengths), I realized I just didn't fit there anymore.

Although the job started out as a good fit, within the year, that good fit simply vanished overnight, due to external forces that were completely out of my control. Therefore, I intentionally began seeking opportunities outside that company to better match my preferred work environment. I began looking for an organizational construct that would be complementary to my design. To be intentional, I had to overcome my initial reluctance to leave the safety of the familiar (even though it shifted toward the worse) and move forward. Ironically, my concerns were validated when an organizational psychologist was brought in to reside on the premises to help improve the ensuing dysfunctional culture. I soon landed a much better job fit at another company. Paradoxically, the company I was hired by was interested in the exact skills I had just recently developed at the job I was leaving.

Knowing what you were designed for allows you to confidently make correct choices. In this case, the choice meant moving on to greener pastures with another company instead of getting mired down in a situation that wasn't suited to me and would have eventually limited my career growth. In contrast, one of my close coworkers stayed with the company and was able to accomplish his annual goals in that environment. Obviously his design was very different than mine. *Vive la différence!*

Incidentally, my friends I left behind at that company (which you should always stay in contact with as part of your networking) confirmed that the organizational psychologist was still sorting things out eighteen months later. By understanding this one key factor from my personal inventory, I was able to advance my career and avoid being trapped in a frustrating job situation. I would have spent a lot of my vocational energy just surviving at the expense of forfeiting opportunities for prospering.

As the old cliché goes, "If you wrestle with a pig you both get muddy, but the pig is happy to be muddy." Sometimes it is better to avoid the mess and just move on. Knowing your design will help you determine where you best fit. Incorporating your unique design information into your career-development plan will establish the solid foundation needed for courageously moving forward to pursue new opportunities. Planning gives you the confidence and freedom to make career choices that best allow you to multiply your *talents* over the long term.

On the other hand, an example of an employee not fully aware of his strengths and weaknesses occurred during a mid-year performance review I conducted with a management-level employee. He was requesting additional responsibilities in the business development arena. I was surprised and actually a little taken back because this employee hadn't showed any prior interest or aptitude (introverted personality) for external involvement with our customer base. I ascertained from the ensuing conversation that the motivation for this new vocational thrust was for career advancement and not driven from a deep passion or love for business development.

The employee went on to explain that the only way he knew to advance in the organization was by bringing in new business. Because of this misconception, he was willing to try something different to achieve that goal. After discussing all the business development role would require—attendance at many after-hour social functions, meeting and greeting company executives, cold calling customers, trade show participation, weekends dedicated to proposal writing, and on-call help for any other department needing proposal surge capability—we concluded there was probably a better opportunity for advancement elsewhere within the organization. This employee had good analytical-critical thinking skills for problem solving and was very detailed and thorough. Therefore, we focused on those strengths and how those skills could be leveraged for increased responsibilities and career advancement for this highly capable employee.

Having a good grasp of your areas of strength, passions, and weaknesses is essential for planning your long-term career path. Plan to maximize your energy and time spent toward your strengths and passions to maximize your opportunities for success. Conversely, plan to limit your energy and time spent toward developing weaknesses areas to minimize any limitations.

To help you further, many more of these useful assessment tools are included in books on career planning and are available online for free or a nominal cost. Specifically the *Make Your Way Design Profile* was developed as a special application by Dr. Maris and Dr. Jerry C. Richardson for *Make Your Way Resources* from *The Servants by Design* inventory and profile assessment. The *Make Your Way Design Profile* can be found at: www.ServantsByDesign.com (login required). The results of this profile will allow you to match your Data-People-Things (DPT) results with published US Department of Labor job codes. I would recommend trying one of the self-assessments now so you can incorporate what you discover into the materials in the upcoming chapters on job capture. You can also find various state Employment Development Department websites that offer assessment tests at no charge. A free *Skill Profiler* assessment provided by CareerOneStop can be found at: http://www.careerinfonet.org/skills/default.aspx?nodeid=20 which will create a list of your skills and match them to job types that use those skills. You might also try the State of California's Employment Development Department (EDD) website or the US Department of Labor's O*Net (www.onetonline.org) as a starting point.

Whichever tool or set of tools you try, the important thing is to understand your strengths, passions, and weaknesses so you are better equipped to successfully accomplish your ultimate career journey. Use the tools that are most helpful for you, and don't hesitate to collaborate with your friends. Ask them for their candid feedback as a confirmation of your self-assessment results. We all have blind spots, and drawing feedback from trusted others will enhance your understanding of yourself. Once you've determined your strengths, passions, and weaknesses, you can effectively plan and begin the job searching strategies outlined in the upcoming chapters.

CHAPTER 8

Career Development Planning

Your career development plan—what exactly is it?

Career development planning is an iterative process of establishing goals for your long-term career vision. These goals form an overall plan that provides the framework for making intentional choices for achieving that vision. Your vocational vision is based on your unique design and your passions. Measureable milestones are established for each goal to help you evaluate your progress and focus your energy. "The mind of man plans his way, but the Lord directs his steps" (Prov. 16:9). The iterative nature of planning allows for God to direct your steps. Life is a journey, and every journey has a destination. Your vocation path is a part of that journey with a destination. Even though we may not know every step of that journey beforehand, we seek the Lord's direction as we plan our way. "For we are His workmanship, created in Christ Jesus for good works, which God prepared beforehand so that we would walk in them" (Eph. 2:10).

The book of Nehemiah tells us that Nehemiah, as an exile, had never actually been to Jerusalem. Yet upon hearing about the distress among the remnant in Jerusalem and the shambles the city walls and gates were in, Nehemiah wept, mourned, fasted, and prayed before the God of heaven. His passion for helping his people led him to prayer, and that prayer led him to a plan. After four months had passed, Nehemiah presented his plan to the king. As King Artaxerxes's cupbearer, Nehemiah had a very trusted relationship with the king. Even so, Nehemiah's decision to make such a request of the king was a huge risk. The Bible says that Nehemiah, "being very much afraid," asked the king to:

1) send him to Judah to rebuild the city of his fathers;
2) write letters for safe passage;
3) and authorize the keeper of the forest to provide him timber.

King Artaxerxes granted these requests and sent Nehemiah with officers of the army and horsemen (Neh. 1:1–2:10). Nehemiah was passionate about repairing the wall and the gates of Jerusalem. He prayed and fasted, made a plan to repair Jerusalem's walls, and was granted favor to accomplish this plan.

As you read on in the book of Nehemiah, you will find there was a struggle. We read, "But when Sanballat the Horonite and Tobiah the Ammonite official, and Geshem the Arab heard it, they mocked us and despised us …" (Neh. 2:19). But despite the mocking and threats, Nehemiah pressed on and completed his mission of rebuilding the wall around Jerusalem. He found a way to accomplish his passion despite opposition. With prayer we seek God's direction for our plans, God grants us favor, and change comes through our faithfulness and hard work. This is a wonderful picture of how we *Make Our Way* vocationally.

The best way to lay out a plan is with the end in mind. How do you want to finish? I once had the privilege of visiting England, and I remember seeing gravestone markers inside the old church buildings. I could not help to wonder how the presiding archbishops' perspectives must have been influenced by the constant reminder of those buried saints just under the floor stones, knowing that someday their own bones would be joining the others in that row. They must have contemplated how they would be regarded by their successors. As I looked at the dates and the span of years of these buried saints, it was evident that they all had lived and served a relatively short period of time in comparison to the history of the church building.

Today in our fast-paced society, graveyards and tombstones are often tucked away, out of sight and out of mind. We tend to think only of the here and now. Instead I ask you to consider for

Career Development Planning

a moment what you would like to accomplish in the end. What would you like others to say that you accomplished? Was it important? What relationships did you have? How did you help others? How did you finish? As uncomfortable as those questions may be, consider this admonishment: "Behold, I am coming quickly, and My reward is with Me, to render to every man according to what he has done" (Rev. 22:12). Remember, it is important to finish well; therefore take courage and plan how you can successfully reach your final destination.

As we begin to put together the plan, the steps, specific dates, and times aren't as important as determining the sequence of major milestones. Combining what you have learned about your unique design with the vast array of other career resource information, such as your state government's Employment Development Department's (EDD) Labor Market Information (LMI) (which we will look at in detail in the next part), will allow you to leverage your strengths and passions toward planning for your long-term career success.

Regardless of whether your career plan is rigorously entered in a planning tool like Microsoft Project or scratched out on tablet paper, any plan that is going to be effective must be written down. As you continue to learn about your career field, your plan will evolve with more details. The short-term milestones will become more finite and well defined, while the longer-term specifics will remain a bit fuzzy, with some unknowns (and realistically, some unknown unknowns). But that is okay; it is a plan. And plans will inevitably change as new information becomes available. The benefit of the plan is that you will now have direction and a yardstick to measure your progress. The plan will keep you career choices intentional, thus avoiding the dreaded and pernicious *uninspired drift* that robs us of our God-given potential.

As a reminder, let's reflect on our opening quote by C. S. Lewis: "The future is something which everyone reaches at the rate of sixty minutes an hour, whatever he does, whoever he is." There-

MAKE YOUR WAY

fore, let's be intentional with the sixty minutes of each hour that we will spend on our vocation.

Remember as with any journey, start your plan with a destination in mind. Ask yourself, "How do I want to end my vocational journey"? Then work backward from your desired end state to the next logical position and so forth until you arrive at where you are today. For each *desired position* consider what *milestones* would need to be met. This initial sequence of desired positions and associated milestones establishes the long range steering vector for our vocational planning.

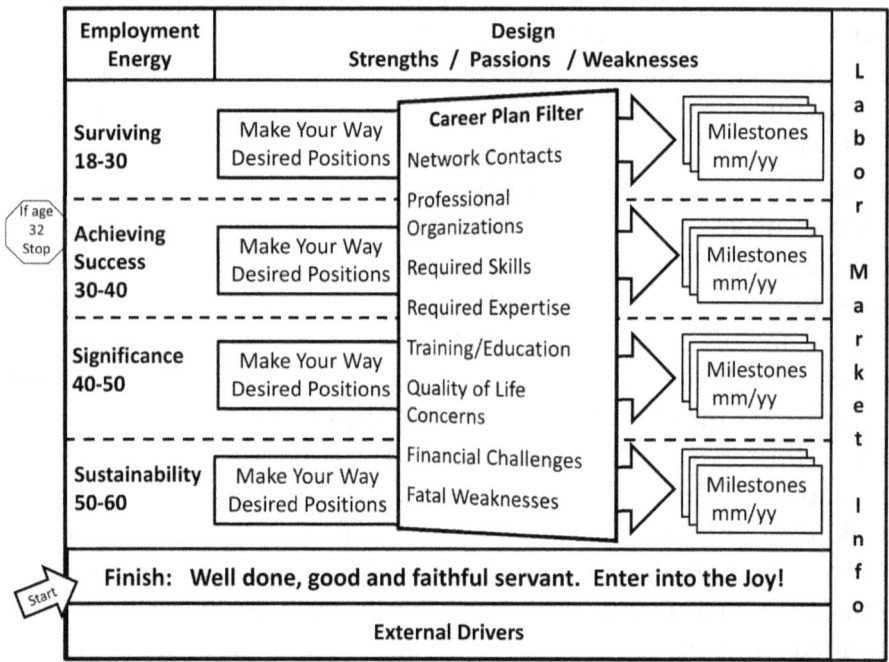

Process for Establishing Career Milestones

There is a conventional technique used for project planning called the *rolling wave*. This technique emphasizes detail planning for the near-term events and less-defined planning in the out years.

Career Development PLANNING

You can apply this method to your career plan by establishing the initial five-year portion of your plan with detailed steps and time spans while at the same time planning with less scheduling rigor beyond the initial five-year period. As each year passes, *roll* the details for the next fifth-year into the plan. Think of the detailed five-year portion as consisting of shorter planning steps that can be seen as inch stones while the remaining out-years of your plan will involve longer-term milestones.

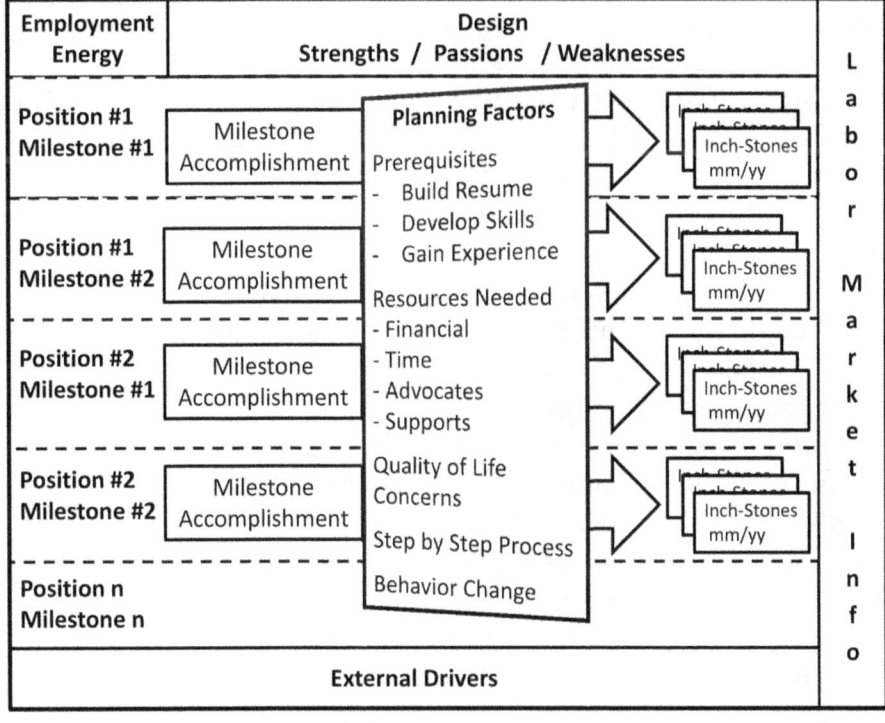

From Career Milestones to Inch-stones

The beauty of having a career plan is that you can track and measure your progress while focusing on solutions to accomplish the remaining milestones. Much more will be addressed about harnessing the power of your creative mind to complete your plan in the last part of this book.

What are some of the considerations for deriving the details of an effective career plan? This is your plan, so it must be developed with you in mind. That means your plan should include all of your nonvocational interests as well. Quality of life considerations probably drive the scheduling of the milestones more than any other factor. Your plan simply will not be realistic without quality of life considerations embedded within your milestones and inch stones.

There must be a clear balance between vocational commitments and quality of life choices (e.g., marriage, child-raising, financial obligations, medical or physical limitations, retirement plans, etc.). Therefore evaluate how well your career plan synchronizes with your quality of life issues. Do these complement each other or compete against each other? Would the cost of completing an additional degree place you in a negative financial position that could restrict your long-term success options? (By the way, student debt has become a real problem for many people.) Carefully weigh the advantages of potential salary increases or additional career opportunities before incurring a large family debt from additional training.

Another of the many quality of life issues worth considering is your commuting time or time away from home on travel. Your family won't wait for you forever. Holiday seasons zip by, kids grow up, and missed vacations can never be brought back. By having a plan, you bring awareness to how you are spending your time, energy, and resources. Seeking the correct balance and planning to maintain that balance is essential to your long-term success. As the cliché goes, "Failure to plan is a plan for failure."

These are just some of the considerations that must be incorporated into your planning.

The LMI (as the next chapter will examine in greater detail) provides a generous amount of information to help you start putting the details of your plan together. You can begin to include the what that you will need to achieve your goals, such as additional training, certificates, experience, and skills as you *Make Your Way* toward your goals. Then determine how to achieve those steps by evaluating all the options available. As an example, if you need additional education, the how might be: after-hours classes sponsored by your company, community college courses, professional organization–sponsored conferences, enrolling in a correspondence-style MBA program, or online training for a specific knowledge area. Which of these options works best for you must be assessed in the context of the work-life balance for your current season of life and circumstances.

In addition to training, seriously consider doing volunteer work. Volunteer work can often provide a shortcut for accomplishing your goals. My daughter volunteered to work preparing food in a high-end restaurant two days a week. After only three weeks of volunteering, there was an opening. She was then provided with training for a planned trial opportunity on the dinner shift. She passed and became a full-time employee. She definitely had a passion for cooking and probably learned a great deal from the many hours she dedicated to watching food shows on TV. However, she did not have any chef (or cooking) work experience, and she had never attended a culinary school. Through volunteering, however, she quickly became a pantry chef at a prestigious, nationally recognized restaurant in Santa Monica!

Volunteering can also give you a chance to gain multiple years of experience while only working on a part-time basis. For example, volunteering to be a committee chairperson for a two-year term at a nonprofit organization may only require a few hours of your time each month, but your resume can truthfully state that you have two years of management experience (e.g., from 2010 to 2012).

While we are on the subject of volunteer work, let me just say that volunteering provides excellent training in people skills. Working with other volunteers can be more challenging than working with employees or coworkers. After all, you usually can't reward them monetarily (with bonuses or pay increases), and neither can you fire them; they volunteered. You work with what you are given. You must totally rely on your leadership skills to motivate other volunteers to help accomplish the tasks at hand. The volunteers you are working with will have their own interests and reasons for participating; you have to unite everyone around common objectives that will provide the intrinsic value for their continued service. Furthermore, as Professor Morris Okun discovered through his research at Arizona State University, there very well may be health benefits from volunteering. It is a good practice to carefully consider how you might be able to volunteer as part of your career plan.

Yet, any plan is only as good as the information you plan with. This is where your network really pays off. First, identify three to five contacts that are absolutely essential to help you achieve your career plans. If you are not already connected, begin to connect with them now. If you are not sure how to get connected with those key people, add the task of finding a way to get connected as part of your career planning. Next, determine three to five companies that you favor as possible employers someday. Then add three contacts for each of those companies as part of the detailed rolling wave portion for your near-term planning. Use your network as an enabler for the accomplishment your career goals.

Think of your career development plan as an overarching integrated plan, with sub-plans for networking, education and training, financial objectives, skills development, quality of life issues, etc. All the sub-plans should be interrelated and need to be in sync by flowing up into an overall master plan. Developing your plan will compel you to slow down and think through exactly what you would like to achieve and how to proceed. Taking ownership of your career by developing and executing your plan will empower you to serve as the CEO of *YourName*, Inc.

The effort that you need to put into the plan doesn't end with the career plan. What you will discover about yourself through career planning will be reused, repackaged, and incorporated into many areas of your life:

- Vocationally for serving as the blueprint for building a resume for the future and for equipping you to effectively respond to those tough interview questions.
- Socially for networking and building trusted relationships.
- Personally for intentionally becoming better as a spouse, parent, manager, and well ... any relationship.

Romans 8:28 is a familiar passage that is often truncated as, "And we know that God causes all things to work together for good," but we should not forget the rest of the passage: "to those who are called according to His purpose." Constantly seek God's direction for your plans as you *Make Your Way*. We read the words of Jesus in the Gospel of John, "I am the vine, you are the branches; he who abides in Me and I in him, bears much fruit, for apart from Me you can do nothing" (John 15:5). Stay connected to the vine.

Slowing down long enough for a time of honest self-reflection, while seeking God's purpose for your life, brings a peace that is often forfeited by reacting to the expectations of an overly busy, highly caffeinated society where having 4G connectivity to coworkers, bosses, family, and friends twenty-four/seven is expected. Resist the temptation of allowing yourself to be constantly distracted. Purposefully disconnect yourself, turn off your phones, avoid the Internet, find a quiet place, and then take a deep breath; relax and enjoy the silence. This is going to be your plan, and it is going to be very good.

In summary, combining your *network advantage*, unique design, life passions, and labor market information into a career development plan that incorporates your individual quality of life considerations is a powerful instrument for you as the CEO of *YourName*, Inc.

Notes:

See Appendix A *for a specific example of career planning with milestone and inch-stone tracking.*

Make Your Way—myPlanner

Provides your personal online working environment for career planning complete with book summaries and step-by-step instructions for developing, assessing, editing, and storing your: design strengths and passions; desired positions; career milestones; network contacts; and much more. It also includes up-to-date recommendations and links to additional tools to help you with your career planning and goal achievement. Visit www.MakeYourWayResources.com for a free trial membership.

Part IV

Job-Capture Coaching

Part IV brings us to job capture, the boot camp for how to identify that good-fitting job based on your unique design and how to take the necessary steps to successfully attain an employment contract. We've already learned quite a bit about how to build a personal network consisting of long-term relationships. Networking will open the doors in the job-capture phases of your career plan.

Before we start the job capture discussion, a word of caution and encouragement is in order. Reaching out to the possibilities that are awaiting you will require some hard work and unfortunately some disappointments along the way. Despite the occasional setbacks, which are inevitable anytime you stretch yourself, being intentional about your career development is a very worthwhile and rewarding endeavor in the long term.

I remember a surprisingly upbeat statement from a friend of mine who had had a string of employment interviews and subsequent rejections. He said, "You know, getting a job is really a lot of fun. You learn a lot about yourself." And it is fun because it is so exciting! Being intentional with your God-given talents and taking control of your vocation is a real adrenalin rush. But stepping out is not for the faint of heart; it takes courage. Your Return On Investment (ROI) for taking control of your career is very high, meaning the time and emotional energy you put into it will result in enormous long-term dividends—for you! I will promise you this: taking control of your career development by seeking God's purpose for your life will definitely be an adventure full of excitement, many new opportunities, and some good challenges as you *Make Your Way*.

CHAPTER 9

Effective Job Searching

An effective job search incorporates both your *networking advantage* and an understanding of your personal strengths and passions as you focus your efforts toward that good *fit*. The fit has to be good but not necessarily perfect. Working in a position that requires a skill set aligned with your current abilities while providing opportunities for personal growth will keep you motivated and energized for success. That is a good fit. Keep in mind the enthusiasm and motivation that a good fit provides at the time of hire may very well wane as your competency increases and your skills broaden over time. As we discussed earlier, external forces can also generate changes that affect your fit within the organization or the industry at large.

Career planning involves the ongoing effort to recognize, assess, and initiate the steps toward the next better fit for your career growth. Since you are always growing and the market is always changing, keep vigilant and be ready to seize the moment toward the next better fit when it presents itself. Avoid the trap of passively waiting for that elusive perfect fit at the expense of allowing good growth opportunities to pass you by. This chapter will explore how to effectively search for and find opportunities that are a good fit for your career.

Recently my wife, Jeanie, and I went on a vacation back east to visit family and friends, with a side trip to New York City to celebrate my birthday. I refer to this vacation as our *trip on the fly* since we used our iPhone apps to get us where we were going in lieu of preplanning or even making reservations ahead of time.

One particularly useful app was AroundMe. We could easily review a list of nearby coffee bars, restaurants, theaters, stores, etc., all in the palm of our hands. The GPS-aided map feature provided walking, driving, or bus routes to wherever we wanted to go, along with a 360-degree panoramic video clip for a visual preview of the destination locations. The amount of information available today—literally at our fingertips—is remarkably helpful. The question then is, "Where do I find the equivalent smartphone app for locating that good job fit?" You know—an app that would conveniently point me to the current open positions with the salary, work environment, and growth opportunities that I am seeking. Or is there an Internet job board that I can spam with my resume and then screen calls from a flood of excited recruiters wanting to set up interviews with me?

Unfortunately, the answer to those questions is that there isn't an app or job board that can do the work for you. It will take some hard work on your part despite available employment data and the many tools that can help you today. To get a perspective on the sheer volume of resumes floating around in cyberspace, Northrop Grumman's Information Technology (NGIT) Sector, reported recently that it received over 720,000 resumes for 3,600 jobs in one year. That equates to over 200 resumes per position advertised. Therefore, simply submitting your resume to many companies or posting your resume on numerous job boards is statistically a long shot. Furthermore, as you can surmise, relying on the odds can become very discouraging for the job seeker. Typically most submittals only receive an electronic acknowledgment of receipt, without the candidate ever hearing from a real, live person who is associated with the company.

Let's take a look at how we can better focus our search efforts to achieve the results we want. Most states have websites for employment development, with tons of useful data waiting to be extracted. These public organizations are big business, with big budgets and huge resource pools that can provide helpful employment information to you. It is interesting to note that the amount of tax revenue collected by the California Employment Development Department (EDD) is approximately $5 billion annually, which, as a government agency, is second only to the Federal Internal Revenue Service (IRS). The California EDD's annual tax revenue funds five units: 1) Disability Insurance; 2) Unemployment Insurance; 3) Employment Tax (collections); 4) Labor Market Information (LMI); and 5) Work Force Services. The latter two are important to job seekers for drawing out relevant career information available online.

In addition, the US Labor Department's information is incorporated and links are available directly to the Occupational Network O*Net: http://onetonline.org. We definitely should be tapping into these public resources to help us with our career planning. Other states have similar resources available to their citizens; however, you do not have to be a California resident to access the California site. Therefore, for brevity's sake, let's limit our discussion to just the California website resources located at: http://www.caljobs.ca.gov/.

We'll start with a top-level, forty thousand–foot view of the California site, including the O*Net data, which will provide you with an appreciation of the type of information that is available and how to apply these resources to your job search. Your individual state website can then be accessed to provide the particulars for your local area, such as: nearby employers that hire for a specific skill, contact information of local businesses, local networking organizations, etc.

The following section will provide a step-by-step overview of the California EDD LMI. Each state's employment department functions independently from other states, so adapt your data mining as appropriate for your preferred work location.

Starting at the CalJobs site, http://www.caljobs.ca.gov/, observe the links along the left side of the page. Notice that you do not have to log in to the site for access to this information. Under the "How To" tab, find a link entitled "Labor Market Information" (LMI). As mentioned, LMI is one of the five funded sections of California's EDD, staffed to provide information for job seekers. Select "Labor Market Information" once there you will find a "Featured LMI Publications" box, select "California Occupational

Guides"; from there select "Keyword Search." For demonstration purposes, enter "Property Manager," which will bring up "Property and Community Association Manager"—close enough. After selecting "Los Angeles County" and "View the Guide"—voila! The information is organized into these six relevant questions:

1. What would I do?
2. Will this job fit me?
3. What wages and benefits can I expect?
4. What is the job outlook?
5. How do I qualify?
6. Finding a job (in this occupation)

By quickly reviewing this kind of information, we can see how a person's skills and strengths (unique design) could easily be compared and matched to those identified by the occupational guide for any specific career field of interest. Since our example is for a property manager, most of us will want to merely skim the categories. The important takeaway from this property manager example is the depth and breadth of practical career planning information that is available with just a few mouse clicks. The excerpt below is taken directly from the website (including link references).

> Property, Real Estate, and Community Association Managers in Los Angeles County
>
> **May also be called:** Apartment Managers; Community Managers; Condominium Managers; Landlords; Leasing Managers; Mobile Home Park Managers; and On-Site Managers

What Would I Do?
Property and Real Estate Managers oversee the performance of income-producing commercial or residential properties and

ensure that real estate investments achieve their expected revenues. Community Association Managers manage the common property and services of condominiums, cooperatives, and planned communities through their homeowners' or community associations.

Property, Real Estate, and Community Association Managers typically work in offices that are comfortable and well lit. Their schedules are usually flexible; however, many work long hours during the week, often working evenings or weekends, and may spend a great deal of time away from their desks.

Will This Job Fit Me?

The job of Property, Real Estate, and Community Association Manager will appeal to those who like activities that have to do with starting up and carrying out projects, persuading and leading people, making decisions, and taking risks for profit.

What Wages and Benefits Can I Expect?

The median wage in 2010 for Property and Community Association Managers in California is $49,691 annually, or $23.89 hourly. The median wage for Property and Community Association Managers in Los Angeles County is $45,020 annually, or $21.65 hourly. The median is the point at which half of the workers earn more and half earn less.

Change to Hourly Wages

Annual Wages for 2010	Low (25th percentile)	Median (50th percentile)	High (75th percentile)
California	$30,619	$49,691	$74,818
Los Angeles County	$24,216	$45,020	$68,662

Source: EDD/LMID Occupational Employment Statistics Survey, 2010 Wages do not reflect self-employment.

View Wages for All Areas

Change to Annual Wages

Hourly Wages for 2010	Low (25th percentile)	Median (50th percentile)	High (75th percentile)
California	$14.72	$23.89	$35.97
Los Angeles County	$11.65	$21.65	$33.01

Source: EDD/LMID Occupational Employment Statistics Survey, 2010. Wages do not reflect self-employment.

View Wages for All Areas

Most employers provide vacation, sick leave, and medical insurance. Some provide dental and life insurance, and a few also offer retirement plans and vision insurance. Property and Community Association Managers may receive a rent-reduced or rent-free apartment and a utility allowance as part of their compensation package. Those who are self-employed must provide their own insurance and retirement.

What is the Job Outlook?

Employment opportunities for Property and Community Association Managers fluctuate from year-to-year because the strength of the economy affects their demand. Growth of an older population will increase the need for specialized housing, such as assisted-living facilities and retirement communities, which requires property management.

In California, the number of Property and Community Association Managers is expected to grow slower than average growth rate for all occupations. Jobs for Property and Community Association Managers are expected to increase by 0.5 percent, or 300 jobs between 2008 and 2018.

In Los Angeles County, the number of Property and Community Association Managers is expected to decline between 2008 and 2018.

Estimated Employment and Projected Growth
Property and Community Association Managers

Geographic Area (Estimated Year-Projected Year)	Estimated Employment	Projected Employment	Numeric Change	Percent Change	Additional Openings Due to Net Replacements
California (2008-2018)	56,900	57,200	300	0.5	9,800
Los Angeles County (2008-2018)	17,230	17,190	-40	-0.2	2,970

Source: EDD/LMID <u>Projections of Employment by Occupation</u>

<u>View Projected Growth for All Areas</u>

How Do I Qualify?

The job of Property, Real Estate, and Community Association Manager generally requires a bachelor's degree in business administration, accounting, finance, real estate, public administration, or a related field. Previous work-related skills, knowledge, or experience is also preferred by employers.

Finding a Job

Prospective Property and Community Association Managers may apply directly to property management firms or condominium homeowner associations. They should also check newspaper classified ads and the Internet for current job listings. Job referrals may also be found through the California Apartment Association. **Online job opening systems** include JobCentral at <u>www.jobcentral.com</u> and CalJOBS^{SM} at <u>www.caljobs.ca.gov</u>.

To find your nearest One-Stop Career Center, go to <u>Service Locator</u>. View the <u>helpful job search tips</u> for more resources. (requires <u>Adobe Reader</u>).

<u>Learn More About Property and Community Association Managers</u>

But let's not stop with just this top-level information from the occupational guide. Going back to the LMI page, select "Occupations" under the header "LMI by Subject" once there locate the "Occupational Profile," tab and perform another search by entering the same "Property Manager" position, still in "Los Angeles County." This provides us with a profile for this occupation including the following additional topics:

1. Industries employing this occupation with links
2. Training program links
3. About this Occupation
4. Top Skills used in this Job
5. Top Abilities
6. Top Work Values
7. Top Interest
8. Related Links

Again, we only need to quickly review these topics for an appreciation of the kind of information readily available for any desired occupation. Unless, of course, you were pursuing a property manager position; then takes notes, my friend, because all of this career information will be directly applicable to your career planning, job search, resume building, interviewing, negotiating, and network management.

Effective Job Searching

Industries Employing This Occupation
(click on Industry Title to View Employers List)

Industry Title	Number of Employers in Los Angeles County	Percent of Total Employment for Occupation in State of California
Activities Related to Real Estate	1,245	25.3%
Lessors of Real Estate	5,117	12.9%
Offices of Real Estate Agents & Brokers	11,165	4.3%
Professional and Similar Organizations	1,781	2.1%
Land Subdivision	797	1.9%
Management of Companies and Enterprises	189	1.2%
Office Administrative Services	460	1.0%
Residential Building Construction	2,450	1.0%

About Staffing Patterns

Training Programs (click on title for more information)

Program Title
Business Administration and Management, General
Health/Health Care Administration/Management
Logistics, Materials, and Supply Chain Management.
Office Management and Supervision
Public Administration

About Training & Apprenticeships

MAKE YOUR WAY

About This Occupation (from O*NET – The Occupation Information Network)

Top Tasks (Specific duties and responsibilities of this job.)

Meet with prospective tenants to show properties, explain terms of occupancy, and provide information about local areas.

Direct collection of monthly assessments, rental fees, and deposits and payment of insurance premiums, mortgage, taxes, and incurred operating expenses.

Inspect grounds, facilities, and equipment routinely to determine necessity of repairs or maintenance.

Investigate complaints, disturbances, and violations, and resolve problems following management rules and regulations.

Manage and oversee operations, maintenance, administration, and improvement of commercial, industrial, or residential properties.

Plan, schedule, and coordinate general maintenance, major repairs, and remodeling or construction projects for commercial or residential properties.

Maintain records of sales, rental or usage activity, special permits issued, maintenance and operating costs, or property availability.

Negotiate the sale, lease, or development of property and complete or review appropriate documents and forms.

Determine and certify the eligibility of prospective tenants, following government regulations.

Prepare detailed budgets and financial reports for properties.

More Tasks for Property, Real Estate, and Community Association Managers

Top Skills used in this Job

Speaking – Talking to others to convey information effectively.

Active Listening – Giving full attention to what other people are saying, taking time to understand the points being made, asking questions as appropriate, and not interrupting at inappropriate times.

Negotiation – Bringing others together and trying to reconcile differences.

Reading Comprehension – Understanding written sentences and paragraphs in work related documents.

Coordination – Adjusting actions in relation to others' actions.

Critical Thinking – Using logic and reasoning to identify the strengths and weaknesses of alternative solutions, conclusions, or approaches to problems.

Writing – Communicating effectively in writing as appropriate for the needs of the audience.

Social Perceptiveness – Being aware of others' reactions and understanding why they react as they do.

Monitoring – Monitoring/Assessing performance of yourself, other individuals, or organizations to make improvements or take corrective action.

Persuasion – Persuading others to change their minds or behavior.

More Skills for Property, Real Estate, and Community Association Managers

Top Abilities
(Attributes of the person that influence performance in this job.)

Oral Comprehension – The ability to listen to and understand information and ideas presented through spoken words and sentences.

Oral Expression – The ability to communicate information and ideas in speaking so others will understand.

Written Expression – The ability to communicate information and ideas in writing so others will understand.

Written Comprehension – The ability to read and understand information and ideas presented in writing.

More Abilities for Property, Real Estate, and Community Association Managers

Top Work Values (Aspects of this job that create satisfaction.)

Independence – Occupations that satisfy this work value allow employees to work on their own and make decisions.

Achievement – Occupations that satisfy this work value are results oriented and allow employees to use their strongest abilities, giving them a feeling of accomplishment.

More Work Values for Property, Real Estate, and Community Association Managers

Top Interests
(The types of activities someone in this job would like.)

Enterprising – Enterprising occupations frequently involve starting up and carrying out projects. These occupations can involve leading people and making many decisions. Sometimes they require risk taking and often deal with business.

Conventional – Conventional occupations frequently involve following set procedures and routines. These occupations can include working with data and details more than with ideas. Usually there is a clear line of authority to follow.

More Interests for Property, Real Estate, and Community Association Managers

Alternate Titles

Apartment Managers; Community Managers; Condominium Managers; Landlords; Leasing Managers; Mobile Home Park Managers; and On-Site Managers.

Related Links

Career Information

Local Area Profile

Compare Occupations

View Similar Occupations

O*Net – The Occupation Information Network

You may have noticed the numerous links permitting you to drill down to more specific information. Let's explore just one for instructional purposes. Within the first topic, "Industries Employing This Occupation," select the industry listed on top which is entitled "Activities Related to Real Estate." Selecting this brings up information on sixty companies in Los Angeles County, with one of the employer's details shown as an example below:

Employer Name:	**324 STATE STREET PARTNERS LLC**
Business Description:	REAL ESTATE BUYERS & BROKERS
Employer Address:	1448 15TH ST # 100 SANTA MONICA, CA 90404-2756 <u>Map This Address</u>
Mailing Address:	N/A
Contact:	CHERYL MACARTHUR, MANAGER
Telephone:	310-458-9800
Website:	Not Listed
Employer Size Class:	1-4 Employees
Industry Description:	Residential Property Managers (NAICS code: 531311)

Now we have a plethora of information available to us about any occupation we desire to investigate for our career planning. Also provided is industry-relevant business contact information, even for a company category as small as one to four employees. Amazingly, all this information is available with just a few minutes of research. This is an exceptionally effective method of mining data for any occupation you may choose to examine. My intent is to spark your interest by starting with the California EDD site, which I happen to be most familiar with. This is only the starting point. There are many other equally effective resources. A couple more for your perusal should include directly accessing O*NET online at http://online.onetcenter.org/find/ and the US Department of Labor's Occupational Outlook Handbook (OOH) at http://www.bls.gov/oco/.

We will return to these resource sites as we build our resumes, prepare for interviews, equip ourselves for salary negotiations, and further refine our career plan. As you click away, you will discover even more tools, guides, related links, and helps for your career planning.

Before we leave the O*Net data, select between seven to ten of the top tasks, top skills, top abilities, top work values, or top interests from occupations that coincide with your strengths and passions. These are your attributes that will be used as the foundation blocks in the resume-building section coming up next.

Make Your Way—myPlanner

Due to the dynamic nature of the various referenced websites throughout this book, we have developed another *Make Your Way* resource which will ensure you have convenient direct access to our updated resources and online tools. Appropriately called *myPlanner*, provides your personal online working environment for career planning complete with book summaries and step-by-step instructions for developing, assessing, editing, and storing your: design strengths and passions; desired positions; career milestones; network contacts; and much more.

The *Make Your Way—myPlanner* is the perfect complement to *Make Your Way—the Book* because it will keep you updated with new developments and provide direct access to the latest tools at the click of your finger. Visit www.MakeYourWayResources.com for a free trial membership.

CHAPTER 10

Build Your Resume

Although much has been written on to how to write a good resume, the emphasis of this book will be on how to build a great resume. What is the difference? The term *build* implies starting from the ground up, with a solid foundation of capability statements, and then building on top of them.

Speaking of solid foundations, I remember years ago vicariously experiencing the excitement of one of my young sons while he visited a nearby construction site. The sounds of the heavy equipment pushing around massive mounds of earth and the pouring of concrete into the wooden frames were very captivating for him. What I found fascinating was how very deep the foundational structure was and how the initial framing and protruding rebar (reinforcing bar) from cement posts didn't appear to be forming anything resembling the end design. Somehow all the foundational groundwork would prop up what the artist's sketch depicted as a finished parking structure. A good deal of time and effort was invested in laying that solid foundation before there was any inkling of what the finished structure above would be.

Similarly, the solid foundational building blocks of your resume will allow you to build and adapt your resume in a way that meets any number of specific requirements for future employment opportunities. The building blocks will demonstrate your capabilities for future roles and responsibilities. Many resumes I have reviewed have not been capabilities based but just a historical record of past employment responsibilities. Often they are void of any noteworthy accomplishments. The hiring manager is then forced to *connect the dots* between the listed employment history and the candidate's actual capability to successfully perform in a new role. Our objective is to connect the dots for the hiring manager and show relevant capabilities for success in the next position being sought. If we have the capability to manage a complex software project for the airline industry, then we can manage a complex system for the trucking industry. By developing capabilities-based statements, we open doors to many more opportunities.

As a preview of the next chapter, this upfront capabilities-based resume work will also serve as the underpinnings for equipping you to confidently answer the most challenging of interview questions. Therefore developing capability-based statements will be time well spent!

Returning to the resume, the very notion of *building* your resume also implies *intentionality* about your work, training, time investments, and desired accomplishments. Essentially, *building your resume* forces you to expand your expertise and experience for future career opportunities. If your goal is to become a math teacher within the community college system, you will need to be aware of and plan to accomplish those specific requirements for that teaching position. The community college requirements may be quite different from those of a private four-year college.

If you aspire to reach the director-level of management in your engineering firm within the next five years, you will need to determine (among other things) if there is a minimum number of management years required for that position. If so, will your experience leading a small technical group suffice, or should you seek another broader management position to enhance your qualifications? Or would serving in a management role for a professional organization (volunteering) help you qualify more quickly? By anticipating what emphases a compelling resume should have, you can begin to complete the steps toward that end. We will discuss *goal getting* later in part V. Suffice it to say that having control over your career-development path necessitates having control over your resume experiences. Therefore, plan to build your resume with capability-based accomplishments that will open future positions along your desired career path.

Place yourself in the hiring manager's shoes. Consider what you would want an employee to be capable of. What important skills are needed? What training is required? How much experience is needed? You can probably think of some more requirements for your particular field. The *how* you will build your capabilities to address these types of questions is what you will need to incorporate into your career-development plan. Build your capabilities now in anticipation for future positions. "Do you see a man skilled in his work? He will stand before kings; he will not stand before obscure men" (Prov. 22:29).

We build our resumes for one purpose: to get an interview. That sounds obvious enough, but job seekers can lose sight of this fact as they attempt to jam every bit of work experience into one omnibus resume. All that data won't get you an interview; the hiring manager needs information. Compelling, relevant information about your capabilities will get you an interview. Today's social media websites give us the freedom to post as much about ourselves as we want to, with absolutely no expectation that anyone will actually read any of it. That "take it or leave it" posting approach is fine for Facebook or MySpace, but it is totally inadequate for something as important as your resume. You want your potential employer to be drawn to read your resume and to find your capabilities and skills so relevant to their needs that you get an interview.

To get started, we first must ensure that all of the minimum requirements listed in the job requisition are addressed in a concise and clear manner. All of the minimum requirements have to be met just to get past the *gatekeeper*—a.k.a., the Human Resources (HR) recruiter or an outsourced recruiter firm assigned by the HR department to screen the multitude of incoming resumes.

After the recruiter confirms that the minimum standards have been met, the resumes are typically prioritized, with the top candidates being forwarded to the hiring manager. The hiring manager will need a concise, easy-to-read resume that clearly demonstrates how your capabilities match the requirements of the open position. After this review, the hiring manager is now ready to invest the time into interviewing the top candidates. The HR department then begins scheduling the interviews. The exception to this approach might be with some public institutions that have a policy of interviewing all candidates that meet the minimum requirements. However, industry normally wouldn't invest the resources or time for more than a handful of interviews for a given position.

The astute reader now realizes that an effective resume (compliant, concise, and compelling) is only effective for the one job requisition it was crafted for. Yes, the naïve notion of just updating your resume with some current information probably won't get you the interview at the end of the day. My wife's college placed a job requisition for an administrative assistant position and received over four hundred applications in a two-week period.

With the sheer number of resumes that recruiters are bombarded with from day to day, your resume has to be tailored for the open position and compelling enough to get through the initial recruiter's screening, forwarded to the hiring manager, and selected from the others as a candidate for an interview. If your skills are buried within your resume work history, it can easily get passed over. Therefore, when someone asks you for a copy of your resume, remember that there is no such thing as *your resume* to copy. You must interpret this request as, "Please send me a concise, well-written summary of your capabilities and compelling skill set that will help meet (*some need*) contributing to the success of our company." Of course, we don't have to start from scratch with each and every resume request, but we do have to work hard to tailor our foundational capabilities-based resume statements to the needs of the hiring manger.

Let's go back to building that foundation. We will start with the use of a very effective tool to help develop each of our work experience capability-based statements. That tool is the PAR statement consisting of three parts: 1) the Problem (Task or Challenge); 2) the Action (What did you do?); and 3) the quantifiable Results.

PAR statements are in contrast to the typical work experience statement that reads something like this: "Responsible for the training of a newly formed audit department." Notice that this historical statement does not depict any capabilities that would be transferrable to a new assignment. Let's embellish this statement using the PAR format as our model. What is the Problem or Situation? A newly formed department needed to be trained to accomplish its tasks. What was the Action? Training was provided. And finally, what were the Results? The results were not included in the original resume statement. We will want to provide the prospective employer with more information.

Let's use our creativity, along with the assumption that this person kept very good records for all the training classes, the number of attendees, course evaluations, written kudos for tasks well done, annual appraisals, spot awards, etc. Uncovering facts by digging through past records and applying the PAR format, we can then come up with a statement like:

- Successfully developed and presented five training courses, certifying all thirty employees of a newly formed Internal Audit department three months ahead of the target completion date.

This statement begins with an action verb phrase—"successfully developed"—to describe the development (*Action*) of compliance courses to address the newly formed department's training (*Problem*) requirements, which resulted in everyone being certified ahead of schedule (*Results*). This PAR statement clearly relays the candidate's capabilities for developing training classes, meeting schedules, solving problems, taking initiative, and becoming a Subject Matter Expert (SME) (i.e., audit compliance).

We all solve problems, take action, and influence results as part of our jobs. But sometimes trying to recollect specific, quantifiable examples from past projects is difficult unless we have kept good records. Keep in mind that it is always easier to build these statements as they are occurring so you can add them to your resume along the way.

Once I was helping a salesperson develop his resume PAR statements, but unfortunately, he never kept any specifics of his accomplishments and was at a loss for accurate sales numbers and sales goals percentages. His statements simply stated something to the effect, "Received outstanding unit award for exceeding revenue goal." He ended up going back to his former employers and asking them for specifics. Fortunately, he had left on very good terms and was able to obtain quantifiable data validating his accomplishments. Now one of his PAR-formatted resume statements reads:

"Initiated a mentoring program that resulted in our unit exceeding their annual revenue goal by 215 percent% and being awarded the outstanding unit in 2009 from among 23 units nominated."

This statement is powerful—not only for the sake of describing a past job accomplishment but also because it clearly demonstrates what this person is capable of doing for the next hiring manager. Who wouldn't want to employ a salesperson who could achieve twice his unit's annual revenue goal! Remember the hiring manager's perspective; he has organizational goals to meet that your goals will be a subset of. When you can convey capabilities that would bring success toward accomplishing those goals, then the hiring manager can easily see the value you would add. This is a winning perspective.

So now comes the really tough part—coming up with three or four compelling PAR statements for each past employment position you plan to list on your resume. It takes a lot of brainwork to recall relevant deeds, creatively format them, and accurately quantify these past accomplishments into PAR statements. The historical specific data might not be available anymore, but that is okay. Do the best you can. Build as many statements as compellingly and as specifically as you possibly can! And don't stop there.

It is important to keep building these statements with your current work, volunteer work, or any other activity that is relevant to the capabilities needed for future positions you could be interviewing for someday. Keep a *living resume* by adding your new accomplishments formatted in PAR statements as they occur over time. This practice will provide you with a wonderful gourmet buffet of compelling PAR statements for you to choose from when tailoring future resumes. As a result of this work, not only will you be able to efficiently build tailored resumes, but you will also have excellent anecdotal examples for answering interview questions. You will get a big bang for your buck by diligently doing the hard upfront work now. Below are a few examples of good PAR statements:

- Initiated scheduling changes (A) to accommodate a greater number of students (P) during the busy lunch period between classes, which accounted for reducing the negative suggestion box entries by more than 50% (R).
- Developed and implemented an enterprise-wide channel sales plan (A), resulting in quota goals exceeding 200% (R) while reestablishing lost accounts (P) with Chevron, Northrop Grumman, and the city of Manhattan Beach.
- Reduced the annual office supply costs 18% (R) by developing cost-saving ordering procedures and generating store recycling credits (A) to meet the department's overhead budget challenge (P).
- Received the 2009 Outstanding Administrative Assistance Award from over 275 applicants across the country for my contributions to the successful startup of our training center. (This is not in the PAR format, but it effectively demonstrates proven administrative assistance capabilities by receiving an award from over 275 applicants.)

Be creative in describing your capabilities by leveraging your past successes to show your potential for helping the hiring manager achieve successes in the future. Always think of your capabilities in the present tense as being easily transferrable directly from job to job.

The rule to remember for getting interviews is to help the hiring manager help you. In the infamous scene from the movie

Jerry McGuire, Tom Cruise is pleading with his client, the mediocre professional football player, by dramatically repeating, "Help me help you; helllp me helllp you; help ... me ... help ... you." HR recruiters and hiring managers are busy people. Help them help you by submitting a compliant, concise, and compelling resume—a resume that connects the dots between your capabilities and the requirements of the job requisition.

Returning to the Labor Market Information (LMI) we previously discussed, review and incorporate the following Occupational Profile elements into your resume with PAR statements addressing your capabilities for the specific requirements in your career field:

1. Training programs
2. Top Tasks (Specific duties and responsibilities of this job)
3. Top Skills used in this job
4. Top Abilities (Attributes of the person that influence performance in this job)
5. Top Work Values (Aspects of this job that create satisfaction)
6. Top Interests (Types of activities someone in this job would like)

The LMI also provides names of companies in your field that you can target for your career opportunities. Researching those companies provides market information and trends that can be very useful for understanding the Industry and ultimately the hiring manager's needs.

And finally, when you are deciding what and what not to include in your resume, keep in mind what has been stated earlier: The purpose for submitting your resume is to get an interview. The range of suitable information expands once you arrive at the

Build Your Resume

interview and begin receiving feedback from the hiring manager (or hiring panel, as the case may be). Then you can open the conversation to broader tangential topics that may be of interest.

For example, a friend of mine asked if he should include his favorite sports and recreational activities on his resume. "Only if it will help you get an interview," was my response. I've advised a salesperson to list his golf credentials, including working as a golf instructor at a prestigious Florida golf course. Since his job *duties* included playing golf with his clients, golf was very relevant. In his industry, this is commonly referred to as *duty golf*. On the other hand, had he been applying for an engineering or technical position, golf most likely would not have been relevant. Any information that is not relevant to the job should not be included on a resume. Irrelevant information acts as a distracter from what you want the hiring manager to find out about you.

Listed below are some guidelines to help you build your resume. First, we will take a look at the *dos* and *don'ts* for resumes, and then we will follow up with some format considerations.

Starting with the *dos*:

1. Incorporate the job requisition language and LMI occupation attributes into your resume. Your resume will then clearly fulfill the job requirements, which is exactly what the HR recruiter and hiring manager are looking for.
2. Open your resume with a brief Work Summary Statement. The more specific the statement is toward the position you are applying for, the better. Incorporate as much of the job description as possible into the open statement. As an example, if the job description states, "A minimum of ten years' experience with ..." Open your Work Experience Summary statement with, "I have ten years' experience with ..." (assuming, of course, that you have ten years' experience or you would not be applying for this position; always be truthful). The idea is to help the recruiter

immediately match your qualifications to the published job description.
3. Use twelve-point font. Anything smaller is hard for people over the age of forty to read. The exception to this rule would be if you were trying to limit your opportunities to working only for bosses in their mid-thirties or younger. Let's not limit our opportunities; keep it readable.
4. It should be no more than two pages, ever. For CEOs, CFOs, and presidents, just one page is sufficient. If you can't make a compelling case for your ability to address the needs of an employer in two pages or less, don't expect to be rewarded for your capacity to ramble on. Remember, hiring managers are busy—no more than two pages.
5. Use bulleted PAR statements, starting with action verbs, like accomplished, achieved, created, developed, enhanced, exceeded, implemented, increased, reduced (expenses, waste), saved, validated, etc. Stay away from long text paragraphs. Build the resume in a way that looks crisp and inviting.
6. In addition to your complete contact information and the page number on the first page, include your name and the page number on the second page as well (John Jones, Page 2 of 2). Resumes often arrive on the hiring manager's desk in bulk after someone in HR has printed, reviewed, sorted, and copied many resumes of qualifying candidates. You want to ensure your resume pages stay together during this process.
7. Emphasize industry-peculiar discriminators for that job. If security clearances are needed in your line of work, place that information right up front to pique the reviewer's interest. If you are in the education field, your degrees should be right on top. Always list your highest degree first, so it stands out! Other discriminators could be: certifications, company affiliations (client intimacy), foreign language proficiency, sales quota performance, military experience,

etc. Your research will enlighten you to the discriminators for your field.
8. Have many sets of eyes review your resume; fight for feedback. Find people within the industry, friends, relatives, and anyone else who can check spelling and punctuation and help ensure clarity by reviewing those succinct, powerful, and ever-evolving PAR statements.
9. Use a basic font, either Times New Roman or Arial, because these fonts will maintain their integrity while being electronically forwarded either as an attachment or pasted into a HTML format. And finally, save your resume as a .pdf file. The .pdf is basically a picture of your resume and cannot be edited. I've noticed that some of the industry Internet security firewalls occasionally strip or disable Microsoft Word content from emails, but they allow .pdf files to open normally.
10. When attaching a resume, cover letter, or other reference materials, use professional and descriptive titles for your attached documents. Titles such as *Jones, Thomas—Prog Mgr Resume* or *Jones, Thomas—Cover Memo* are descriptive and much more professional titles than simply *Jones version 32*.

Now for a few *don'ts*:
1. There is absolutely no need to include an "Objective" statement. Your objective is obvious—to get an interview. Not only is this statement a waste of real estate on your resume, but it is also self-centered, focused away from the hiring manager's needs and therefore wasting his precious time. Remember, the hiring manager has a need, often an urgent need. He or she isn't really interested in your stated objective of, "A challenging career opportunity in a fortune five hundred company that can use my skills and … blah, blah, blah …" Sorry to be so frank, but at this point in the hiring process, it is all about finding a candidate who can do the job. Hypothetically, say the hiring manager really just needs

a proficient accounts receivable manager early next week to alleviate his cash flow deficit! It is about screening the candidate resumes for those who can do the job. Get the interview, and then rest assured that you will have a chance to fully discuss the opportunity and ask questions relative to your personal objectives and goals at the time of the interview and HR processing. Remember—first get the interview!

2. Do not include political affiliations, controversial activities, or religious preferences. The exception, of course, would be if you are applying for a job with a political organization such as the Democratic National Committee. Then it would be totally appropriate to list volunteer fundraising activities supporting that political party. The same is true if you are applying for a position in a religious organization; certainly include your years of serving as a deacon in your local church. But unless the affiliation is directly relevant to the opportunity, avoid anything that could be construed as controversial by the resume screeners. Your objective is to get an interview, not make a political or religious statement. Just as Jason Alba teaches in regard to social media, keep it *On Brand and On Purpose*.

3. Do not include any personal information that an employer is not allowed to ask for by law. This includes federal laws and state laws (which differ from state to state). Generally it is illegal for an employer to ask questions about age, gender, race, religion, national origin, disabilities, and sexual orientation. In addition, except for jobs requiring security clearances, arrests, garnishments, and citizenship information cannot be requested. You can find a particular state's hiring regulations on their Labor Department (or equivalent titled) website. Simply put, a hiring manager may personally not want to hire a perfectly qualified older person (or younger person). Therefore, there is no need to put the year of your graduation from high school or colleges. Nor is there a need to list all of your employment, especially

Build Your Resume

early employment that isn't relevant to the position. State laws prohibit an employer from seeking the above types of information; you should help the employer and yourself by avoiding these topics as well. The last thing the HR department wants is a time-consuming and expensive lawsuit for allegations of discriminatory hiring practice due to having too much information from the candidates.

4. Do not include salary requirements. After you get an interview and after you receive an offer is time for you to start negotiating salary. We will discuss salary requirements more in a later chapter. The important thing for the resume is to get the interview. Salary discussions are premature until after you get a job offer.

5. Do not have any misspelled words or use any unfamiliar acronyms or jargon on your resume. Your resume represents the best document you are capable of producing, the harbinger of the quality of products an employer can expect from you. It has to be very good. It is you!

6. Do not include statements like, "Reference upon request." That statement can be an affront to a hiring manager, as if someone might have the audacity to not comply with such a basic request. Of course you will provide references, so it goes without saying. Not only is this statement meaningless and taking up valuable real estate on your resume, but it just isn't appropriate at this phase of the hiring process. The HR department will not spend their time or money on reference checks and background checks until the final candidates are selected. Therefore, save the space on your resume for those compelling PAR statements you worked so hard to develop; the PAR statements are what will get you the interview.

7. Do not misrepresent yourself. Case in point, Mr. Gregory Probert, former president and Chief Operations Officer (COO) for Herbalife, Ltd., fraudulently listed a MBA degree from California State University, Los Angeles, on his initial

employment application in 2003. It turned out years later, in 2008, that Herbalife was involved in a lawsuit defending their products against fraudulent claims. The plaintiff accessed the public records of the chief officers (Securities and Exchange Commission [SEC] disclosure reports) and very easily verified that the COO had "lied" about his MBA on his employment application, in effect supporting their accusations of Herbalife's pervasive fraudulent culture. This prompted an inquiry from the *Wall Street Journal*, which Herbalife later responded to by issuing this press release:

Chairman and CEO Michael O. Johnson accepted President and COO Gregory L. Probert's resignation effective April 30, 2008. The misstatement of Probert's academic credentials has been a matter under review by the board of directors. Given the company's unwavering commitment to the highest standards in business ethics, the company had no other choice but to accept the resignation.

Today there are businesses that do nothing but background checks for new hires. These companies have huge databases and can access all kinds of information that wasn't available before the information explosion of the Internet age. Many employers utilize these relatively inexpensive outsourcing services.

Anecdotally, in 2009 I was informed of a recently hired employee who was going to be terminated for misrepresenting his education—a violation of our company's policy regarding fraudulent employment application information. I wanted to understand how we could have hired someone and actually had him working without properly verifying his education beforehand. I found out that this person had previously worked for us, and he had listed all the same education information that was on file from the previous application years earlier. To expedite the hiring process, and to meet our customer's urgent need, the HR department manager elected to proceed with a job offer prior to receiving the results of the background check.

Ironically, the contested education was a master's degree that was not a requirement for this job. However, by company policy, falsifying an employment application requires termination of the employee. This employee lamented to our HR representative that he was surprised since the company hadn't previously questioned that degree. He even went on to say that he had been working for the CIA, and they had never questioned his education degrees. But times had changed; today employers have the ability to easily access databases and verify information by outsourcing background checks. In essence, for $150, companies can verify data that ten years ago slipped by the CIA! The takeaway is that there are companies that do nothing but background checks for employers, and they are pretty good at what they do. Remember, an employment agreement is a legal contract between the employer and the employee that is valid for the entire period of employment.

Employment Applications

Some employers use online applications and do not accept stand-alone resumes. No worry—the resume information must simply be entered into the online application. It is the same information, and the same powerful PAR statements should be pasted into the appropriate field for work experience. The work you put into building your resume from the foundation up will supply compliant, concise, and compelling submittals for the online application process as well! A word of caution: Never, never submit an incomplete application containing a field with "see attached resume." That shows lack of initiative on your part and certainly does not help the hiring manager help you.

Resume Formats

Frequently I have been asked the question, "What is the best resume format?" The answer to that question is: it depends. The chronological format, which, by the way, is the most widely used format by far, is very effective for some. The chronological format lists your most recent work experience and continues in reverse chronological order as far back as necessary. The advantage of a chronologically formatted resume is the logical flow that can showcase steady growth through promotions and also demonstrate your company loyalty. However, a chronological listing of your accomplishments can hide past relevant capability statements within the resume body. Another potential disadvantage of this format is that it will highlight any career setbacks, frequent job changes, and gaps in employment. On the other hand, this format is highly recommended for people who have demonstrated continuous increased levels of responsibility in their career field and who has not had any lapses in employment. An example can be found in Appendix D.

The second most widely used format is the functional resume. This format showcases your capabilities within functional skill areas without linking them to any particular time period or employer. The advantage of the functionally formatted resume is the ease of emphasizing relevant functional capability right up front versus potentially having it concealed somewhere within the chronological sequence. This format also de-emphasizes, maybe even obscures, employment gaps. Disadvantages are that it is often viewed with suspicion and secondarily de-emphasizes growth progression. The functional format is recommended for someone with frequent job changes or gaps in employment. The functional format is also ideal for incorporating volunteer work or for someone returning back to the workforce. An example can be found in Appendix D.

Are you unsure of which of the two formats will work best for you? How about a combination of both, using the best attributes of each to make your resume even more compelling? The combined format, sometimes referred to as the hybrid resume format, can be very effective. Selectively choose the strongest PAR statements relevant for the job position, regardless of the company or functional area. The PAR statements are then listed, with the strongest and most relevant up front, for the hiring manager to key right in on. Following your compelling PAR statements, simply list your employers and dates of employment. There is no need to link experience by company or include company job titles.

The advantage of the hybrid format is that it highlights your most relevant capabilities while directly connecting them to the position you are seeking, at the same time de-emphasizing less-relevant experiences and gaps in employment. The biggest disadvantage is that the hybrid format can be confusing. This format may require more effort on your part to build your resume because it is so adaptive—which is a very good thing. The hybrid format is ideal for someone who is changing or transitioning into another field, returning after an absence, or pursuing work he or she has done in the distant past. An example can be found in Appendix D.

I have found the hybrid to be the most effective resume format for my current situation because I can draw on many years of experience and list the most relevant capabilities first—on page one of my resume—rather than having relevant experience scattered by functional areas throughout the document or buried chronologically somewhere on page two. It also has the great advantage of being an easy reference source for developing talking points and responding to interview questions, which we will discuss in the next chapter.

It should be pointed out that the PAR statements, education, training, certifications, awards, and professional organization information are exactly the same for any of these formats. The selection rests solely on whatever format will best showcase your capabilities in the most concise and compelling presentation for the position you are seeking.

Have References Ready before They Are Needed

Although references should not be listed on the resume, have at least three strong references in your hip pocket. I would recommend having one at a level above you (previous boss or supervisor), one reference at your peer level (coworker or colleague), and one at a level below you (supervised employee or junior level coworker). Include diversity wherever possible. If you are a male and you had a female boss, list her. It is even better if she happens to have a Hispanic surname and you are not Hispanic.

Before using someone as a reference, respectfully ask his or her permission in advance. Based on your relationship with the person and his or her reaction to your request, you will have a good idea as to whether or not to use this person as a reference. Keep your references' contact information handy and current for that next great opportunity that comes along. Later, once you have provided their names to the HR representative, be sure to inform your references and give them some information about the position. This will not only prevent them from being caught off guard when a recruiter calls, but it will also give you a chance to remind them of your strengths relative to this position. People naturally want to help when they can. Your task is to help them help you.

What about a Cover Memo?

Rule 1: Never submit a resume without a cover memo. The cover memo substantiates and personalizes your resume for a particular position or opportunity. Whether submitting a resume from your own research or through a referral from your network, the cover memo provides the context and reason for reviewing your resume.

If the resume submittal happens to be in response to a referral or as a follow up from an informational interview, the cover memo is even more necessary. You will want to capture and focus the reader's attention on the opportunity you are interested in. Incidentally, referencing a common contact is the strongest approach you can use. However, submitting a cover memo and a resume without a referral can still be effective if you do your homework. When resorting to the cold-call approach, you can still demonstrate your knowledge of the industry and your ability to express yourself. The cover memo may only address one or two of the company's needs that you were able to ascertain, but that is okay. After you have connected to others within the organization, you will have opportunities to more fully understand the needs of the hiring manager.

It is most likely, however, that a cover memo would be accompanying a resume for a particular job posting. As with all cover memos, keep it to one page. Open with a short paragraph telling why you are writing and the specific position you are interested in. Follow with a paragraph on *how* you are qualified. The third paragraph should state *why* you are right for the position. Close with a proactive statement letting the reader know how and when you will be following up (e.g., call next week, schedule a meeting with their administrative assistant, etc.). Use the cover memo to provide a personalized touch to your pithy, bulleted (word-limited) resume. To help you get started, take a look at forty free cover letter samples posted at Quintessential Careers: http://quintcareers.com/cover_letter_samples.html.

Traditionally, cover memos were delivered as a formal business letter through the mail, addressed to the hiring manager or HR representative. Today it is more expedient to incorporate the cover memo into the body of an e-mail, with a resume included as an attachment. The same rules apply for writing an e-mail cover memo as a hard copy memo. Carefully craft the memo on a Word document program (with spelling and grammar checkers on). When you have sufficiently reviewed the wording and the message, cut and paste the text into the e-mail.

There are several advantages to sending the cover memo via e-mail. First, it can be delivered instantaneously and directly to the hiring manager, without the snail mail delay or being stuck away in a cubbyhole somewhere in the company's mailroom. Consider how often a busy hiring manager would have a chance to sit down and open snail mail letters. E-mail is checked much more frequently and can be acted on very quickly. Second, e-mail addresses are much easier to obtain than an office or mail stop addresses. You can easily check the company's website contact link for the company e-mail address convention (e.g., Tom.Jones@abc.com or tjones@xyz.org). Third, by including your referral on the distribution (CC line), you create an immediate intimacy or bond with the recipient while at the same time making it very convenient for him or her to connect on your behalf.

Incidentally, a little research can go a long way in warming up the cold-call approach by simply expressing a deeper knowledge and understanding of the industry, company, and people when you are reaching out to them. Use the cover memo to warm up your resume transmittal. Warm Call Toolbar is a free application that can reside on your tool bar for effectively searching for this kind of information. Try it by searching your own name to see what you can find out about yourself. You might be surprised. Of course, if you are willing to pay a little bit, you can get the full edition with more detailed information. To download the application, go to: www.warmcallcenter.com.

Cover Memo Dos:

1. It should be only one page in twelve-point font.
2. Make first paragraph compelling, stating why you are writing.
3. Be specific toward a job or the information requested.
4. Incorporating action verbs:
    a. State how you are qualified.
    b. Tell why you are right for the position.
5. Make it personal and interesting; reference a common contact as appropriate.
6. Include your follow-up action (e.g., I will contact you next week.).

Tying back to the "Network Advantage" material, it is commonly recognized that 75 percent of all job offers are a result of networking, not *spamming* job boards with a generic resume. This is not to imply that you have to know someone important at the top to land a job, but it is valuable to have coworker-level contact(s) in the organization to help you get your resume directly to the hiring manager. Hiring managers actually prefer referrals by rank-and-file employees rather than from someone at the CEO level. Can you imagine the awkwardness of having the CEO's niece working for you? You better be very careful with that annual performance review! And besides, who would better know the capabilities and fit needed for a position than the actual employees that are currently working in that department? Contacts are critical; statistically, job board submittals alone are not enough.

Don't forget to post your cover memo on social media sites. Once again, the more specific your posted cover memo and resume titles are on LinkedIn, Monster, or a company's career page, the better. You will end up with more hits and will receive more calls by being specific. Hypothetically consider searching for a car to purchase online. With so many websites to review, how often would you open a link with the subject line "2009 car for sale"? Probably not very often, because this is too vague to spark your interest. But if you saw a subject line such as "2009 white Jeep Cherokee—low mileage—for sale" and you were considering that model of vehicle, you would naturally take a deeper look and investigate that listing. The same is true for your cover memo and resume. The more specific (job position, industry, years of experience) it is, the more hits you will get from recruiters searching for that specific skill set. The paradox of attempting to cast a bigger net with a broad-spectrum resume actually results in getting ignored by busy recruiters who have deadlines to meet and openings to fill. An example cover memo can be found in Appendix C.

CHAPTER 11

Tailor Your Resume

Your resume foundational building blocks consist of: compelling PAR statements demonstrating your capabilities, LMI-derived terminology, and relevant training that will provide a solid foundation. With that foundation, you can easily tailor your resume to a detailed job opening in your career field or an unposted opportunity you discovered through networking.

- Job openings will have specific requirements, such as proficiency with a certain software language or tool, number of years of experience, required certifications, and other *keyword* requirements. It is important to rigorously incorporate the job specifics as *searchable* terms into your resume. Since the purpose of submitting a resume is to get an interview, those key terms must jump out at the recruiter with either electronic or human initial screening.

If the job requisition requires proficiency in MS Excel, any similar term other than MS Excel won't be picked up in a search (e.g., "proficiency with spreadsheets or pivot tables"). The search engine will not recognize any terms other than those exact search words entered by the recruiter. So where does a recruiter get the terms? The search words come from the job requisition provided to HR by the hiring manager. Therefore, be sure to use the job requisition terms verbatim.

This is equally true for the manual screening of candidate resumes, since this task is typically performed by junior-level HR personnel who are supporting a hiring manager. These junior employees may not have the broad domain knowledge spanning the company's many job categories, enabling them to immediately recognize relevant experience, unless the same keywords listed in the job requisition are incorporated into your resume. The more technical the position, the more critical the tailoring of your resume is to the terms contained within the job requisition.

For example, say the position calls for experience with HTML and your PAR statements include the wonderful results you achieved with JAVA scripts for web-based marketing applications. The search engine won't necessarily know JAVA and web-based have anything to do with the HTML search word. Therefore, simply rewrite your PAR statement for this job requisition to include HTML somewhere; help the screening process (recruiter) help you.

Sample Resume, Candidate Scenario

Applying what was learned about PAR statements to a hypothetical situation will give you a better appreciation for how to build and tailor your own resume. This scenario has our candidate, Ms. Sandra Beck, pursuing a management position in marketing after a short break from her primary marketing field. During this short break, she has been working as a real estate agent. She now realizes she misses the marketing aspect of her job and believes she has the qualifications and capabilities to be a good marketing manager. Ms. Beck sits downs and develops the first cut of several PAR statements for each job she has had:

Temporary Position as Receptionist

- Worked closely with office staff (A) to establish an electronic library (R) and in the process eliminated twenty-five file drawers of paper copies (P).

- Effectively implemented standard operating procedure changes (A) leading to the reinstatement of a satisfactory rating (R) after having had two major audit findings the previous year (P).

- Efficiently utilized online travel voucher system (A) to accommodate all travel requests of an additional department (R) during the absence of their travel coordinator (P).

Full-Time Receptionist
- Developed an electronic spreadsheet (A) that organizes customer product preferences (P) producing customized address lists (R) for future mailings.

- Earned exemplary ratings for three of the last four company procedure compliance audits (R).

- Effectively planned and coordinated (A) a successful company off-site strategy session (R) at a nearby facility for over seventy-five attendees (P).

- Received outstanding annual performance ratings (R) for initiating corrective actions (A) and displaying ability to handle customer complaints (P).

- Ensured all company-related activities were posted on a central online calendar (A), increasing facility utilization (R) and reducing schedule conflicts (P).

Administrative Assistant to Vice President of Marketing
- Initiated an employee survey (A) that resulted in the implementation of an employee recognition program (R) to increase employee morale (P).

- Developed and maintained a calendar of industry marketing and business development events (A) to effectively plan activities (R) and eliminate redundant expenses (P).

- Hand selected to mentor new administrative assistants (A), resulting in a 25% reduction (R) in first-year turnover (P).

- Designed three invoicing training classes (A) that were presented to over fifty students annually, significantly reducing (R) unbillable (P) expenditures.

- Prepared agenda and coordinated (A) executive-level meetings between company vice presidents and civic leaders, ensuring effective use (R) of their meeting time (P).

- Initiated and maintained a tracking system (A), which provided status of all staff meeting action items (P) and highlighted resultant progress (R).

- Effectively maintained marketing expenses summaries (A) for presentation at corporate budget reviews (P), ensuring the efficient use of funds (R).

Customer Service Representative

- Received the 2007 Outstanding Customer Service Representative of the Year award from among 165 nominees nationwide (R).

- Established an intra-company tracking tool (A) to leverage exhibit contact information between divisions (P), resulting in over $2.4 million additional cross-division sales for 2006 (R).

- Developed online customer feedback survey (A), which resulted in seven product improvements (R, P).

- Effectively researched growth areas (P) and developed a marketing plan, leading to successful exhibits at three new trade shows (A), reaching hundreds of new customers (R).

- Established trusted relationships (A) within industry; (R) elected to serve on the board of directors for the local chapter of the National Marketing Representatives (NMR).

Manager Trade Show

- Oversaw the development of marketing media (A) for use on ultra-definition video wall displays that eliminated the need for expensive product mock-ups (P), resulting in an annual savings of $74,000 (R).

- Effectively managed (A) a department of twelve customer representatives, increasing annual follow-on sales (P) from 75% to 93% over a three-year period (R).

- Initiated medical equipment market research (A), which led to implementing new pricing options (R) for a more competitive approach in a changing market (P).

- Established marketing policy (A) that leveraged quantity buys of corporate and division exhibit materials (P), reducing annual trade show expenditures by 22% (R).

- Managed multiple advertising agencies' contracts (A) within budget and on schedule (R) while ensuring a consistent corporate brand across all product lines (P).

Realtor, Manager for Wells Fargo Account

- Successfully closed escrow (A) on 75% of properties (R) prior to foreclosure auction, saving client over $3 million (P) annually.

- Established a program (A) to fast-track VA and FHA qualification (R), resulting in eight additional sales for homeowners not having a down payment (P).

Developing this list of PAR statements took some head scratching and mind searching for past accomplishments. Our Ms. Beck also went to the LMI during the process to jog her memory of what these types of jobs typically entail. These initial PAR statements will continue to develop as new requirements become known for future positions.

The next step is to review an example of an actual job description in your field and tailor the PAR statements for that position. Sales Careers Online at www.salescareersonline.com provided our example for a marketing manager job description as the basis for this exercise (See Appendix B: Marketing Manager—Job Requisition #98765). Formatting your resume to meet the requirements of an actual job requisition that is typical for your field is a great way to get started with your resume building. As you later focus your job search toward a particular location or company, you can easily tailor your resume to a specific requisition (or the requirements of an internal opening not yet advertised). The internal opening may not even have a published job requisition when you are first hearing about the need (referring back to the networking advantage), therefore offering your *built resume for a typical position* may actually help shape the employer's thinking toward your resume and the subsequent job description.

We'll get started with the following job requisition:

Job Objective:
Responsible for developing and maintaining marketing strategies to meet organizational objectives. Evaluates customer research, market conditions, and competitor data, and implements marketing plan changes as needed. Oversees all marketing, advertising, and promotional staff and activities.

Responsibilities:
- Responsible for the marketing of medical equipment and services tailored exclusively to the needs of the geriatrics market.
- Demonstrates technical marketing skills and product knowledge of medical type products.

- Develops annual marketing plan in conjunction with sales department, which details activities to follow during the fiscal year, which will focus on meeting organizational objectives.
- To manage the marketing department budget. Delivery of all marketing activity within agreed budget. Direction of marketing staff where budgets are devolved.
- To manage all aspects of print production, receipt, and distribution.
- The achievement of frequent, timely, and positive media coverage for products across all available media.
- Managing the entire product line life cycle from strategic planning to tactical activities.
- Specifying market requirements for current and future products by conducting market research supported by ongoing visits to customers and non-customers.
- Driving a solution set across development teams (primarily development/engineering, and marketing communications) through market requirements, product contract, and positioning.
- Developing and implementing a company-wide go-to-market plan, working with all departments to execute.
- Analyzing potential partner relationships for product lines.

Relationships and Roles:

Internal/External Cooperation
- Demonstrate ability to interact and cooperate with all company employees.
- Build trust, value others, communicate effectively, drive execution, foster innovation, focus on the customer, collaborate with others, solve problems creatively, and demonstrate high integrity.
- Maintain professional internal and external relationships that meet company core values.

- Proactively establish and maintain effective working team relationships with all support departments.

Job Specifications:
- Four to six years of sales experience in the marketing industry.
- Extensive experience in all aspects of developing and maintaining marketing strategies to meet organizational objectives.
- Strong understanding of customer and market dynamics and requirements.
- Willingness to travel and work in a global team of professionals.
- Proven ability to oversee all marketing, advertising, and promotional staff and activities.

That is a lot to digest, so we will parse it out and include as much as we can into our resume and cover memo. Incidentally, just as I have cut and pasted this job description from the Sales Careers Online website to use as a starting point, many hiring managers will start with a sample or previously written job description. Therefore, to ensure all aspects of the job are met, reference the LMI information and the O*Net data. Job descriptions are only the starting point for the hiring manager and HR recruiters as they initiate the screening process. As the process continues, the hiring manager will gain a better feel for what is needed and available. You can be one step ahead of the hiring manager by doing your research.

Note keywords such as: marketing, strategies, competitor data, research, budget.

Marketing Managers
(SOC Code : 11-2021)
in California
Determine the demand for products and services offered by a firm and its competitors and identify potential customers. Develop

pricing strategies with the goal of maximizing the firm's profits or share of the market while ensuring the firm's customers are satisfied. Oversee product development or monitor trends that indicate the need for new products and services.

Employers are usually looking for candidates with a work experience, plus bachelor's or higher degree.

About This Occupation
(from O*NET - The Occupation Information Network)

(Top Tasks (Specific duties and responsibilities of this job.)

Formulate, direct, and coordinate marketing activities and policies to promote products and services, working with advertising and promotion managers.

Identify, develop, and evaluate marketing strategy, based on knowledge of establishment objectives, market characteristics, and cost and markup factors.

Direct the hiring, training, and performance evaluations of marketing and sales staff and oversee their daily activities.

Evaluate the financial aspects of product development, such as budgets, expenditures, research and development appropriations, and return-on-investment and profit-loss projections.

Develop pricing strategies, balancing firm objectives and customer satisfaction.

Compile lists describing product or service offerings.

Initiate market research studies and analyze their findings.

Use sales forecasting and strategic planning to ensure the sale and profitability of products, lines, or services, analyzing business developments and monitoring market trends.

Coordinate and participate in promotional activities and trade shows, working with developers, advertisers, and production managers, to market products and services.

Consult with buying personnel to gain advice regarding the types of products or services expected to be in demand.

More Tasks for Marketing Managers

Top Skills used in this Job

Critical Thinking - Using logic and reasoning to identify the strengths and weaknesses of alternative solutions, conclusions, or approaches to problems.

Active Listening - Giving full attention to what other people are saying, taking time to understand the points being made, asking questions as appropriate, and not interrupting at inappropriate times.

Speaking - Talking to others to convey information effectively.

Persuasion - Persuading others to change their minds or behavior.

Social Perceptiveness - Being aware of others' reactions and understanding why they react as they do.

Monitoring - Monitoring/Assessing performance of yourself, other individuals, or organizations to make improvements or take corrective action.

Judgment and Decision Making - Considering the relative costs and benefits of potential actions to choose the most appropriate one.

Coordination - Adjusting actions in relation to others' actions.

Reading Comprehension - Understanding written sentences and paragraphs in work related documents.

Active Learning - Understanding the implications of new information for both current and future problem-solving and decision-making.

More Skills for Marketing Managers

Top Abilities (Attributes of the person that influence performance in this job.)

Oral Comprehension - The ability to listen to and understand information and ideas presented through spoken words and sentences.

Oral Expression - The ability to communicate information and ideas in speaking so others will understand.

Deductive Reasoning - The ability to apply general rules to specific problems to produce answers that make sense.

Written Comprehension - The ability to read and understand information and ideas presented in writing.

More Abilities for Marketing Managers

Tailor Your Resume

Top Work Values (Aspects of this job that create satisfaction.)

Working Conditions - Occupations that satisfy this work value offer job security and good working conditions.

Achievement - Occupations that satisfy this work value are results oriented and allow employees to use their strongest abilities, giving them a feeling of accomplishment.

More Work Values for Marketing Managers

Top Interests (The types of activities someone in this job would like.)

Enterprising - Enterprising occupations frequently involve starting up and carrying out projects. These occupations can involve leading people and making many decisions. Sometimes they require risk taking and often deal with business.

Conventional - Conventional occupations frequently involve following set procedures and routines. These occupations can include working with data and details more than with ideas. Usually there is a clear line of authority to follow.

To get even more information about this type of position, refer to the Standard Occupational Code (SOC) for a marketing manager, 11-2021.00 (listed on the above EDD report) to search the Occupational Informational Network, O*Net at: http://www.onetonline.org/, which produces the following summary.

Summary Report for:

11-2021.00 - Marketing Managers

Plan, direct, or coordinate marketing policies and programs, such as determining the demand for products and services offered by a firm and its competitors, and identify potential customers. Develop pricing strategies with the goal of maximizing the firm's profits or share of the market while ensuring the firm's customers are satisfied. Oversee product development or monitor trends that indicate the need for new products and services.

Sample of reported job titles: Marketing Director, Marketing Manager, Vice President of Marketing, Business Development Manager, Marketing Coordinator, Account Supervisor, Business Development Director, Commercial Lines Manager, Commercial Marketing Specialist, Market Development Manager.

Tasks

- Formulate, direct, and coordinate marketing activities and policies to promote products and services, working with advertising and promotion managers.
- Identify, develop, or evaluate marketing strategy, based on knowledge of establishment objectives, market characteristics, and cost and markup factors.
- Direct the hiring, training, or performance evaluations of marketing or sales staff and oversee their daily activities.
- Evaluate the financial aspects of product development, such as budgets, expenditures, research and development appropriations, or return-on-investment and profit-loss projections.
- Develop pricing strategies, balancing firm objectives and customer satisfaction.
- Compile lists describing product or service offerings.
- Initiate market research studies or analyze their findings.
- Use sales forecasting or strategic planning to ensure the sale and profitability of products, lines, or services, analyzing business developments and monitoring market trends.
- Coordinate or participate in promotional activities or trade shows, working with developers, advertisers, or production managers, to market products or services.
- Consult with buying personnel to gain advice regarding the types of products or services expected to be in demand.

Tools & Technology

Tools used in this occupation:

Facsimile machines — Fax machines

Notebook computers

Personal digital assistant PDAs or organizers — Personal digital assistants PDA

Photocopiers

Scanners

Technology used in this occupation:

Analytical or scientific software — Lyris HQ Web-Analytics Solution; Minitab software; Nedstat Sitestat; Online advertising reporting software

Customer relationship management CRM software — Oracle Siebel Server Sync; QAD Marketing Automation; Sage Sales-Logix; Salesforce.com Salesforce CRM

Database user interface and query software — ClearEDGE software; Fast Track Systems software; Microsoft Access; Structured query language SQL

Electronic mail software — Email software; Listserv software; Microsoft Outlook

Graphics or photo imaging software — Adobe Systems Adobe Photoshop software; Graphic presentation software

Knowledge

Sales and Marketing — Knowledge of principles and methods for showing, promoting, and selling products or services. This includes marketing strategy and tactics, product demonstration, sales techniques, and sales control systems.

Customer and Personal Service — Knowledge of principles and processes for providing customer and personal services. This includes customer needs assessment, meeting quality standards for services, and evaluation of customer satisfaction.

English Language — Knowledge of the structure and content of the English language, including the meaning and spelling of words, rules of composition, and grammar.

Administration and Management — Knowledge of business and management principles involved in strategic planning, resource allocation, human resources modeling, leadership techniques, production methods, and coordination of people and resources.

Communications and Media — Knowledge of media production, communication, and dissemination techniques and methods. This includes alternative ways to inform and entertain via written, oral, and visual media.

Computers and Electronics — Knowledge of circuit boards, processors, chips, electronic equipment, and computer hardware and software, including applications and programming.

Skills

Active Listening — Giving full attention to what other people are saying, taking time to understand the points being made, asking questions as appropriate, and not interrupting at inappropriate times.

Critical Thinking — Using logic and reasoning to identify the strengths and weaknesses of alternative solutions, conclusions, or approaches to problems.

Persuasion — Persuading others to change their minds or behavior.

Social Perceptiveness — Being aware of others' reactions and understanding why they react as they do.

Speaking — Talking to others to convey information effectively.

Judgment and Decision Making — Considering the relative costs and benefits of potential actions to choose the most appropriate one.

Monitoring — Monitoring/Assessing performance of yourself, other individuals, or organizations to make improvements or take corrective action.

Active Learning — Understanding the implications of new information for both current and future problem-solving and decision-making.

Coordination — Adjusting actions in relation to others' actions.

Operations Analysis — Analyzing needs and product requirements to create a design.

Abilities

Oral Comprehension — The ability to listen to and understand information and ideas presented through spoken words and sentences.

Oral Expression — The ability to communicate information and ideas in speaking so others will understand.

Deductive Reasoning — The ability to apply general rules to specific problems to produce answers that make sense.

Written Comprehension — The ability to read and understand information and ideas presented in writing.

Fluency of Ideas — The ability to come up with a number of ideas about a topic (the number of ideas is important, not their quality, correctness, or creativity).

Speech Recognition — The ability to identify and understand the speech of another person.

Written Expression — The ability to communicate information and ideas in writing so others will understand.

Inductive Reasoning — The ability to combine pieces of information to form general rules or conclusions (includes finding a relationship among seemingly unrelated events).

Originality — The ability to come up with unusual or clever ideas about a given topic or situation, or to develop creative ways to solve a problem.

Problem Sensitivity — The ability to tell when something is wrong or is likely to go wrong. It does not involve solving the problem, only recognizing there is a problem.

Work Activities

Communicating with Persons Outside Organization — Communicating with people outside the organization, representing the organization to customers, the public, government, and other external sources. This information can be exchanged in person, in writing, or by telephone or e-mail.

Communicating with Supervisors, Peers, or Subordinates — Providing information to supervisors, co-workers, and subordinates by telephone, in written form, e-mail, or in person.

Getting Information — Observing, receiving, and otherwise obtaining information from all relevant sources.

Thinking Creatively — Developing, designing, or creating new applications, ideas, relationships, systems, or products, including artistic contributions.

Establishing and Maintaining Interpersonal Relationships — Developing constructive and cooperative working relationships with others, and maintaining them over time.

Developing and Building Teams — Encouraging and building mutual trust, respect, and cooperation among team members.

Making Decisions and Solving Problems — Analyzing information and evaluating results to choose the best solution and solve problems.

Organizing, Planning, and Prioritizing Work — Developing specific goals and plans to prioritize, organize, and accomplish your work.

Interacting With Computers — Using computers and computer systems (including hardware and software) to program, write software, set up functions, enter data, or process information.

Developing Objectives and Strategies — Establishing long-range objectives and specifying the strategies and actions to achieve them.

Work Context

Electronic Mail — How often do you use electronic mail in this job?

Telephone — How often do you have telephone conversations in this job?

Face-to-Face Discussions — How often do you have to have face-to-face discussions with individuals or teams in this job?

Contact With Others — How much does this job require the worker to be in contact with others (face-to-face, by telephone, or otherwise) in order to perform it?

Letters and Memos — How often does the job require written letters and memos?

Work With Work Group or Team — How important is it to work with others in a group or team in this job?

Duration of Typical Work Week — Number of hours typically worked in one week.

Structured versus Unstructured Work — To what extent is this job structured for the worker, rather than allowing the worker to determine tasks, priorities, and goals?

Spend Time Sitting — How much does this job require sitting?

Freedom to Make Decisions — How much decision-making freedom, without supervision, does the job offer?

Job Zone

Title	Job Zone Four: Considerable Preparation Needed
Education	Most of these occupations require a four-year bachelor's degree, but some do not.
Related Experience	A considerable amount of work-related skill, knowledge, or experience is needed for these occupations. For example, an accountant must complete four years of college and work for several years in accounting to be considered qualified.
Job Training	Employees in these occupations usually need several years of work-related experience, on-the-job training, and/or vocational training.
Job Zone Examples	Many of these occupations involve coordinating, supervising, managing, or training others. Examples include accountants, sales managers, database administrators, teachers, chemists, environmental engineers, criminal investigators, and special agents.
SVP Range	(7.0 to < 8.0)

Education

Percentage of Respondents	Education Level Required
84 ▬▬▬▬▬▬	Bachelor's degree
4 ▪	High school diploma or equivalent
4 ▪	Some college, no degree

Interests

Interest code: EC

Enterprising — Enterprising occupations frequently involve starting up and carrying out projects. These occupations can involve leading people and making many decisions. Sometimes they require risk taking and often deal with business.

Conventional — Conventional occupations frequently involve following set procedures and routines. These occupations can include working with data and details more than with ideas. Usually there is a clear line of authority to follow.

Work Styles

Dependability — Job requires being reliable, responsible, and dependable, and fulfilling obligations.

Attention to Detail — Job requires being careful about detail and thorough in completing work tasks.

Cooperation — Job requires being pleasant with others on the job and displaying a good-natured, cooperative attitude.

Integrity — Job requires being honest and ethical.

Leadership — Job requires a willingness to lead, take charge, and offer opinions and direction.

Initiative — Job requires a willingness to take on responsibilities and challenges.

Persistence — Job requires persistence in the face of obstacles.

Achievement/Effort — Job requires establishing and maintaining personally challenging achievement goals and exerting effort toward mastering tasks.

Adaptability/Flexibility — Job requires being open to change (positive or negative) and to considerable variety in the workplace.

Independence — Job requires developing one's own ways of doing things, guiding oneself with little or no supervision, and depending on oneself to get things done.

Work Values

Working Conditions — Occupations that satisfy this work value offer job security and good working conditions. Corresponding needs are Activity, Compensation, Independence, Security, Variety, and Working Conditions.

Achievement — Occupations that satisfy this work value are results oriented and allow employees to use their strongest abilities, giving them a feeling of accomplishment. Corresponding needs are Ability Utilization and Achievement.

Independence — Occupations that satisfy this work value allow employees to work on their own and make decisions. Corresponding needs are Creativity, Responsibility, and Autonomy.

Furthermore, the O*Net site has a "Detail" tab that can then drill down further to assess any of the above areas. For demonstration purposes, I've only included the job skills (thirty-five skills) and the abilities (fifty-three abilities) for you to scan through. These attributes are listed by importance, with the highest on top.

Abilities

Importance	Ability
78 ▬▬▬▬	**Oral Comprehension** — The ability to listen to and understand information and ideas presented through spoken words and sentences.
75 ▬▬▬▬	**Oral Expression** — The ability to communicate information and ideas in speaking so others will understand.

Tailor Your Resume

72 ▬▬▬ **Deductive Reasoning** — The ability to apply general rules to specific problems to produce answers that make sense.

72 ▬▬▬ **Written Comprehension** — The ability to read and understand information and ideas presented in writing.

69 ▬▬▬ **Fluency of Ideas** — The ability to come up with a number of ideas about a topic (the number of ideas is important, not their quality, correctness, or creativity).

69 ▬▬▬ **Speech Recognition** — The ability to identify and understand the speech of another person.

69 ▬▬▬ **Written Expression** — The ability to communicate information and ideas in writing so others will understand.

66 ▬▬▬ **Inductive Reasoning** — The ability to combine pieces of information to form general rules or conclusions (includes finding a relationship among seemingly unrelated events).

66 ▬▬▬ **Originality** — The ability to come up with unusual or clever ideas about a given topic or situation, or to develop creative ways to solve a problem.

66 ▬▬▬ **Problem Sensitivity** — The ability to tell when something is wrong or is likely to go wrong. It does not involve solving the problem, only recognizing there is a problem.

66 ▬▬▬ **Speech Clarity** — The ability to speak clearly so others can understand you.

60 ▬▬▬ **Category Flexibility** — The ability to generate or use different sets of rules for combining or grouping things in different ways.

60 — **Information Ordering** — The ability to arrange things or actions in a certain order or pattern according to a specific rule or set of rules (e.g., patterns of numbers, letters, words, pictures, mathematical operations).

56 — **Near Vision** — The ability to see details at close range (within a few feet of the observer).

56 — **Selective Attention** — The ability to concentrate on a task over a period of time without being distracted.

50 — **Flexibility of Closure** — The ability to identify or detect a known pattern (a figure, object, word, or sound) that is hidden in other distracting material.

50 — **Visualization** — The ability to imagine how something will look after it is moved around or when its parts are moved or rearranged.

47 — **Mathematical Reasoning** — The ability to choose the right mathematical methods or formulas to solve a problem.

47 — **Number Facility** — The ability to add, subtract, multiply, or divide quickly and correctly.

47 — **Perceptual Speed** — The ability to quickly and accurately compare similarities and differences among sets of letters, numbers, objects, pictures, or patterns. The things to be compared may be presented at the same time or one after the other. This ability also includes comparing a presented object with a remembered object.

44 — **Far Vision** — The ability to see details at a distance.

44 — **Visual Color Discrimination** — The ability to match or detect differences between colors, including shades of color and brightness.

Tailor Your Resume

41 ▬ **Memorization** — The ability to remember information such as words, numbers, pictures, and procedures.

41 ▬ **Speed of Closure** — The ability to quickly make sense of, combine, and organize information into meaningful patterns.

41 ▬ **Time Sharing** — The ability to shift back and forth between two or more activities or sources of information (such as speech, sounds, touch, or other sources).

28 ▬ **Finger Dexterity** — The ability to make precisely coordinated movements of the fingers of one or both hands to grasp, manipulate, or assemble very small objects.

25 ▬ **Auditory Attention** — The ability to focus on a single source of sound in the presence of other distracting sounds.

25 ▬ **Hearing Sensitivity** — The ability to detect or tell the differences between sounds that vary in pitch and loudness.

19 ▬ **Depth Perception** — The ability to judge which of several objects is closer or farther away from you, or to judge the distance between you and an object.

6 ▪ **Spatial Orientation** — The ability to know your location in relation to the environment or to know where other objects are in relation to you.

3 ▪ **Arm-Hand Steadiness** — The ability to keep your hand and arm steady while moving your arm or while holding your arm and hand in one position.

3 ▪ **Glare Sensitivity** — The ability to see objects in the presence of glare or bright lighting.

3. **Response Orientation** — The ability to choose quickly between two or more movements in response to two or more different signals (lights, sounds, pictures). It includes the speed with which the correct response is started with the hand, foot, or other body part.

3. **Trunk Strength** — The ability to use your abdominal and lower back muscles to support part of the body repeatedly or continuously over time without 'giving out' or fatiguing.

3. **Wrist-Finger Speed** — The ability to make fast, simple, repeated movements of the fingers, hands, and wrists.

0. **Control Precision** — The ability to quickly and repeatedly adjust the controls of a machine or a vehicle to exact positions.

0. **Dynamic Flexibility** — The ability to quickly and repeatedly bend, stretch, twist, or reach out with your body, arms, and/or legs.

0. **Dynamic Strength** — The ability to exert muscle force repeatedly or continuously over time. This involves muscular endurance and resistance to muscle fatigue.

0. **Explosive Strength** — The ability to use short bursts of muscle force to propel oneself (as in jumping or sprinting), or to throw an object.

0. **Extent Flexibility** — The ability to bend, stretch, twist, or reach with your body, arms, and/or legs.

0. **Gross Body Coordination** — The ability to coordinate the movement of your arms, legs, and torso together when the whole body is in motion.

0. **Gross Body Equilibrium** — The ability to keep or regain your body balance or stay upright when in an unstable position.

- **Manual Dexterity** — The ability to quickly move your hand, your hand together with your arm, or your two hands to grasp, manipulate, or assemble objects.
- **Multi-limb Coordination** — The ability to coordinate two or more limbs (for example, two arms, two legs, or one leg and one arm) while sitting, standing, or lying down. It does not involve performing the activities while the whole body is in motion.
- **Night Vision** — The ability to see under low light conditions.
- **Peripheral Vision** — The ability to see objects or movement of objects to one's side when the eyes are looking ahead.
- **Rate Control** — The ability to time your movements or the movement of a piece of equipment in anticipation of changes in the speed and/or direction of a moving object or scene.
- **Reaction Time** — The ability to quickly respond (with the hand, finger, or foot) to a signal (sound, light, picture) when it appears.
- **Sound Localization** — The ability to tell the direction from which a sound originated.
- **Speed of Limb Movement** — The ability to quickly move the arms and legs.
- **Stamina** — The ability to exert yourself physically over long periods of time without getting winded or out of breath.
- **Static Strength** — The ability to exert maximum muscle force to lift, push, pull, or carry objects.

Granted, that is a lot of information about our position. However, the O*Net occupational information provides you with a very high level of confidence because you know exactly what the expectations for this position are. By incorporating the high importance areas into your PAR statements, you can start to build your resume for the marketing manager position. For all subsequent marketing manager positions, your marketing manager resume will only need to be tailored to incorporate the peculiar requirements for that job. That is, it needs to include the key searchable words for that position and place emphasis on those areas emphasized in the job description.

To get started with your resume, include complete contact information in the header of the first page. I recommend using the left and right sides of the page to save vertical space on your resume for your important PAR statements, in essence using three lines rather than the six lines if everything were to be centered on the top.

Sandra Beck	**Sandra.Beck@yahoo.com**
123 Main Street	**(408) 555-7777 Mobile**
Phoenix, AZ 85037	**linkedin.com/in/SandraBeck**

Next is the Work Experience Summary, which incorporates as many of the job description's key requirements as possible to capture the recruiter's attention. Also include the keywords and phrases for the search engine to find electronically. Ms. Beck's summary follows:

Work Experience Summary: Over seven years' experience developing and maintaining marketing strategies to meet the objectives of the medical product and services unit. Researched and evaluated market conditions and competitor data and implemented marketing plans within budget. Oversaw all marketing and advertising activities for the medical products division.

Since this is a management position in the private sector, follow this with work accomplishments. If this were for an academic position or a college-hire position, then it would be more appropriate to begin with education credentials. For this scenario, we will begin by chronologically formatting the capabilities, starting with the most recent employment.

2010–Present: Seaside Realty, Manager, Wells Fargo Account

- Successfully closed escrow on 75% of properties prior to foreclosure auction, saving over $3 million annually
- Established a program to fast-track VA and FHA qualification resulting in eight additional sales to homeowners not having a down payment

2006–2010 Johnson's Medical, Inc., Manager, Trade Show

- Oversaw the development of marketing media for use on ultra-definition video wall displays, eliminating the need for expensive product mock-ups, resulting in an annual savings of $74,000
- Effectively managed a department of twelve customer representatives, increasing annual follow-on sales from 75% to 93% over a three-year period
- Initiated medical equipment market research, which led to implementing new pricing options for a more competitive approach in a changing market
- Established marketing policy that leveraged quantity buys of corporate and division exhibit materials, reducing annual trade show expenditures by 22%
- Managed multiple advertising agencies' contracts within budget and on schedule while ensuring a consistent corporate brand across all product lines

**2002–2006 Johnson Medical, Inc.,
Customer Service Representative**

- Received the 2007 Outstanding Customer Service Representative of the Year award from among 165 nominees nationwide

- Established an intra-company tracking tool to leverage exhibit contact information between divisions, resulting in over $2.4M in additional cross-division sales for 2006
- Developed online customer feedback survey, which resulted in seven product improvements
- Effectively researched growth areas and developed a marketing plan, leading to successful exhibits at three new trade shows, reaching hundreds of new customers
- Established trusted relationships within the industry; elected to serve on the board of directors for the local chapter of the National Marketing Representatives (NMR)

2000–2002 Johnson Medical, Inc. Administrative Assistant to Vice President Marketing

- Initiated an employee survey that resulted in the implementation of an employee recognition program to increase employee morale
- Developed and maintained a calendar of industry marketing and business development events to effectively plan activities and eliminate redundant expenses
- Hand selected to mentor new administrative assistants, resulting in a 25% reduction in first-year turnover
- Designed three invoicing training classes that were presented to over fifty students annually, significantly reducing the unbillable expenditures
- Prepared agenda and coordinated executive-level meetings between company vice presidents and civic leaders, ensuring effective use of their meeting time.
- Initiated and maintained a tracking system that provided the status of all staff meeting action items and highlighted resultant progress
- Effectively maintained marketing expense summaries for presentation at corporate budget reviews, ensuring the efficient use of funds

Tailor Your Resume

1997–2000 Johnson Medical, Inc., Receptionist

- Developed an electronic spreadsheet that organized customer product preferences, producing customized address lists for future mailings
- Earned exemplary ratings for three of the last four company procedure compliance audits
- Effectively planned and coordinated a successful company off-site strategy session at nearby facility for over seventy-five attendees
- Received outstanding annual performance ratings for initiating corrective actions and displaying ability to handle customer complaints
- Ensured all company-related activities were posted on a central online calendar, increasing facility utilization and reducing schedule conflicts

1996–1997 Advantage Temps, On-Call Receptionist

- Worked closely with office staff to establish an electronic library and eliminated twenty-five file drawers of paper copies
- Effectively implemented standard operating procedure changes, leading to the reinstatement of a satisfactory rating after having had two major findings the previous year
- Efficiently utilized online travel voucher system to accommodate all travel requests of an additional department during the absence of their travel coordinator

From this preliminary layout, notice that the first employment listed chronologically—that of a realtor—isn't relevant to the marketing manager position. Furthermore, some very strong PAR statements relevant to this position are listed toward the bottom of the first page, which is not particularly good for capturing a busy hiring manager's attention. Therefore, we might want to consider trying a functionally formatted resume as an alternative.

The functional areas we need to consider are those rated high in importance from the O*Net data. The top rated skills were: Active Listening, Critical Thinking, Persuasion, Social Perceptiveness, Speaking, and Judgment and Decision Making. The top-rated abilities were: Oral Communications, Oral Expression, Deductive Reasoning, Written Comprehension, Fluency of Ideas, and Written Expression. Let's combine these into broader categories: Management (Decision Maker/Judgment/Deductive Reasoning), Marketing Products (Fluency of Ideas/Critical Thinking/Persuasive), and Communications (Written/Oral/Social Perceptiveness). Let's move on to the functional format using these categories as functional areas.

Marketing Management
- Effectively managed a department of twelve customer representatives, increasing annual follow-on sales from 75% to 93% over a three-year period
- Managed multiple advertising agencies' contracts within budget and on schedule while ensuring a consistent corporate brand across all product lines
- Established an intra-company tracking tool to leverage exhibit contact information between divisions, resulting in over $2.4 million additional cross-division sales for 2006
- Initiated and maintained a tracking system that provided the status of all staff meeting action items and highlighted resultant progress
- Effectively maintained marketing expense summaries for presentation at corporate budget reviews, ensuring the efficient use of funds

Marketing Medical Products
- Oversaw the development of marketing media for use on ultra-definition video wall displays, eliminating the need for expensive product mock-ups, resulting in an annual savings of $74,000

- Initiated medical equipment market research, which led to implementing new pricing options for a more competitive approach in a changing market
- Established marketing policy that leveraged quantity buys of corporate and division exhibit materials, reducing annual trade show expenditures by 22%
- Effectively researched growth areas and developed a marketing plan, leading to successful exhibits at three new trade shows, reaching hundreds of new customers
- Received the 2007 Outstanding Customer Service Representative of the Year award from among 165 nominees nationwide

Communications

- Developed online customer feedback survey, which resulted in seven product improvements
- Established trusted relationships within the industry; was elected to serve on the board of directors for the local chapter of the National Marketing Representatives (NMR)
- Developed and maintained a calendar of industry marketing and business development events to effectively plan activities and eliminate redundant expenses
- Hand selected to mentor new administrative assistants, resulting in a 25% reduction in first-year turnover
- Designed three invoicing training classes that were presented to over 50 students annually, significantly reducing unbillable expenditures

This seems to have solved the chronological sequence problem by categorizing capability-based PAR statements into buckets that clearly present relevant skills and abilities. Also notice that the dates are no longer associated with the accomplishments; therefore, you have the freedom to list your accomplishments in the order that best highlights your capabilities for that opportunity. The number of PAR statements was reduced, since they were not relevant to the marketing manager position (nor were they for the chronological format). As an added note, the functional format can eliminate accomplishments that don't fit well into the functional *buckets*. So far so good, but we still need to massage the PAR statements for the requirements of this position, so let's go back to the job description and see how close we are.

Although the functional format captured most of the requirements, due to the broad responsibilities of this marketing manager position, we would need to add several more categories to address all of the requirements (i.e., cooperate well with all company employees, build trust, maintain external professional relationships, demonstrate high integrity, and analyze partnering relationships). Including that many functional buckets tends to look a little awkward. You want your capabilities to be presented as eloquently as possible. Therefore, let's take a look at the hybrid format to see if that will capture everything we need.

Immediately after the Work Experience Summary paragraph, list your PAR statements with the strongest statements first.

- Effectively managed a department of twelve customer representatives responsible for increasing annual follow-on sales from 75% to 93% over a three-year period
- Oversaw the development of marketing media for use on ultra-definition video wall displays, eliminating the need for expensive product mock-ups, resulting in an annual savings of $74,000
- Managed multiple advertising agencies' contracts within budget and on schedule while ensuring a consistent corporate brand across all product lines
- Effectively researched growth areas and developed a marketing plan, leading to successful exhibits at three new trade shows, reaching hundreds of new customers
- Established an intra-company tracking tool to leverage exhibit contact information between divisions, resulting in over $2.4 million additional cross-division sales for 2006

- Established trusted relationships within the industry; was elected to serve on the board of directors for the local chapter of the National Marketing Representatives (NMR)
- Developed online customer feedback survey, which resulted in seven product improvements
- Initiated medical equipment market research, which led to implementing new pricing options for a more competitive approach in a changing market
- Established a marketing policy that leveraged quantity buys of corporate and division exhibit materials, reducing annual trade show expenditures by 22%
- Effectively maintained marketing expenses summaries for presentation at corporate budget reviews, ensuring the efficient use of funds
- Designed three invoicing training classes that were presented to over fifty students annually, significantly reducing the unbillable expenditures
- Received the 2007 Outstanding Customer Service Representative of the Year award from among 165 nominees nationwide

The hybrid format gives the freedom to list your PAR statements by strength and relevancy, regardless of a functional category or date. The hybrid is a very effective format for this candidate. Once the format has been decided, it is time to put our thinking caps back on and revisit each of the PAR statements relative to the job position. As an example, the job description lists the following requirement:

- Develops annual marketing plan in conjunction with sales department, which details activities to follow during the fiscal year, which will focus on meeting organizational objectives

Rework the first PAR statement from:

- Effectively managed a department of twelve customer representatives, increasing annual follow-on sales from 75% to 93% over a three-year period

To include your marketing plan experience:

- Effectively developed annual marketing plans and managed the detail sales activities to achieve an increase in annual follow-on sales from 75% to 93% over a three-year period.

With strong relevant PAR statements, your resume will be getting the attention it deserves and you will be getting an interview. For either the hybrid or the functional formatted resume, follow the PAR statements with a chronological listing of your employers. There is no need to list job titles or positions held at those companies. Ms. Beck's short list follows:

2010–Present	Seaside Realty
1997–2010	Johnson's Medical, Inc.
1996–1997	Advantage Temps

Next, list your education and training, with the highest level first. Conclude each of the formats with any special certifications, professional organizations, published papers, awards, or other relevant information. There are many websites to help you with sample resumes and tips so you can pick and choose what works best for your circumstances.

Before we complete this resume-building exercise, draft a sample cover memo for this sample job requisition. Having a boilerplate cover memo in your hip pocket makes it easier to personalize it later for the particular opportunity you will be pursuing.

A sample cover memo and all resume formats (chronological, functional, and hybrid) for this exercise are located in Appendices B and C. Additional resources are listed at the end of part IV.

Resume Building and Tailoring Summary

1. Effective career planning includes building your resume capabilities in anticipation for your future positions.
    a. Research your state Employment Development Department's Labor Market Information to find what skills you will need, where to network, what training is needed, etc.
    b. Complete career development milestones (e.g., training, certificates, experience, etc.) to strengthen your resume.
    c. Volunteer work can broaden your experience level and rapidly build your capabilities.

2. Consider what the hiring manager and organization need from an employee.
    a. Have the attitude of, "How can I make my boss successful?"
    b. Help them help you.

3. Continually develop and refine those Problems, Action, and Results (PAR) capabilities-based statements.
    a. Identify and quantify PAR statements with material from your past employee evaluations, weekly activity reports and accomplishments, organizational achievements (inspection results, audits, etc.), awards and recognition letters (ask for feedback; don't be shy), spot award bonus for meeting departmental goals, etc.
    b. Continually develop new PAR statements as you go.
4. Never misrepresent yourself. Your signed employment application is considered part of your employment contract for the duration of your employment.
5. Determine the most effective resume format for your situation: chronological, functional, or hybrid.

6. Tailor your foundational building block resume for each job opening by incorporating key searchable words and language from the job requisition.
7. Always include a cover memo to personalize your submittal.
8. Establish your references before you need them, and keep them informed of any upcoming interviews.

Finally, remember your resume's primary purpose is to get you an interview; tailor it for that. There is no need to include work history or accomplishments that are not relevant to the current position. A history dump is counterproductive; rather, showcase your capabilities with a compliant, concise, and compelling resume. There is one additional or secondary function for your resume: helping the hiring manager get approval from his manage to hire you. Remember, everyone reports to someone, so the easier you make it for the hiring manager, the better it will be for you. We will discuss this last point more in the post-interview discussion in the next chapter.

CHAPTER 12

Confident Interviewing

Just as the resume has the explicit purpose of getting an interview, the interview has the explicit purpose of getting an initial job offer (an offer that will later be negotiated). Let's take a look at the interview process and how to increase the likelihood of receiving an offer.

Preparation is absolutely the essential key for successful interviewing. Just as a foundational resume has to be tailored to a specific job requisition, the employee candidate has to be prepared to address the specific needs of a given job interviewer. Our preparation begins by expanding upon the earlier information and research we used for developing our resume for that position. However, now that we have an interview scheduled with real people (e.g., a hiring manager or possibly a panel of interviewers), we need more exact information about the roles of these individuals and the organizations or disciplines they represent.

Try Google and LinkedIn searches by the name or company or both. The information that pops up can be surprising. Often the trick is to figure out which of the many (hypothetically speaking) *Bill Johnson* references is actually the *Bill Johnson* you are scheduled to interview with. You will often discover papers authored by your interviewer, conferences attended, previous positions held, and sometimes even a photo giving you a preview of whom you will be meeting. Combining this information with the company's website information, its products and services, SEC reports, and Annual Shareholders Perspective prepares you to better understand their needs when responding to questions during the interview. Think of mining this information for the idea of *getting into their heads*. And yes, how impressive would a job candidate be who is mentally in sync with the interviewers' needs? Ask yourself, "If I were the hiring manager, what would I be looking for?"

Next, leverage the contacts you earlier established for those targeted companies of yours. Those *insider* contacts can really help you identify changes, thrusts, hot buttons, and challenges within the company relative to the open position. The inside contacts are helpful because they often have knowledge of the organization's challenges and immediate access to current information.

A word of caution: Be careful not to request or use information that is not releasable to the public. Never ask a contact for information that could be considered company-private or sensitive material. This could provide you an unfair competitive advantage at your contact's expense, and it would be considered ethically unacceptable. However, company bulletins, organization charts, recent reorganizations and promotions, titles of interviewers (internal auditor, community outreach representative, capture manager, etc.), new business, and recent contract awards are the types of information that are often releasable or within the public domain. This information gives you an inside perspective that will be very helpful during your preparation for the interview. Remember, however, that you want an advantage but never an unethical advantage.

Interview Types and Purposes (Three General Types)

Let's start with the most overlooked and untapped interview type: the informational interview. Informational interviews can be very beneficial, particularly if you are new to a field or are a recent graduate looking for career information or connections to get started. An informational interview is also a great way to get interview practice (this can be a great confidence builder) if you have not been job hunting for some time. The purpose of the informational interview is to get information about your career field regarding potential opportunities, required qualifications, available training, upcoming events, and most importantly—referrals.

Confident Interviewing

Although you are not interviewing for a specific job opening, think along strategic lines for your career development planning. You will find that people who are excited about their work and their contributions are usually quite happy to take twenty or thirty minutes out of their day to help others get established in their field. Being prepared and showing your interest and passion for their career field will leave a very positive impression about you with the interviewer. These impressions are the seeds for growing long-term networking relationships in your chosen career field.

As part of your preparation, have several open-ended questions about the industry, such as: "What are some of the biggest challenges in the industry today?" or "How did you get started?" Listen for any possible job opportunities during the interview. Then find out as much as you can about those opportunities and contacts while making the best use of your time together. Be sure to remain aware of the time allotted for the interview. By all means, do not be afraid to ask for a referral if the opportunity arises. As with any interview, be sure to thank the interviewer and follow up with a thank you note within the next three business days. Having a referral from an informational interview is a sure sign that the interview was a success!

The second type of interview is focused on an actual job opening and makes use of the traditional line of interviewing questions. The traditional interview questions are characteristically broad-based and start with some form of opener: "What can you tell me about yourself?" or "How would you describe your ideal job?" These questions provide an open door for you to own the interview. By being prepared, you can take the "What can you tell me about yourself?" question and present three or four of your strengths right off the bat. However, this is not a green light to get long-winded; rather, it is your chance to deliver a well-crafted *elevator pitch* that contains your top three or four strengths germane to the job opening. Expect that question!

As popular as the traditional style of interviewing questions have been in the past, employers are realizing that interviewing with these broad-based types of questions has favored candidates with better communication skills. The candidate with the best capabilities for success on the job may be passed over for a better-rehearsed candidate. As an evaluator, accurately differentiating a candidate's capabilities in a brief interview by relying on rehearseable, broad questions is at best difficult.

Exacerbating the difficulty for the hiring manager who is trying to differentiate one candidate's qualifications from another's are the many interview-coaching resources now available to candidates online and in job placement books. These resources provide excellent *canned* answers for candidates to practice beforehand. Therefore, the bar has been raised. It is now expected that all candidates will answer the traditional questions very well. Ensure that you are just as well prepared. A particularly good website for help practicing your responses to interview questions is provided by Quintessential Careers at: www.quintessentialcareers.com. You will find a bank of 150 interview questions with good answers, plus many other resources for the job seeker. Below is a sampling of some of those questions to give you a feel for good answers.

How would you describe yourself?

Sample excellent response:

    My background to date has been centered around preparing myself to become the very best financial consultant I can become. Let me tell you specifically how I've prepared myself. I am an undergraduate student in finance and accounting at _____ University. My past experiences have been in retail and higher education. Both aspects have prepared me well for this career.

What specific goals, including those related to your occupation, have you established for your life?

Sample excellent response:

    I want to be working for an excellent company like yours in a job in which I am managing information. I plan to contribute my leadership, *interpersonal, and technical skills. My long-range career goal is to be the best <u>information systems</u> technician I can for the company I work for.*

What specific goals have you established for your career?

Sample excellent response:

 My goals include becoming a Certified Financial Advisor so I can obtain a better working knowledge of financial research analysis, which would allow me contribute to my client base as a better financial consultant since I would have that extra insight into the companies they are seeking to invest in. Also this is the foundation block to advancing my career to portfolio manager or even branch <u>office manager</u>.

What will it take to attain your goals, and what steps have you taken toward attaining them?

Sample excellent response:

 I've already done some research on other workers at Merrill Lynch to see how they achieved similar goals. I know that Merrill Lynch encourages the pursuit and will reimburse for tuition of a graduate degree. I plan on pursuing a MBA to give me an even more extensive knowledge of business and financial analysis.

How would you describe yourself in terms of your ability to work as a member of a team?

Sample excellent response:

 I have had many opportunities in both athletics and academics to develop my skills as a team player. My tenure as a rower with my college's crew team serves as a good example. I learned a great deal about teamwork while rowing because all the rowers in the boat must act as one, which meant that we incessantly worked to keep each movement in the boat synchronized. On an individual basis, we still worked toward group goals through weightlifting and land-rowing. My experience as a marketing research team leader also helped me to learn the role of "team player." I viewed my position as that of group leader and of group member. I ensured that everyone in the group had equal opportunity to contribute, maintained excellent <u>com-</u>

munication among group members, and coordinated their energies toward reaching our team's goal.

What motivates you to put forth you greatest effort?

Sample excellent response:

You would think that because I am interested in sales, only financial compensation would motivate me to achieve. Although monetary rewards are important to me, I am driven to succeed internally. More than anything, I want to be respected by my friends and coworkers for being the best at what I do. Whether I am considered to be the best car detailer in my hometown or the best columnist for my college newspaper, I want to be recognized as the best.

Given the investment our company will make in hiring and training you, can you give us a reason to hire you?

Sample excellent response:

I sincerely believe that I'm the best person for the job. I realize that there are many other college students who have the ability to do this job. I also have that ability. But I also bring an additional quality that makes me the very best person for the job—my attitude for excellence. Not just giving lip service to excellence, but putting every part of myself into achieving it. In college and at my previous jobs, I have consistently reached for becoming the very best I can become. I think my leadership awards from my college, and my management positions are the result of possessing the qualities you're looking for in an employee.

What do you expect to be doing in five years?

Sample excellent response:

Although it is hard to predict the future, I sincerely believe that I will become a very good financial consultant. I believe that my abilities will allow me to excel to the point that I can seek other opportunities as a portfolio manager (the next step) and possibly even higher. My ultimate goal continues to be—and will always be—to be the best at whatever level I am working at within Merrill Lynch's corporate structure.

What do you see yourself doing in ten years?

Sample excellent response:

Ten years from now I see myself as a successful consultant for a world-class firm like yours. I want to have developed a wonderful bond with my employer. I will have proven myself a highly competent systems analyst and will represent my company in helping others find solutions to their <u>information-systems</u> needs in a professional and timely manner.

How would you evaluate your ability to deal with conflict?

Sample excellent response:

I believe I am quite good at handling conflict. Working in retail and in the residence halls required that I make many unpopular decisions at times, whether it was terminating an associate or taking judicial action on a resident. Often the person in conflict with me would be upset and sometimes physically outraged. I would always make sure that I fully explained the situation, the policies behind my decision, and why those policies exist. Usually by the end of the conversation, the person could see the other side of the situation.

What personal weakness has caused you the greatest difficulty in school or on the job?

Sample excellent response (shows how he recognized his weakness and worked to improve):

My greatest weakness had been delegation. I would take it upon myself to do many small projects throughout my shift as a manager that could have been done by others in an attempt to improve my workers' efficiency. Once I realized that I was doing more work than the other assistant managers, and they were achieving better results, I reevaluated what I was doing. I quickly realized that if I assigned each person just one small project at the beginning of their shift, clearly stated expectations for the project, and then followed up, then everything would get done, and I could manage much more efficiently and actually accomplish much more.

Student examples were provided to demonstrate that, even with very limited work experience, one can effectively showcase one's capabilities. I encourage you to review these and the remaining questions. Practice by incorporating your own work experience to embellish the responses, showcasing your capabilities. With a little practice and rehearsal, you too will be able to confidently answer these broad, traditional-type questions very well. The general nature of these questions allows you to easily incorporate your PAR statements to emphasize your capabilities.

The third type of job interview utilizes behavioral-based interviewing questions. This is becoming more popular because it addresses the shortcomings of the well-rehearsed, traditional-style questioning by fostering a deeper inquiry and subsequent discussion of the candidate's capabilities. Behavioral-based, open-ended questions are structured to generate follow-on questions, drilling down a layer or two toward the heart of the matter.

Examples of behavioral questions are, "Tell me about a time when you were confronted with …" or "Give me a specific time when you managed a difficult employee …" Based on your answer, the interviewer will then ask, "Tell me more about that; how did you …?" The interviewer can continue asking questions about the problem, the action you took, and the result of that action.

"Ahhhh," you say, "That all sounds very familiar—just like those PAR statements I spend so much time developing." Exactly! The PAR statements provide the stories and *discriminators* for you. They showcase your ability to deal with Problems, take Action, and achieve Results. Armed with a quiver of PAR statements, you can hit the target and confidently answer any of those challenging behavioral-based questions. If candidates have not invested the time to search out experiences for developing good examples of their capabilities, validated by past performance effectiveness, they will be at a huge disadvantage. The behavioral interview question can make the unprepared candidate's work experience appear shallow and weaker than the well-prepared *Problem/Action/Results* focused candidates. There is no fudging with these types of questions, no prefabricated book answers. Your capabilities will be revealed through your selection of your individual and unique PAR statements. When you select the PAR story for your answer, you now own the interview!

Review the below behavior-based interview questions and prepare your own answers by incorporating your PAR examples. But this time, take it a step further and drill down another layer or two in your preparation. What would be the next logical question that an interviewer would ask you about the particulars of your examples? After practicing with a few of the behavioral-type questions, you will get the hang of it. When you get to the interview, your answers will flow off your tongue as you confidently incorporate and enhance those powerful PAR statements, conveying your capabilities for the job through your responses. Below are sample behavior-based questions and responses taken directly from the list of 150 interview questions posted at: www.quintessentialcareers.com.

Describe a situation in which you were able to use persuasion to successfully convince someone to see things your way?

Sample excellent response:

Recently my company asked for bids on a phone system. Two <u>companies</u> came in very close with their bids, and most of my department wanted to go with a vendor that we have used in the past. After I looked over the proposals, it was clear that this was the wrong decision. So, I talked individually with each member of our staff and was able to change their minds and get the best product that would save money and provide the highest quality.

Describe a time when you had to use your written communication skills to get an important point across.

Sample excellent response:

As an Administrative Coordinator, I had a staff of 27 <u>students</u>. Having such a large student staff all working different shifts and having varying class schedules meant that meetings could not be held with everyone at one time. I needed to communicate with everyone about important policies and information often, so I came up with the idea of designing a Web page for my staff with written announcements. Each Desk Assistant was required to check the Web page daily at the beginning of his/her shift. I also sent email <u>communications</u> by a distribution list that allowed each Desk Assistant to keep informed about anything. The one situation that stands out in my mind is a last-minute summer camp that decided to come in a day early with only one day's notice. I had no staff scheduled to check in the campers or to organize the keys. I posted an update to the <u>Web page</u> and sent an email. Within four hours, I had the following day completely staffed and desk assistants there to organize room keys for the campers that night.

Give me a specific occasion in which you conformed to a policy with which you did not agree.

Sample excellent response:

When I worked at Home Depot as an assistant manager, I was always looking for way to boost my <u>employees</u>' morale. Unloading trucks is a very routine and physical job and can become very boring and exhausting, so to improve the unloaders' attitude toward their duties and make the best of the situation, I put a radio in the receiving dock. It worked; however, the district <u>manager</u> did not approve of the radio in the workplace even though it did not interfere with any set policy of company objectives. The radio was also out of any areas where customers would hear the music. I did not agree with my DMs decision to remove the radio; however, I understood his point of view once he explained it to me and promptly complied with his request. The employees were not happy that their radio was gone, so I found an alternative method of reward and morale boosting by implementing a program in which we provided lunch for the unloaders from any restaurant of their choice if they unloaded the trucks faster than normal. This program succeeded by increasing their unloading time from 2 1/2 hours to only 1 1/2, a savings in <u>payroll</u> of 8 percent of sales for that shift.

Describe a situation where others you were working with on a project

Confident Interviewing

disagreed with your ideas. What did you do?

Sample excellent response:

I was on a project team in a business class in my freshman year in college. The group brainstormed ideas for the video we were assigned to produce, and everyone but me was leaning toward an idea that would be easy. I suggested instead an idea that would be more difficult but would be something different that no other group would be doing. I used my communications skills to persuade the rest of the group to use my idea. During the project, we really learned what teamwork was all about, became a close team, and ended up putting a lot of hard work into the project. All the team members ended up feeling very proud of the video, and they thanked me for the idea—for which we earned an A.

In a supervisory or group leader role, have you ever had to discipline or counsel an employee or group member? What was the nature of the discipline? What steps did you take? How did that make you feel? How did you prepare yourself?

Sample excellent response:

As president of a community-service organization, I was faced with a board member not carrying out his duties as <u>management development</u> vice president. I consulted with him as to what we could do together to fix the problem. We agreed that he really couldn't devote the time that it took to carry out certain projects, and he ended up resigning his position, but he also stated he would help his replacement in whatever capacity he could. It made me feel as though we had come to the conclusion together, rather than him thinking I was criticizing his <u>performance</u>, which was not the case. I had a plan of action and carried it out successfully.

Describe some projects or ideas (not necessarily your own) that were implemented, or carried out successfully primarily because of your efforts.

Sample excellent response:

I had been recently given the duty of being the head swim team coach for the YMCA I was employed with. A swim meet was just around the corner, but only five swimmers had enrolled for the program, none of whom had ever been a part of an organized team. Funding would be cut for the team if more interest could not be generated. So I decided that I would take action and actively <u>recruit</u> people to join. Not only did I have to run the practices and correct any technical mistakes the swimmers were making, but I also had to contact other local swim teams to invite then to join the meet. I had to meet with the parents and the children separately and organize a way to help pay for t-shirts, swimsuits, goggles, and swim caps. By the third week of the program, I had gained 15 more swimmers and every single one had beat his or her own time in practice. When the meet came, I organized the events, ordered ribbons, and recruited volunteers. At the end of the meet, my team had come in first place among four other teams. The parents were delighted, and the profits from the swim team had skyrocketed to the approval of the board of directors.

Tell me about a time when you came up with an innovative solution to a challenge your company/class/organization was facing. What was the challenge? What role did others play?

Sample excellent response:
    The trucks at Wal-Mart come loaded by personnel at a distribution center, box-by-box. After receiving a few trucks, I noticed that my employees were unloading broken merchandise that took a lot of time to clean up before the rest of the truck could be finished. The broken glass, paint, or whatever material it was, prevented the employees from preceding farther into the truck, causing more person-hours than normal. I noticed that the merchandise was broken because heavier boxes were on top of lighter boxes. After a couple of days of this situation, productivity decreasing, I learned that the rest of the stores in my district faced the same problem. As a result, I asked each store to take pictures of the mess so the distribution centers could see exactly what was happening. I also asked each one to write down how many additional person-hours it took to clean up the mess. After we gathered this information for a four-week period, we had a pretty a good estimate of how much the company was losing, approximately $9.50 per person-hour... an average of $125 per store times 15 stores times 30 nights a month amounted to a substantial sum. We took the information as a group to our district manager. Once he realized how much money his dis-

trict was losing each month because of broken merchandise in the trucks, he contacted his regional manager, and the trucks were loaded more carefully after that. The district made our Profit and Loss the next month by a 9 percent increase.

Tell about a time when you built rapport quickly with someone under difficult conditions.

Sample excellent response:

While managing a high-end mall jewelry store in which the clientele are usually quite well-mannered and soft-spoken, I returned from a lunch break to find one of our newer sales associates struggling with an irate and somewhat irrational customer. Voices were escalating, with the customer spewing negative comments that could be heard from within the mall. While maintaining good relationships with our customers is a hallmark of our company, this particular situation was not ordinary by any means. I could tell the sales associate was in over his head with this encounter, so I quickly walked into the conversation—argument—and proceeded to ask the customer several key questions so that I could calm her down while also discovering more about her situation. I could then defuse the confrontation and restore order in the store. In the process of talking with her, I found we had a common love of dogs and were able to talk about our dogs—sharing some funny stories—before getting back to her specific problem with the store. In the end, it turns out the company that handles our credit card had been double-billing her account, and I was able to make a phone call and solve her problem.

Recall a situation in which communications were poor. How did you handle it?

Sample excellent response:

I worked on a team with several members, and while we worked in the same building, we often used email to communicate with each other. One of the members was not as comfortable with email as the rest of the team, and would always slow the team process down by repeatedly asking people to repeat or rephrase their emails—always reading way too much *into whatever was written in the emails. At one point, after an agonizing day of emails back and forth trying to explain a critical part of the work, I decided I simply needed to go to her office and talk with her about the problem. We met, and I listened to her issues, and together we worked out a solution in which the team still did most of its communications via email, but whenever this team member did not understand something, instead of sending a confusing collection of emails, she would either pick up the phone or walk to the other person's office and solve the miscommunication quickly and efficiently.*

On occasion we are confronted by dishonesty in the workplace or in school. Tell about such an occurrence and how you handled it.

Sample excellent response:

I worked for a magazine that had two main competitors, and at the time I worked there, the economy was a bit slow, and the competition for readers and advertisers among these three publications was fierce. We had just finished a market-research study that showed that our audience was just a bit larger and more attractive (better educated, <u>higher incomes</u>) than our competition. We sent the good news to our publisher, who called us in for a meeting to tell us he wanted to combine some numbers to make our position appear even stronger—and then put those numbers in an ad campaign touting how much better we were than our competition. We told the publisher that he was mistaken and that you could not combine the numbers the way he suggested, but he replied he knew that, but no one else would, and it would strengthen our position in a bad market. It took a lot of courage, but after the meeting, I went back and talked with him one-on-one so as not to embarrass him in front of my colleagues, and told him that what he was doing was dishonest—and could get us all fired. I knew I risked getting fired for even talking to him this way, but I felt pretty sure he was not dishonest at heart. He did not decide right then, bit he did call back the next day to say he had decided not to run the ad.

From reading these questions, you can appreciate how an interviewer can ask more detailed questions based on your initial responses. As you work through these questions, your PAR statements will continually be developed and refined to adapt to new scenarios. Your past efforts focused on developing PAR statements will help you recall previous accomplishments. The prepared interviewee will then be able to respond straightforwardly, using the answer to place the interview back squarely on familiar turf. Having this familiarity allows you to be yourself and confidently respond to the interviewer.

Interview Settings

Interview settings can vary widely, and generally speaking, private industry is less standardized than the public sector. Variations that are common include: a single one-hour interview with the hiring manager, a series of one-on-one interviews with key stakeholders, or a panel interview with typically four to six interviewers. And if you just happen to be a general flag officer being considered for a major military command, you can expect to have a Senate hearing with potentially one hundred interviewers (senators), along with C-SPAN coverage. Yikes!

Public institutions tend toward a more structured group interview process, utilizing the same questions for each candidate and keeping tight control of the allotted time. One advantage of such a structured process is the transparent fairness of the selection process, which reduces the likelihood of discriminatory hiring lawsuits or the perception of unfair favoritism.

To find out what to expect for your career field, ask your network contacts in the field, and don't forget to include questions about the hiring process during those early informational interviews. Just knowing a little about the interview setting will help you with your preparation. Definitely ask the recruiter as much as you can about the interview beforehand, including the names of the people you will be meeting, their positions, the scheduled length of the interview, and any other questions peculiar to this job. Simply knowing who will be interviewing you and their roles in the organization can give you clearer insights into their needs when responding to their questions.

However, don't be discouraged if the recruiter doesn't supply you with everything you asked for. Outsourced recruiters are often used to schedule interviews, and they may have only limited corporate knowledge or understanding of the roles and responsibilities of the organization you will be interviewing with. For the more structured interview processes, you may be fortunate enough to receive an information packet with detailed instructions about the interview process. The interview details will eliminate some of your unknowns and help you to be better prepared.

The setting you want to avoid, if at all possible, is a telephone interview, particularly if other candidates will be interviewing face-to-face. I have never seen a telephone candidate do as well as the live candidate when interviewing for the same position. The difficulty with a phone interview is the limited feedback received compared to the many nonverbal communication cues received during a face-to-face meeting. Studies have shown that communication is roughly 20 percent verbal and 80 percent nonverbal—meaning micro-expressions, vocal inflections, and body language. Those important nonverbal messages are often not easily discernible, and therefore missed, in a telephone conversation. Without the nonverbal signals, your ability to listen and appropriately respond is diminished, thus making it harder for you to be in sync with the interviewers and their needs.

In an effort to mitigate the shortcomings of a telephone interview, some companies have supplied computer-mounted camera packages to interview remotely with candidates. A word of caution here: First, be aware of what will be projecting behind you. If you will be interviewing from your home, you may want to re-locate your computer. Keep the look professional. Second, realize that the little camera that mounts on top of your computer monitor will be staring at the top of your forehead. However, your audience will appear on your monitor directly in front of and below your forehead. Therefore, remember that if you have relative eye contact with the interviewers' eyes on your monitor, they in turn will be looking at the top of your forehead and not your eyes. Be sure to look up into the camera as you speak. I know it is unnatural, and that is another reason face-to-face meetings are preferred, even with the *help* of technology.

If it is just not possible to schedule a face-to-face meeting with the interviewers, help to level the playing field by acting on these tips. First, set the environment. If you are going to be at your work location, find a place where you will not be interrupted. If you are at home, let the other household members know when the interview is scheduled, and find a quiet place away from barking dogs, lawn mowers, etc. For clearer voice reception, use a landline telephone instead of a cellular phone.

Take advantage of the distant interview situation by having your notes spread out in front of you for easy reference. Consider dressing up for the interview to feel the part, and try standing rather than sitting so you can better project your voice. Trust me—lounging in bed, propped up on pillows, in your casuals, with dim lighting, will broadcast a less-professional persona to the person listening on the other end of the line. Think, act, and look professional for all interviews. As with any interview, practice first with a friend or family member. Practice getting your message across while using only 20 percent of the communication resources you usually have at your disposal.

Silence is okay in a phone interview. Do not feel compelled to keep talking after you have given your answer, even if there appears to be an awkward silence on the phone. The interviewer may be writing down your answers and may simply need some quiet time to catch up. Also, he or she may be carefully deciding which question to ask you next. The employer is facilitating the meeting; pause after your answers, and let the interviewer have all the time needed to ask the next question.

Frequently the initial screening by HR recruiters is performed over the telephone for the purpose of verifying the candidate's qualifications for the job, ensuring that the candidate is still interested, and answering any questions about the published job requisition. A telephone interview with the screener doesn't need to be avoided; just remember this is the gatekeeper and your purpose is to get past the gatekeeper and meet with the hiring manager.

Remember, what the hiring manager is actually looking for may not be accurately portrayed in the short job description. Bear in mind that everyone is busy, and it is much easier to cut and paste from a previous job requisition, with similar requirements, to get the hiring process underway. Incidentally, often the hiring manager learns what is needed by interviewing candidates and discovering what they have to offer. Your objective is to get the interview; therefore, prepare by setting the environment, reviewing the job requisition, and sounding professional when you return the call. Yes, I said when you return the call, meaning you don't have to answer the phone if you suspect the caller to be a recruiter and you are not prepared, busy in traffic, or just on the go. Simply let the call roll over to voicemail and return the call later, in an environment that allows for your undivided attention. I realize this is contrary to the mindset of the instant text-messaging generation, but if the recruiter has identified you as a candidate, he or she will be grateful to receive your returned call later that day. You won't lose the opportunity by not responding on the spot.

My friend Lewis is in the telecommunications sales business. Telephone interviews are the norm for many of the smaller businesses in that field. He accepted a request for a telephone interview that coincided with his scheduled family vacation. He was so accustomed to interviewing over the phone that he thought he would pick up the call during his five-hour drive up the California coast. In essence, he was not taking charge of the interview setting. In addition to giving up the nonverbal communications cues, he was putting himself at a huge disadvantage.

Can you imagine the distractions in a setting like that? He would have been surrounded by three children in the car, sharing the road with eighteen-wheelers, navigating onto connecting highways, experiencing breaks in cell phone coverage, etc. Fortunately, my friend listened to my advice and rescheduled the interview so he could be there in person after his vacation. And guess what! He was offered the job. I cannot imagine how he could have ever presented himself as well while interviewing during a family road trip.

As an aside, professional airline pilots and copilots share the flying and communication duties between themselves as a standard practice. These well-trained professionals typically do not fly and talk on the radios at the same time. Likewise, despite being *hands free* with an ear device, you are not *head free* while driving. Important conversations require 100 percent of your attention. Own the environment!

Another less-than-favorable setting is the lunch interview. A lunch interview can work very well if a company has already decided that they need you on their team and they are now selling the company and themselves to you. One the other hand, a lunch interview doesn't work very well if you are in a fully fledged competitive interview process, meaning you are selling yourself. If possible, try to get an office interview instead by rescheduling away from the lunch hour. If you cannot avoid it, be sure to eat a snack before you arrive for lunch so you are not overly hungry. This is not the time to gobble, even though the tab is on them.

The challenge is that there is just too much going on to worry about a piece of spinach getting stuck in your teeth. Kidding aside, restaurants have a fairly high-decibel noise level, which always makes communication more difficult. There are also many distractions, including the untimely entrance of the waiter asking if you would like an iced tea refill at the very moment you are going to deliver your clincher of a strength attribute for their job opening. Then, of course, there is the distraction of your interviewer as he waves the waiter over to order the crème brûlée. With so many variables and unpredictable distractions to manage, I would suggest avoiding such settings altogether. Protect your important interview from the casual but often distracting atmosphere of a lunch setting. There will be time for casual lunches once you have the job.

Looking back on my career, I have good memories of each of these interview settings and the relationships that developed from them. However, I can definitely conclude that by far the best setting to present your powerful PAR accomplishments is in a controlled environment that allows you to capture the complete attention of the interviewer(s) and take ownership of your interview's surroundings. Furthermore, as a hiring manager, I have always tried to provide the best possible environment for candidates to express themselves so I could make the most informed decision. After all, hiring is the most important of the managing functions. Getting the staffing right makes everything else possible. Despite the relatively short interviewing and hiring process, the decisions have long-term consequences. Therefore, do your part. Help the hiring manager by understanding how best to present your capabilities.

Taming the Tough Interview Questions

As we addressed earlier, the behavior-type questions demand a more thoughtful, personalized response if you are going to score well. Therefore, we will focus our efforts on answering these more-challenging questions, with the realization that the less-challenging, traditional-style questions will also be tamed in the process. By knowing our strengths, we can use the very popular opening question, "Tell me a little about yourself," to deliver three or four of our strengths relative to the job description. This response should be a short elevator pitch, with enthusiasm for the opportunity at hand.

As the interview progresses, behavioral questions can be best addressed by leveraging your bulleted resume PAR statements. The PAR statements can be expanded into a more-detailed story of accomplishments. This will allow you to deliver two very powerful messages. First, your responses will demonstrate your strengths through your past successes. Second, and even more important, your responses will highlight your capabilities for future positions. Your capabilities, not your past history, are what the hiring manager is interested in. It is your capabilities that will get the hiring manager's needs met and goals accomplished. Your capabilities are what will directly contribute to the overall success of the organization. As the interviewer digs deeper into the scenario you provided through your PAR statements, you will be able to confidently answer those probing questions because, after all, this is your success story. Now you will own the perspective!

Consider your repertoire of PAR statements as a dynamic resource that are always in a state of development and improvement and that are very alive! As you see different ways to apply your experiences, add new PAR statements or tweak the Problem, Action, and Result to make it relevant to different questions. Depending on your level of experience, have six to ten PAR statements that showcase your strengths ready for each interview.

Conversely, along with the strength statements, you can expect to be asked one or two *weakness-type* questions. Let's rename the weakness questions from this point forward with the phrase "used to be a weakness" questions. A couple of examples of such questions are, "Tell me about a weakness and how it could impact your work here" or "What is the biggest mistake you have ever made on the job?" The rule is to always take the weakness and show how you learned from the situation or overcame the limitation. Therefore, if you are a real go-getter and have a tendency to take on too many projects (weakness), then you learned to prioritize (strength) your work. If you realize that you sometimes get so focused on completing a task on schedule that you have develop blind spots (weakness) to the needs of others on your team, then you learned to seek regular feedback (strength) from each of your team members. And if you needed additional training (weakness) to perform your job, then you attended training classes (strength) at the local college. With a little preparation and thought, you can be ready and circumvent the awkwardness of these weakness-type questions.

From the interviewer's perspective, a candidate who answers a "used to be a weakness" question well by turning it into a strength answer demonstrates more about his or her initiative and ability to prepare for the interview than an actual weakness or liability that would affect performance on the job. Personally, I have tended to not ask weakness questions but to use the interview time to assess a person's strengths and potential contribution to the organization instead. However, I probably won't be interviewing you. Therefore, be prepared and do very well. These questions are freebees!

Let me say a bit about any salary and benefits negotiations before or during the interview, keeping in mind that the objective of the interview is to get a job offer. It is in your best interest to delay salary discussions until you have been made an offer. The win-win negotiation strategies for a fair compensation package will be addressed later. Suffice it to say, the interview is not the place to discuss salary. If asked about salary, you can delay answering directly with statements such as, "Salary is important, but a good fit is more important to me …" or "It shouldn't be an issue." Also if you can, avoid telling them what your present salary is or what your previous salary was. Most employers have a salary range in mind, based on industry standards and published market trends. If you are still pressed with salary questions, you can always come back with, "You must have a salary range for this position in mind. Would you mind sharing your range with me?" That at least puts it back on them to give you their starting point; you can only go up from there.

The problem with providing your desired compensation too early in the selection process is that you could be eliminated if it is deemed too high. However, after they decide you are the right person for the job, they will be far more inclined to work toward a deal with you. On the other hand, if you offer something lower than what they were prepared to offer, you will leave money on the table. Mum's the word with salary and benefits negotiations until after you receive a formal offer.

It may come as a surprise to some that the number-one discriminator for hiring one applicant from among a group of screened qualified applicants is whether that candidate will be happy in the job. You say, "Happy? What does happy have to do with meeting the hiring manager's needs and the organizational goals?" The answer is everything, because if the applicant doesn't appear to fit well with the culture, is overly qualified, or lacks enthusiasm for the position, that person will most likely become dissatisfied and begin to look for other opportunities. High employee turnover is very disruptive to an organization. It increases training costs and drains precious company resources to re-staff positions. Hiring organizations want employees who are a good fit and who will basically be happy on the job.

The happiness assessment may provide little solace to the rejected applicant at the time, but in the long term, if the assessment was accurate, it is for the best. Studies have shown that employees who are happy on the job actually perform better, have better work habits (arrive on time, follow policy, etc.), get along better with their coworkers, and remain longer with the company. What is not to like?

I recently received an e-mail message from a recruiter for a position I had applied for stating, "Spencer, your background looks great and very relevant for what we need, but I need to ask you straight up: You look like director material. This is a level-lower, senior manager position. Why would you be interested in this position?" The recruiter was concerned about my long-term happiness. Yes, I fit the requirements, but she was questioning why I wanted the job and was not simply focused on filling a vacancy in the short term.

The *why* of interview questions is best answered by referring back to your career-development plan. Let me introduce the acronym WIFM, meaning, "What's in it for me?" Knowing how your WIFMs fit with a particular position provides the answer to how well you will be motivated and why you would want a position. Questions such as, "Where do you see yourself in five years, ten years?" or "Describe a short- (or long-) term goal you have," are best answered with your WIFMs and their WIFMs in mind.

If you assess that you might be slightly underqualified, you will want to emphasize your current skills and strengths, and you will also want to include the importance of developing new skills (your WIFM) in accordance with your career-development plan. Or express an enthusiasm and willingness to grow and contribute more than you ever have before (their WIFM). If, on the other hand, you feel you might be a little overqualified for the position, you can emphasize how your years of experience and your passion (your WIFM) will make a difference in impacting their bottom line (their WIFM), etc. Enthusiasm and positive energy sell; however, be careful not to be overly aggressive. I heard of a candidate responding to the hiring manager's question, "Where do you see yourself in three years?" with an arrogant snip, "In your office." Humility is a very attractive virtue; arrogance, not so much. Be attractive!

In order to get a handle on the dissimilar types of interview questions, organize them in your mind into Strength (leverage PAR statement), Weakness (used to be weakness), and WIFM (*your* career plan objectives and *their* needs) type questions, and then provide compelling and personalized responses. Personalizing your responses will leave an impression; you will be remembered!

A less frequently used question style that is worth mentioning is referred to as the *hypothetical.* Hypothetical questions can sometimes be off the wall. They are useful to evaluate your integrity, judgment, and analytical skills. The answer to a particular hypothetical question often isn't as important as the process and steps you demonstrate to get to your answer. An example question might be, "If you were a school administrator, how would you thwart a student protest over tuition increases?" As any successful politician knows, you don't have to answer the question in the same way it was presented to you; you can rephrase it to your advantage. (After all, this was a hypothetical question in the first place.) You may say something like, "Well, I have never worked in the education field, but this is similar to the time when our company's contributing percentage to the employees medical benefits was reduced ..."

Voila, now you are back to a familiar PAR statement, and once again—you own the perspective!

At the Interview

We've dedicated the major portion of this chapter to interview preparation, which corresponds to the ratio of prep time required for the succinct interview session that will last only an hour or so. Typically, the number of applicants selected to be interviewed for a job will range anywhere from three to as high as ten. If you happen to be highly qualified for a position but as a result of not being fully prepared, you finish as only the second or third choice, you won't receive an offer. Furthermore, finishing second or third, no matter how many times you are interviewed, won't get you an offer. Finishing on the top is what it is all about—and that takes preparation. Think quality over quantity when preparing for interviews.

Having prepared the best you possibly can, you are now ready to meet the interviewer(s)! Dress one level up from what you would be expected to wear on the job. For a company that is very casual, go with a business casual sports jacket with a dress shirt. If the company's dress code is business casual, wear a coat and tie. First impressions count; not that this is fair, it's just the way it is. Be well groomed, and dress conservatively. Wear nothing provocative (avoid low-cut blouses, short skirts, or silly ties), don't forget to polish you shoes, and look your best. Have a notebook and pen in hand, along with copies of your resume ready to help an interviewer who may have come less than fully prepared.

The hiring manager is expecting you to look your best and can only assume your day-to-day job attire won't be any better than this first impression; this is as good as it gets. Therefore, being slightly overdressed is perfectly fine. Even if you are interviewing on *casual Friday*, do not consider your interview as something that is a part of the company's Friday casual dress policy. Important visits from customers will trump a company's casual Friday policy in a heartbeat. Managers get dressed to sell to their customers. In the same way, you should be dressed to sell your capabilities to your customer—the interviewer(s).

Be sure to arrive with plenty of time to spare. You might even want to check out the location prior to the interview to make sure you know where it is and what to expect as far as traffic and parking. Planning some time margin in your arrival is a wonderful idea. It gives you the luxury of a relaxed arrival and a chance to calmly review your notes, glance over your PAR statements, meditate on your favorite Scriptures, and say a short prayer—a prayer asking that you will be able to represent yourself very well and for favor during the interview. All this can be done in the privacy of your car. Also, plan adequate time for a stop in the rest room to freshen up (check your hair, tie, collar, etc.). Arrive at the interview a little early, yet not earlier than ten minutes, as this can inconvenience the office staff. And never, never, never be late—never!

Be of the mindset that you are going to make a positive first impression with all the people you meet at the interview (everyone is special), not just the hiring manager. Use the ten-minute-early arrival interval to establish a rapport with the receptionist (or administrative assistant), collect business cards, obtain the contact information of your interviewers (needed for later follow-ups), and collect any company publications that may be available to visitors on coffee tables or countertops.

Of course you can expect to be a bit nervous, and that is quite normal. Professional speakers and actors get anxious before their performances as well. Use this adrenalin-producing situation to your advantage. Smile as you meet people, make eye contact, give a friendly but firm handshake, and be alert to names and titles. Let your enthusiasm and excitement shine, leaving a good impression. Bear in mind that most days in the office entail interacting with familiar faces, familiar tasks, familiar meetings, etc. But today you are new, you are upbeat, and your energy is contagious. You are being noticed. Thank God for the adrenalin rush and that little nervous feeling inside you that is making you wonderfully stand out from the day-to-day routine business!

Confident Interviewing

Once you are introduced to the interviewer or interviewing panel, attempt to match their energy and sense of urgency. For instance, in the structured panel interview, the formal process is controlled by the facilitator, who monitors the time, ensures the same questions are properly asked of each candidate, and affords each candidate a predetermined amount of time to ask questions of the panel. In that situation, you could expect a brief round of introductions and then getting right to the interviewing, with the facilitator following a checklist-like regimen. On the other hand, if you are being interviewed by a hiring manager only, you might be offered a cup of coffee or water and asked about your drive there, the weather, etc. Whatever the situation might be, align your state with theirs to generate an initial chemistry between the interviewer(s) and yourself.

Referring back to the resume chapter, we discussed when it is appropriate to include golf on your resume. Suppose you decided not to include anything about golf on your resume, and after arriving at the interview, you notice the hiring manager has a golf club in his office and a watercolor of Saint Andrew's hole 5 on his wall. If this happens, then by all means bringing up golf before the actual interview questions begin would be appropriate and a great ice breaker. Take the time to look around and observe any clues that might reveal your interviewer's interests that you could then use as openers to initially connect and build chemistry between you both.

Expect the interviewer to open the questioning with the, "Tell me about yourself ..." question. This is your chance to give a brief summary of three to four of your strengths that would apply to this position. It is not meant to be the story of your life or a recital of your resume (which they should have already reviewed). Use it to your advantage with concise, compelling (your passion for the work), and relevant elevator pitch highlights of your strengths and capabilities toward their needs. The remaining questions will be in some form of the Strength, Weakness, Salary, WIFM, or Hypothetical-type questions. Your rigorous preparation will make answering these questions easy and hopefully enjoyable for you and the interviewer(s).

Toward the end, you will have an opportunity to ask your questions of them. This is where you can really own the perspective. Thoughtful questions from your research can be very effective. You can ask questions such as, "I understand you division headquarters will be relocating to … What do you expect will be the impact on the customer base?" or "From the reorganization you explained, what are you expecting more of, and what are you expecting less of?" Questions about the job position can be, "After ninety days on the job, what would the selected candidate need to accomplish for you to say, 'We hired the right person'?" Your questions to them will help you get a better idea of how they are thinking about the role of this position and what they are thinking about you. This is very important to understand, because you will be following up with a thank you note. That follow-up note will address their needs and reaffirm your committed interest in their company (and that you will be happy there).

Being aware of the time and the remaining amount of content you want to convey allows you to gauge your questions and conclude the interview with time to make a closing statement. The closing statement will state your affirmation of interest based on everything you heard today. Remember that they want to hire people who are excited about the company and will be happy! Show your enthusiasm; leave a lasting impression.

Before we leave the topic, one great, and absolutely essential, question to ask is, "Based on everything you have heard from me today, is there anything preventing us from moving forward to the next step?" (whatever that step might be—the next round of interviews or the job offer). This may seem like a gutsy move, but if there is any doubt in an interviewer's mind, it is best to address it right then and hopefully correct it. Any doubt on his or her part will only get worse with time.

As a personal example, I was unaware that one of my responses had left some doubt about my fitness (happiness on the job) for a particular position. I had been asked whether I preferred working with a manager who provided specific or general direction. I had stated that I prefer a more hands-off manager who allows me the freedom to solve problems using my creativity. When I asked my closing question about "any doubt" from any of my responses, the facilitator said he was concerned about my need for creativity on the job because this company had put a lot of effort into standardizing processes and there might not be that much creativity remaining for me in their processes.

Again this was a question of whether I would be happy working for them. I quickly amended my earlier statement with, "Having been a pilot with the Air Force Reserves for thirty years, I am very comfortable following disciplined checklists and organizational procedures." I went on to explain, "The creativity I spoke of was for finding solutions, not circumventing organizational processes. ... I have a great appreciation for the structured approaches (relating back to one of my PAR statements) and the need to obtain repeatable results through approved processes, etc." The lead interviewer let out an audible sigh of relief and said, "Oh, I am glad you clarified that. My only reservation was whether you would be a good fit working within our structured processes, and you answered it very well. Thank you." I thought, **Wow**, *I am so glad I put that question out there. It gave me the chance to clear up that one hanging doubt that I wasn't aware of.*

The bottom line is, job interviewing is an exchange of information. Be sure to ask the interviewer(s) if they have any doubts; it is your chance to mitigate or remove a lingering doubt.

After the interview, when you are back in your car, take a relaxing breath and then jot down everything you can remember about the interview, the interview questions, your answers, their responses to your answers (verbal and nonverbal cues), etc. Every interview is a learning experience; jot down what went well and what you would do a little differently the next time. You will be learning as you *Make Your Way*. Furthermore, these freshly taken notes will help you with your follow-up correspondence, the subject of the next section.

Now would be a good time to contact your references if you haven't already. Let them know you have interviewed for a position and provide them with a little information about why this job is a good match for your capabilities and passions. They will then be prepared when the HR representative calls them. Help them help you.

Follow Up

Follow up using the "every three days" rule. Hiring managers expect you to follow up with a thank you; that is a given. In addition to merely complying with business etiquette, it is very important to include in your follow up thank you any further clarifications or additional points you want to emphasize after you had some time to re-think your answers. You know the feeling, "Ah shucks, I can't believe I didn't mention …" or "I wish I would have said it differently …" A well-constructed follow-up note can be used to clarify those points. Also taking what you learned from their responses to your questions, you can reestablish their perspective and further align your good fit. And always be sure to include a statement showing your enthusiasm for the position. They want to know you are interested!

Also be sure to include a personalized thank you for everyone you interviewed with. You never know who might be advocating on your behalf. Typically, HR procedures require each interviewer to complete a candidate assessment sheet. The hiring decision can be a team effort; this is particularly true for the public sector.

Being the last applicant to be interviewed gives you the advantage of having your strengths fresh in the interviewers' minds as they begin selecting the best candidate from the group. The next-best position would be the first applicant interviewed. Either way, you avoid being caught in the *menagerie of the middle*, where the candidates' strengths and discriminators tend to get blurred over time. Of course, you typically wouldn't have much, if any, control over where in the sequence of interviewees you will land.

To mitigate this leveling effect, politely ping the hiring manager or decision makers every couple of days. The follow-up memos will help differentiate you (and your capabilities) from the others in the days following the interview period. Most likely, the interviewers gave their business cards to you and thus their permission (at least tacit) to call for updates, so use the update opportunities to remain fresh in their memory.

But how do you ping without becoming annoying? Remember two points. First, try to structure every correspondence with information that will help them. And second, include a follow-up action for the next correspondence so they will be expecting to hear from you. In addition to what was stated in the section on building your resume for the purpose of getting an interview, a secondary purpose of the resume is to give the hiring manager the tools to sell you to their management as the next new hire. Therefore, you can refine your resume from the information gained at the interview and resubmit your resume to the hiring manager. A short note explaining that you have included some additional accomplishments based on what you learned of the company's needs at the interview would be appropriate. Now you are helping the hiring manager hire you.

Based on what you learned from the interview, you can use your network to discover information that would be of interest to the interviewer. I once sent a summary of the key points from a keynote address given by a government customer of theirs for a professional organization–sponsored event. Coincidentally, the information was very relevant to the discussion of the company's future business pursuits that we had during the interview. Now was this simply a random coincidence? Or should we expect our network to provide helpful information for others? I believe the latter. Our network contacts and organizations not only help us find the opportunities and prepare us for the interviews, but they also provide us with helpful information for follow-up correspondences.

To make a point of just how adamantly I believe in this *helps principle*, I continued corresponding with a hiring manager by providing helpful information long after the position I applied for was cancelled. That's right. Funding was cut after the lengthy interview process—ouch! Even though the job posting disappeared, and even though I wasn't hired, the job search effort wasn't wasted. I established a key relationship in my industry and now have access for future endeavors, whether within that company or with another company as a teaming partner. At the end of the day, I established a solid relationship within one of my key companies through the interview and follow-up process.

Things to Avoid During the Interview

- Don't discuss salary with the hiring manager. Save that for HR after the offer is made.
- Don't ask about benefits. Benefits are an HR function.
- Don't mention religious or political affiliations unless you are applying as a chaplain, lobbyist, etc.
- Be careful with personal information. Avoid anything that federal and state law prohibits.
- Avoid anything negative. Keep the interview upbeat and positive (particularly regarding past or current employers).
- Don't have your cell phone on (ring or vibrate calls are distractions).

Summary

My hope is that you will approach an interview fully prepared and ready to put forth your best value proposition toward meeting the hiring manager's needs—and then enjoy the adrenalin rush! Knowing that your resume caught their attention, the interview will determine if there is a good fit for the open job position.

If the job just isn't a good match, then that is okay. What you learned can be applied to your career plan to help you to better focus on positions that will be a good fit in the future. You will have learned from the experience. It is very discouraging when you believe the job would have been a great fit but you did not get an offer. Any time you invest your time and energy into something as personal as who you are and what you do and it doesn't work out, it is a disappointment in your career journey—a disappointment that is emotionally painful. Despite the outcome, thank the interviewer for considering you. Let him or her know you are very interested in the company, and stay in touch. Be of good courage; there will be a next time. Your responsibility is to be ready for it.

Incidentally, the hiring manager may not know beforehand exactly what the ideal candidate's capabilities should be. The job requisition was the starting point. Interviewing several candidates could change the interviewer(s) perspective of what capability mix the ideal candidate should possess. Each vacant position can be unique. I've seen concurrent hiring for multiple positions with offers going to the candidates best fitted for the team's pooled ability to work as a cohesive and complementary unit. In essence, your skill set would have to complement some number of other candidates' capabilities that are unknown to you and vice versa.

The lesson to take away from interviewing is to always be prepared and realize there are many variables, some of which are out of your control. Therefore, do the best you can, and then be at peace knowing that you did your best. Career-development planning is a lifelong quest. There will always be new opportunities for those who faithfully seek to multiply their talents. Only be strong and very courageous during your quest, seeking the Master's words, "Well done, good and faithful servant. You were faithful with a few things, I will put you in charge of many things; enter into the joy of your master" (Matt. 25:21).

So hopefully, not too long after your interview, HR will be calling you with the exciting news of an initial job offer. Upon receiving such a call, it is time to earnestly negotiate. Let's learn more about win-win employment negotiations in the next chapter.

CHAPTER 13

Win-Win Negotiating

Just as the resume has the explicit purpose of getting an interview and the interview has the explicit purpose of getting an initial job offer, employment negotiations have the explicit purpose of getting a win-win employment contract between you and your employer.

Once the employer decides you are the best candidate, you are in a strong position to work with the HR department to negotiate a win-win contract. To effectively negotiate, you must consider the offer's entire compensation package relative to your personal career development plan (e.g., educational goals, future opportunities, financial needs, quality of life preferences).

Employee compensation encompasses more than just salary. Unfortunately, salary is often the only portion we wrangle over, so we consequently miss the opportunity to negotiate other benefits. Consider compensation as a total package, including negotiable benefits such as vacation time, health care, tuition assistance, telecommuting options, mileage stipend, mobile phone plan, gym membership, discounts on company services or products, etc. The value of any one of those perks depends on your circumstances. Other perquisites (a.k.a., perks) can include 401K plans with or without matching, profit sharing, retirement plans, bonus pool, sign-on bonuses, and relocation allowances.

Again, the value of any individual perk always depends on your circumstances. As an example, the value of a relocation perk is quite different for a college student moving from a dorm room when contrasted with a family of four moving across the country. Likewise, medical benefits might be a huge plus to someone with a dependent who has costly medical needs. On the other hand, medical benefits may be of little value to someone with a working spouse who already has a great family medical plan in place. And so it goes for each perk. The value is dependent on your individual situation, and therefore there is the need for negotiations to reach a win-win employment contract. As a reminder, signing an employment application and the subsequent job offer constitutes a legal contract between you and your employer. Good contracts require good negotiations.

A word about salary: Many employers have established pay grades with salary ranges or bands. The salary ranges are broad enough that they can span across several pay grades. As a hypothetical example: salary grade 5 has a range of $1,000 to $1,500 per week; grade 6 has a range of $1,200 to $1,800 per week; and grade 7 has a range of $1,400 to $2,000 per week. In practice, employees working similar jobs are earning different pay within the *range* for that job grade or classification. Where you fit within the range is negotiable; salaries are not set in stone.

Veterans of the Human Resources world sometimes refer to the *where* in the range as the penetration percentage. To illustrate, if a pay grade has a $20,000 range starting at $60,000 per year and ending at $80,000, a salary recommendation of $73,000 would penetrate the range by $13,000 or 13/20, equating to a penetration of 65 percent. In practice, to simplify the calculations, quartiles are often used, meaning a recommendation from HR could be to compensate the candidate at the low (0 to 25 percent), low-mid (25 percent to 50 percent), high-mid (50 percent to 75 percent), or high (75 percent to 100 percent) quartile. Again, there is room for negotiating within the quartile.

In the public sector, salary grades often have *steps*, meaning you can enter the job at the beginning step or at a higher step within the pay grade, based on some qualifying criteria. This again gives the candidate room to negotiate. The HR organization has the responsibility to keep salaries in balance and to ensure the fairness of similar pay for similar work (job responsibilities). By analyzing and assessing: 1) the market's competitive conditions (e.g., what is the going salary, LMI); 2) the urgency to fill a position (e.g., lost sales revenue, maintain customer satisfaction, keep production level); and 3) any known constraints of the hiring organization's budget, you can gain an appreciation for the drivers and feasible solutions for negotiating your side of the win-win.

As a case in point, my colleague, Steve, recently retired from the military and had marketing and business development skills that were desired by a small business. The small business wanted to hire Steve to develop new business contracts (this is an overhead cost) with the intent for Steve to later act as the program manager for any new contracts (this is a direct billing charge to the contract). The dilemma for the small business was that they needed Steve's expertise for pursuing new business opportunities and wanted to propose him as the program manager for winning new business, but they couldn't afford to hire him until after they were awarded a new contract. The win-win solution in this case was for Steve to establish himself as a consultant. As a consultant, Steve could receive a higher hourly rate at less cost to the company.

Let me explain. If the company had hired Steve as an employee, the company's cost would have included salary plus medical benefits, the cost of 401K matching, facility costs (offices, labs, corporate HQ, etc.), social security and Medicare taxes (FICA), along with state and federal unemployment taxes. These additional overhead expenses can actually exceed the employee's salary, depending on the company's infrastructure expenditures and benefit package costs. The accounting term often used is the *multiplier* as the numerical factor to quantify this wrapped-in cost. If the multiplier happens to be 2.0 for employees, assuming an employee is paid an hourly rate of $50 (approximately $100,000 annual salary), the hiring manager's department must have $200,000 budgeted (salary, taxes, and benefits) for a full-time employee for the year.

Remembering that Steve is retired from the military, he already has lifetime medical benefits and is a military retiree receiving a pension, so he would not be eligible to collect unemployment insurance payments; therefore, these perks are of little value to him. During the two-week interval before negotiations were completed, Steve established himself as "Steve's Consulting" by paying nineteen dollars for a city business license and another twenty dollars for a stack of "Steve's Consulting" business cards. Steve then contracted with that small business at seventy-five dollars per hour for thirty hours per week. Doing the math, that is $112,500 annually, which was within the small business's overhead budget. As a consultant, Steve will be earning a higher hourly rate (and annual salary was $112,500 versus $100,000). This was possible by not charging the company for costly, unneeded benefits that are standard for full-time employees. Steve not only is making $12,500 more annually, but he also has ten additional hours per week available for other clients, or maybe just to spend with his family enjoying his "retirement."

By using the consulting approach, the small business gained a formidable business development capability and a qualified program manager for proposing and executing the anticipated contract awards—at a price they could afford immediately. This was a win-win for both.

By the way, once Steve captures that new business (as I am sure he will), he will be positioned for renegotiating a win-win for his role as program manager for the new work. His client will have gained an additional revenue stream, and this will allow Steve to open negotiations to increase his hourly rate while performing in the new role. Life is good!

Your long-term career path and how best to accomplish the incremental steps along the way should be the prime driver in determining the importance of elements within your compensation package. For instance, airline pilots have a mandatory one-year probationary period where they earn meager wages and are assigned the least-desired schedules and routes. On the surface, you would wonder why anyone would accept those lousy airline industry terms. But after the probation period is completed, the recently hired pilot's salary increases significantly. As older pilots retire, or if the airline expands its route structure, more-desirable options become available for the more recently hired pilots. If your career goal is to become a commercial airline pilot, you must *pay your dues* along the way; it comes with the territory. Some form of this is true for many fields, including doctors serving their internships, senior pastors serving as youth pastors, etc. Having a realistic industry expectation is essential for effective negotiations.

Finally, quality of life concerns need to be considered. Consider questions such as these: How long can you sustain a full-time position that entails a ninety-minute commute on congested freeways each way? How much overtime is expected, and how much flexibility is there in the workweek? What is the cost of living in the area you will be moving to? Quality of life concerns can be crucial to your long-term success with a company. Although not all quality of life concerns are quantifiable like the other compensation package considerations, do not underestimate the emotional and physical cost to you and your loved ones.

Accordingly, the trade-offs and options are broad, allowing us room to negotiate toward that optimized win-win contract. Again, I've used the word *contract* because that is exactly what you will be signing—a legally binding agreement between your employer and yourself. Be creative and bold. Make it great!

Be Encouraged

As you progress through the hiring process, starting with the hard work of building a compelling resume and proceeding to a negotiated win-win contract, expect an exciting ride. Some parts of the ride will inevitably end in disappointment. Try to consider yourself to be in *Boot Camp*, as if you are being tested each time. The preparation isn't easy. It is hard work that is often emotionally straining. This makes it all the more discouraging when what you thought to be a good opportunity just doesn't pan out for you in the end. Remember, it is all about the fit. Try to learn from each attempt, but do not take the rejections personally. Keep the doors open; you might be back at that company interviewing before you know it.

Paul's encouragement is applicable: "Be anxious for nothing, but in everything by prayer and supplication with thanksgiving let your requests be made known to God. And the peace of God which surpasses all comprehension, will guard your hearts and your minds in Christ Jesus" (Phil. 4:6–7).

On a personal note, early one morning I had my Bible opened to Philippians 4:6–7 during my devotional time. I noticed that I was unconsciously avoiding reading that Scripture. I had applied for a job, had received a call from HR indicating their interest in my skills, and was now waiting for a confirmation call for the date and time of the interview. But I was afraid. I was afraid this might not be the right job for me, and I was also afraid to ask God to intervene.

Sadly, at the very time when I should have been seeking God's direction, I lacked the faith to boldly trust in His providence. My conundrum was that if I asked for this job and it turned out to be a poor choice on my part, I was stuck with what I had asked for. And if I didn't get the job after I prayed to get it, then I might lose faith or even get a little angry with God (for only a moment, of course). Then suddenly I came to my senses, rose above my anxiety, and earnestly prayed, giving thanks and making my requests known to God. The interview did happen. I believed I did very well, but the funding for the position was eliminated before they could select a candidate. But I had peace through the process! I was able to do my best.

What did I gain? I gained valuable interview experience and learned from the process. It prepared me for an even better fit for another position within that same company. But more importantly, I gained a deeper appreciation for the loving-kindness God showers on us in regard to our vocations (our callings). I realized once again that He definitely is in control. Working to get the right fit during your career development journey is hard work and requires faith, but the payback for your obedience to your calling is phenomenal! You will receive a breathtaking, "Well done, good and faithful servant. You were faithful with a few things, I will put you in charge of many things; enter into the joy of your master" (Matt. 25:21).

The next chapter provides references to some of the many *job-capture* resources that will further expand your knowledge. You will find sample resumes, interview questions, compensation tables, and articles by the experts in career placement. Along with keeping you updated on the latest trends, it will also help you to start networking with people at these sites who share your common career concerns. Enjoy!

CHAPTER 14

Job-Capture Resources

As I have stated in previous chapters, there are so many great career resources available at the click of a mouse that it is difficult to list them all. My hope is that this book will spark your interest to search for more information. In grade school, we learned our math tables and mastered our spelling words through practice and repetition. The teacher didn't just show us long division once and then leave it at that—not at all. Rather, there were many homework sheets requiring practice and re-practice of the learning objectives for that day. Learning is a repetitive process. Likewise, reading this book provides you with an introduction to career development, but really learning the art of resume building, interviewing, and negotiating takes practice. In addition, once you achieve a level of proficiency, you must use your skills to maintain that proficiency and keep abreast of new developments in your industry.

I highly recommend maintaining and refining your career-development skills by joining career groups or blogs. For instance, on LinkedIn I found 13,732 career groups when I last checked. Other social networking sites have many more. New information and new perspectives are always being discussed. Find a few that are useful for you. By constantly re-engaging and stimulating your thinking about the dynamic subject of careers, you will alert your mind to new ideas and become aware of new ways to apply what you already know.

Consider this: I flew the same military aircraft for twenty-eight years while serving in the US Air Force and Air Force Reserve, yet every month I had to maintain my flying currency by performing two takeoffs, two landings, and two precision approaches. You might ask, "Why, after all those years of flying, would you still be required to practice that rigorously?" The truth of the matter is that the monthly currency requirements only provided the minimal level of proficiency (a.k.a., safety). In addition to these monthly currency requirements, there were also many more quarterly, semi-annual, and annual requirements. The consequence of not completing at least two landings in June was that, come July, you would have to be accompanied by an instructor pilot, since you were considered unsafe to fly on your own. Keep yourself proficient by taking advantage of the many career groups, web resources, and blogs available today. And have a great flight!

Research your state's employment development department; be sure to visit the California EDD site at: caljob.ca.gov and their extensive Labor Market Information (LMI) link. If your state employment website incorporates O*Net information, you will be able to search for local, regional, and state companies, as well as positions and employment trends in your area. Some additional state websites for your consideration:

>Alaska Department of Labor and Workforce Development: Almis.labor.state.ak.us
>Arizona Department of Economic Security: www.workforce.az.gov
>Arkansas Labor Market Information: www.discoverarkansas.net
>California Employment Development Department: www.labormarketinfo.edd.ca.gov
>Hawaii Department of Labor and Industrial Relations: www.hiwi.org
>Idaho Department of Labor: www.jobservice.ws
>Kentucky Department of Employment Services: www.workforcekentucky.ky.gov
>Michigan Department of Labor and Economic Growth: www.milmi.org/
>Montana Department of Labor and Industry: www.ourfactsyourfuture.org

Job-Capture Resources

Nevada Department of Employment:
www.nevadaworkforce.com
Texas Workforce Commission: www.tracer2.com
Washington Department of Labor:
www.workforceexplorer.com
Wyoming: doe.state.wy.us/answers

The all-time classic book on job hunting is *What color is your parachute?* by Richard Nelson Bolles (jobhuntersbible.com). This book has sold more copies than any other career-development book ever, and it is available at your public library, on audio, and in paperback. You can complement that book with *Job Search Bloopers* by DeCarlo and Susan Guarneri.

To get you started with online resources, Quintessential Careers at www.quintcareers.com is a must. As noted previous the sample interview questions and answers were provided directly from the Quintessential Career site. I personally have used the Quintessential Career interview question bank for conducting mock interview sessions in preparation for interviews. You can too. Try practicing in front of a video camera for upcoming interviews by either reviewing the video yourself or soliciting a few close friends to help coach you. You will be surprised how quickly you can hone your responses to highlight your strengths and capabilities. In addition to the interview questions found at Quintessential Careers, there is a plethora of job capture resources for your use. Caution: Please note the Quintessential Careers copyright restriction and use appropriately. I would also recommend Job-hunt.org, which identifies the best job sites on the Internet, and rileyguide.com for the online librarian, Margaret Riley. All of these are free!

I also highly recommend a free subscription to a newsletter published by Nick Corcodilos, author and host of *Ask the Headhunter*. Nick provides a wealth of pragmatic advice for the job seeker. Check it out. There are many other online resources (free and for a fee) that can help you with specific employment concerns, such as those for military personnel transitioning to civilian

www.MakeYourWayResources.com 213

careers, career changes, older workers, executive level, entry level, women professionals, etc. Find what works best for your needs.

A few more job sites of note are Usajobs.gov for all federal agency jobs and Jobsearch.monster.com for industry general jobs. As you identify targeted companies, visit their career sites, keep your information updated, and set up automatic notification of new job postings that meet your search criteria. The other advantage of populating the company job career site with your qualifications is that HR recruiters will first search their own site for candidates before paying search firms and outside job boards to purchase your resume from them.

Inevitably, you will receive calls from headhunters and recruiter search firms. Both of these can be helpful. I would recommend that you always welcome calls from headhunters. They get paid to find the right person for their clients. They serve as the middle man between their client and the employee candidate. You want a headhunter who you can trust as your agent. When you have that trust, you can then work with the headhunter toward a win-win contract. The headhunter also requires you to be trustworthy. Never contact the employer directly from his lead or work with two headhunters for the same position. The hiring company does not want to be placed in a predicament between two headhunters seeking commission, and they would most likely rather pursue a less-contentious hire. Relationships matter. Be open and respect the role of the headhunter. Visit Nick Corcodilos's site, *Ask The Headhunter* at: http://www.asktheheadhunter.com/ for a wealth of resources and a free newsletter.

Keep in mind that recruiter search firms have a different role than headhunters. Typically they do not have actual job openings to fill but would like your permission to use your resume so they can search for you. They usually get paid directly by you for their services. The services include consulting, writing resumes and cover memos, and mailing to prospective companies. Caution: There is no guarantee that search firms will find you the job you want after you have paid for the search services. I'm confident that the material we have discussed so far will serve you well in determining if and when you might be in a situation that warrants considering these services.

Make Your Way—myPlanner

We have developed another *Make Your Way* resource to help you bring all your career information into an organized working area appropriately called my*Planner*. This online planner provides you your personal working environment for career planning complete with book summaries and step-by-step instructions for developing, assessing, editing, and storing your: design strengths and passions; career milestones and plans; PAR statements; interview responses; network contacts; and much, much more. It also includes up-to-date recommendations and direct links to our latest resources and tools to help you with your career planning and goal achievement.

The *Make Your Way—myPlanner* is the perfect complement to *Make Your Way—the Book*. Visit www.MakeYourWayResources.com for a free trial membership.

Congratulations! You now have the *Networking advantage* and J*ob-capture* knowledge to determine and incorporate those needed inch-stone planning goals into your career development plan. Next we want to address the intentionality and discipline needed to accomplish those goals as you continue on your career journey. We will dedicate the next part to "Goal Getting".

Part V

Goal Getting

Thus far we have explored the merits of our "Network Advantage" and "Career Planning" for successful *Job Captures*. However, knowledge and enabling techniques alone do not bring about the behavioral change necessary for accomplishing goals. Just as an overweight person doesn't lose those extra pounds simply by knowing about caloric intake, we can't develop our careers simply by knowing about career-development planning. We must act on that knowledge as the Scripture tells us in James 1:22: "But prove yourselves doers of the word, and not merely hearers who delude themselves." So how exactly do we establish and set achievable career goals? And, better still, how do we go about successfully accomplishing our career-planning goals? Part V gives us the actionable methods for accomplishing our career goals.

The exciting part of *goal getting* is the sheer intentionality of it all—that is, your intentionality! It is your career plan, based on your strengths and passions, with you in control of establishing and pursuing your goals—and you take complete ownership of it all. You are the captain of your ship, *Making Your Way* toward your goals. And as any captain knows, the sea's state is constantly changing, and the winds are forever shifting, but through it all you are still at the helm, making the best of the opportunities to leverage your God-given gifts.

I have fond memories of my early days as a young Air Force Captain when I was serving as a commander (a.k.a., pilot) for a large transport aircraft. Reminiscence of those days harkens the thrill of pulling back on the yoke, rotating a 325,000-pound aircraft off the runway, climbing through ten thousand feet, and then accelerating to the desired climb airspeed—knowing that I was in command of the aircraft. As the commander, I was responsible for the safety and success of the flight, while respectfully acknowledging my total dependence on the other crew members. I was not flying solo. It was a team effort, and the more effectively the crew worked together, the higher the probability of a successful mission.

Similarly, as you accept command of your career plans, you must always acknowledge your dependence on a working network to achieve your success. The good news is, you are not doing this alone; you have help! We were created as social beings. Today's social media boom is making our socializing even easier and illustrates the significance of staying connected with popular mottos such as LinkedIn's tagline, "Relationships Matter." Nonetheless, there can never be a greater illustration of the importance of relationships than that of Christ dying for us so we could have a relationship with the Father. Yes, relationships matter; we can't do it alone.

However, in conjunction with managing our external social networking and relational framework, we also need to manage our internal thoughts and our self-talk. We read in 2 Corinthians 10:5 that we are to "take every thought captive." This compels us to take ownership of and responsibility for our thoughts by being intentional about God's purpose for us. And part of being intentional is learning and understanding how our physical brain functions. This is vital to establishing a disciplined and effective approach to achieving His purpose for us. We will explore how to successfully accomplish career goals, or any other goal, such as physical fitness, personal development, or financial stability. However, our focus will be primarily on career goals. In Psalm 139:13, David declares, "For I am fearfully and wonderfully made ..." This recognition of our personal value provides an excellent prelude to exploring the *goal getting* chapters that lie ahead.

CHAPTER 15

What Goal Getting Is Not

Beginning part V with a chapter entitled, "What Goal Getting Is Not" may seem out of place and a bit strange. And of course, you are absolutely correct. However, I am deeply concerned that what I present regarding goal setting—specifically the terms used in the next chapters—will not be misconstrued by any reader. For example, a particular word or term can have different meanings for different people, different cultures, and different times.

For example, in the book of Psalms we read, "Let the words of my mouth and the meditation of my heart be acceptable in Your sight, O Lord, my rock and my Redeemer" (Ps. 19:14). The use of the word *meditation* in this prayer has a very different meaning from that used for today's new age meditation ritual of chanting yourself into a mindless trance. Thus the word meditation could easily mislead people who are dabbling in new age cults into believing that what they are doing is biblical. Therefore, this chapter lays a foundation in the interest of clarifying any terms or ideas that could be misinterpreted.

Furthermore, while I was doing my research for this book, I attended as many career events as I could to learn more and get the latest information available in the field. By and large, listening to most of the sponsored speakers was very beneficial. I can always gain nuggets of wisdom from other points of view. As a practice, I highly encourage seeking and attending career-development events as part of ongoing career planning. However, any idea or claim must be tested against Scripture: "But examine everything *carefully*; hold fast to that which is good; abstain from every form of evil" (1Thess. 5:21–22, emphasis mine). Hence, as a safeguard, I feel compelled to digress for a bit to relate an anecdotal case in point that illustrates what you may encounter regarding false teachings regarding *self-image*. Unless these teachings are based directly on Scripture, they must be soundly rejected.

As a backdrop, I had previously attended a very informative seminar featuring a well-known author on social networking at a local church. Therefore, I was not expecting anything bizarre or shocking to occur at this second meeting. But after the introductory career materials were presented, we were led into a trance by the instructor, who was narrating us through an imaginary journey down below (we rode an elevator down ten floors) to reach a royal throne room complete with a very large throne for us to climb up onto. We were told our inner self would be revealed as we envisioned ourselves upon this glorious throne, while at the same time we were completely opening and exposing our minds to every thought ... and things just got weirder from there. The concept being taught was that you have the power within yourself to shape your future and obtain your desires.

Not being one to shy away from confrontation, I challenged the presenter during the group discussion that followed. After listening to some of the attendees comment on their underground throne experiences and their new self-image, I stood up and questioned whether the presenter could provide any biblical basis for such practices. After all, we were in a church.

That single question halted the momentum of the presentation. Some in attendance looked puzzled and began to show signs of doubt. I continued to describe my self-image during the meditation exercise as that of being on the Los Angeles Lakers basketball team (all five feet five inches of me) and having just received a pass from Kobe Bryant that set me up for the winning score of the final playoff game. A few smiles began to break across the sober but hopeful faces in the room. I went on to ask the group of about fifty participants if any of them thought I could achieve that self-image with chanting and the daily emptying of my mind with the methods being taught by the presenter.

What Goal Getting Is Not

Not surprisingly, I got some resistance from those who actually liked to have their ears tickled (even by their own unchecked imaginations). "For the time will come when they will not endure sound doctrine; but wanting to have their ears tickled, they will accumulate for themselves teachers in accordance with their own desires, and will turn away their ears from the truth and will turn aside to myths" (2 Tim. 4:3–4).

One woman in particular, being very agitated by my challenge, explained that God is a God of love, and He wants us to feel good, and this type of exercise felt very good to her. *Wow*, I thought to myself. I then replied, "But do you think I will be playing for the Los Angeles Lakers anytime soon?" The host facilitator quickly intervened in an attempt to help the silent and now clearly disoriented and confused presenter.

The facilitator explained to me that I might not fully understand how or why this practice works, but if I tried these exercises, as many people had, I would see how good it feels. He went on to explain that the good feeling validates the exercise, even though he didn't know of any biblical basis for this practice (or even one Scripture reference supporting it). Not letting him off the hook that easily, I said, "Well, I'm told heroin feels good, but I don't think I want to try any of that. And sex outside of marriage probably feels good, but I really don't want to do that either." I asked again, "Is there no biblical basis for this practice?"

As an invited guest, I certainly did not want to crash the party. Yet early on in the presentation, I sensed the Holy Spirit was rising up in me to speak out. As I cautiously waited for the right moment, I began crafting some of my words before I spoke. Then I heard more bizarre tales from these genuinely naive attendees expressing their false hopes about what they intended to gain from this meditation exercise. They were being fundamentally deceived by this presenter, and I was highly motivated to speak out to keep these people from locking onto this false teaching.

That is when I stood up and used the LA Laker example to apply humor to help the audience understand the foolishness of it all. Did it work? I suspect that the new image I gave them of a short, older, balding guy chanting his way to eventually playing for the Lakers overrode any newly formed deceptive self-images from this exercise. After all, this meeting was in Los Angeles during the basketball season. Who in LA could possibly muster up enough belief in chanting to override the hilarious image of the short, old, balding guy playing with Kobe?

As an aside, I will tell you that when I stood up to make my challenge, I was nervous. I did not have a completely formed rebuttal memorized and ready. I didn't know what to expect or what the presenter would counter with. As it turned out, there was no counter. My challenge was effective not because it was merely confrontational but because the audience could see the foolishness through my example. Being a fool for Christ was fun and exciting!

On a very serious note, the presenter also exposed the audience to other occult practices, including his daily conversations with dead *mentors*. To this day, I am troubled by this deception in our society. I prayed for those who attended that meeting. I also prayed for the leadership of the sponsoring church, that they would courageously seek the truth and not allow the sheep of their flock to be exposed to harmful deceptions.

Consider earnestly the warning Jesus provides in Matthew 12:45, "Then it goes and takes along with it seven other spirits more wicked than itself, and they go in and live there; and the last state of that man becomes worse than the first. That is the way it will also be with this evil generation." By meditation through hypnosis, we are giving up control of our thoughts and allowing our minds to receive suggestions while ignoring sound doctrine as a filter.

Unfortunately, much of our western society is spiritually ignorant, enthralled by the lure and entertainment of the occult but without the slightest discernment of the impending deception and pernicious nature of it. Any doctrine that leads you away from complete dependence on your Creator through a personal relationship with Jesus Christ is not biblical and not of God. If you are being directed to rely solely on your own inner strength or being led to seek wisdom from departed souls, you are receiving teaching that is surely not from God. The insidious acceptance of occult practices as something that is just harmlessly entertaining actually blinds us to the red flag keywords and activities (e.g., Harry Potter, the vampire craze).

We slowly get inoculated to this evil without recognizing it. It is like the old adage of how best to boil a frog: simply place the frog in a pot of cool water and slowly increase the heat to boiling point. The cold-blooded frog will never recognize the slowly warming water as a danger and will slowly drift off to a sleepy death. However, if the pot has very hot water at the start, the frog will notice the danger and quickly jump out of the pot. If you have any doubt about your ability or a friend's ability to recognize the pervasive occult practices in our society, I highly recommend Johanna Michaelsen's book entitled, *The Beautiful Side of Evil.* This work will enlighten you and reveal the subtle and not-so-subtle deceptions in our culture.

Getting back to *goal getting*, the purpose of this book is to present biblical truths to help you achieve you career-development plan. Aligning your strengths and passions with God's kingdom plan for your life far exceeds anything you could do on your own inner wisdom or strength. Having now established a God's-kingdom frame of reference, I feel confident we can safely proceed without having our message misconstrued or somehow unintentionally validating a variation of the false doctrines of positive thinking, chanting, hypnosis, or new-age meditation. I encourage you to cautiously consider each point and not accept any previously learned interpretation but rather seek only God's truth for accomplishing your vocational goals.

CHAPTER 16

How Our Brain Works

"Where there is no vision, the people are unrestrained ..." (Prov. 29:18). This passage shows us the importance of vision and purpose for our lives. The word *unrestrained* in Proverbs 29:18 has the transliteration *para* (H6544) according to *Strong's Concordance*. This has implication of "avenge" or "perish"—not what you would want for your vocation fulfillment. Having a vision for your career path with specific goals for achieving your God-given potential is very exciting—truly a thrilling lifelong journey. In earlier chapters, we discussed the importance of assessing your unique design to better understand your individual strengths and passions as you seek good (not necessarily perfect) job matches along your career development path. But how do you move forward with a vocational vision? How do you seriously consider new career opportunities (with inherent uncertainties and risks) and leave the security of the familiar present—your *comfort zone*?

Please understand that our natural propensity toward remaining within the familiarity of our comfort zone can actually hinder us from experiencing opportunities that God has in store for us. Remember all the complaining Moses had to deal with as he led Israel out of slavery in Egypt and toward the Promised Land flowing with milk and honey? Moses had to listen to the people complaining about not having the *comfort* of leeks and onions they had back in Egypt. How quickly they forgot how uncomfortable life was as slaves under Pharaoh: "So go now and work; for you will be given no straw, yet you must deliver the quota of bricks" (Ex. 5:18).

Paradoxically, by opting for the comfort of the familiar, we unintentionally turn a blind eye toward the opportunities awaiting us in our Promised Land. Therefore, having a credible vision implies, by definition, that we are not turning a blind eye to opportunities but rather that we are seeing (envisioning) the possibilities. As we will discover throughout part V, we have an exceptional ability to harness our mind's creativity for the achievement of possibilities that are believable. In essence, we have an ability to renew our thoughts intentionally toward the accomplishment of our goals.

Romans 12:2 commands us, "And do not be conformed to this world, but be transformed by the renewing of your mind, so that you may prove what the will of God is, that which is good and acceptable and perfect." Therefore, if we are instructed to renew our minds, we must have already been given authority over our minds sand over our thought lives.

The authority given to us over our thought lives is one of the few controls we have in this life. We plainly do not have control over much else. After all, we didn't choose who our parents would be or the gene pool we inherited; our health can quickly change despite our good efforts to be healthy; accidents happen; global economic conditions change independently of our hard labor; death can take us early; etc. However, embracing control over our thoughts and using our minds to work creatively for us is a very powerful capability we have been given.

As an aside, understanding the power and freedom given to us for controlling our thoughts can only impassion us against the sinister captivity of recreational mind-altering drugs. Forfeiting the freedom and ability to control what we do with our thoughts is not only reckless physically but even more so spiritually. The brain is too magnificent to alter; it is a gift for our use. The freedom to control our thought lives comes with the responsibility to manage our thoughts.

Note: For the purpose of these chapters, there is no distinction between the term brain as an organ and the term mind for generating our thoughts. These terms are used interchangeably, and no distinction of function is intended.

Comfort Zones

First, we must appreciate that our minds seek to keep us protected in our familiar comfort zones where we assume we are safe and protected. The book of Exodus teaches us that the *familiarity desire* can lock a nation's thinking into a captive slave mentality rather than that of a conqueror seeking the Promised Land (our vision). The slave mentality considers the journey to the Promised Land as a bridge too far. Put in another way, we "mind" our comfort zones. Our comfort zone has kept us protected (or at least alive) in the past, so we unquestionably trust it for all future situations. Amazingly, our minds keep us protected without us asking or even being made aware of this instinctual service controlling our thoughts.

Autopilot

Another key aspect of our brains is their sheer efficiency in functioning with an autopilot-like capacity. Autopilot systems that are integrated with flight computers are capable of operating an aircraft from liftoff to landing more accurately and safely than is humanly possible, significantly reducing the pilot's workload. Interestingly, we perform many of our tasks as if our brains were on autopilot. Have you ever arrived at work after driving the same route day in and day out, realizing that you do not actually remember the particulars of the drive that day because you were pretty well wrapped up in a talk radio program? Basically, your brain operated the car safely without you cognitively being aware of navigating, applying the gas, braking, or any steering inputs.

The reason we don't take a different route to work every day is because it would require more thought on our part and would place us outside our comfort zones. Just as aircraft autopilots are programmable, so are our mental autopilots programmable, but we do have to be very intentional about the programming. As an analogy, if the destination weather conditions change while a pilot is flying to the East Coast, he or she might have to reprogram the flight profile and intentionally disengage the autopilot. It sounds simple enough, yet several commercial aircraft flights have had fatal consequences due to the aircrew not being aware that the autopilot was unintentionally still partially engaged, thus counteracting the pilot's manual inputs.

As a case in point, consider the Airbus 320 autopilot. Despite all the other cockpit indicators available, the aircrew let the autopilot continue to take them where they did not intend to go. To address this danger, the Federal Aviation Administration (FAA) issued a Flight Standards Information Bulletin (FSIB) for Air Transportation (FSAT) 95-13, *Autopilot Disconnect Differences.* For the aviation types reading this book, a quick summary of the technical circumstances follows: the countering forces between the autopilot's input on the aircraft's horizontal stabilizer (*trims* aircraft's pitch) and the pilot's inputs on the elevator (*controls* aircraft's pitch) aerodynamically *stalled* the airflow over the surfaces, resulting in a loss of aircraft control. The FAA bulletin is a caution alerting pilots to the dangers of unsolicited autopilot automatic inputs having fatal consequences by countering the pilot's manual inputs.

Likewise, being aware of your thoughts, and therefore being aware of when your internal autopilot is operating to *protect* you (by keeping you within your comfort zone), is critical for moving toward your career path goals. On the other hand, unintentional mental inputs could stall the accomplishments of your career goals and in severe cases even cause a metaphorical *crash and burn.*

A very effective ad campaign for military service recruiting entices young people to "Join the army and see the world." Yet at noncombat overseas military installations, the facilities are not much different from a facility the troops might be assigned to in America. The troops feel comfortable on base (or on the post) because of the familiar McDonalds, Burger King, Starbucks coffee, and Krispy Kreme doughnuts. The Base Exchanges (Air Force) or Post Exchanges (Army) and commissaries attempt to have all the familiar items available to service members overseas. Where is the adventure of living on the local economy? We prefer our comfort zones and seek the familiar things that are different, just as we establish and firmly hold on to our habit patterns.

Because of the global terrorist threat and pockets of American resentment in the world, seeking the security and comfort of a guarded military installation is very understandable. However, in my observations, even in a benign, nonthreatening environment, it is especially interesting how many GIs abroad do not explore the sights or venture out very far from their military installations. Our brains protect us by keeping us in our comfort zones, with familiar surroundings, friends, and activities.

If one is residing abroad in areas on the State Department's travel warning list, it is highly recommended to change one's daily travel routines and schedules to avoid establishing predictable habit patterns. Imagine going to work by a different route each day, not routinely frequenting the same restaurant, and constantly shopping at different stores. You can easily imagine how much time and energy your brain has been saving with incredibly efficient habit patterns. Anytime you consider deviating from your familiar routine, your internal thought resistance can quickly guide you back to the easy *familiar*. And interestingly, we are not consciously aware that this protection phenomenon is even taking place.

One of the downsides of this unsolicited protection is complacency. You may recall the Northwest Airline pilots who overflew their destination by 150 miles due to a *loss of situational awareness* on October 21, 2009. They were comfortably chatting (being complacent) because the autopilot was fully engaged and providing the flight control inputs. In a similar vein, have you ever had an errand to run on the way home from work, but only after arriving at home do you realize that you forgot to pick up the (nonroutine) dry cleaning? Why did you forget? It is because that stop was not part of your normal routine. We can get so comfortable in our comfort zones that we lose situational awareness of our paths and our surroundings.

Potentially much more harmful than just the loss of situational awareness is the reality that this same *protection* the brain so freely provides us by keeping us in our comfort zones also hinders any desired beneficial changes we will want to incorporate into our lives. We may hear the most inspirational message for a very needed positive change that we genuinely desire in our lives and yet fail to change—because changing would require leaving our comfort zones.

So now let's address these questions: How do our individual comfort zones get established? And is there anything we can do to intentionally expand our comfort zones? To answer the first question, the composite of all our past self-images establishes the zone that we operate in comfortably. Therefore, by accepting new self-images, we expand our comfort zones, allowing us to operate effectively in new areas.

Consider the plight of Joseph. First of all, Joseph was sold into slavery by his jealous brothers, eventually ending up in an Egyptian prison for thirteen years because of a false accusation. Scripture tells us he became Pharaoh's second in command because of his consistent obedience and faithfulness. How did Pharaoh elevate young Joseph to this high position? Did he address him as, "Joseph, betrayed by your brothers and longtime prisoner of Egypt …?" Not at all! Genesis 41:45 tells us, "Then Pharaoh named Joseph, Zaphenath-Paneah … And Joseph went forth over the land of Egypt." Pharaoh gave Joseph a new self-image, transforming him from of a prisoner in Egypt to a ruler in Egypt with the name Zaphenath-Paneah, which means *God speaks, He lives*. By changing Joseph's name, and thus his self-image along with it, Pharaoh instituted the process of significantly enlarging Joseph's comfort zone. Joseph went forth over all the land; he wasn't confined to his prison cell anymore.

Self-Images

In today's western society, changing your name with every career change would seem very strange indeed. Can you imagine having

How Our Brain Works

multiple Facebook pages, each with a different name and set of friends? On the other hand, it is not uncommon for a woman to change her last name when she marries, signifying that her self-image is now that of a married woman. Titles such as doctor, sergeant, senator, coach, etc., are not uncommon either. Titles shape the self-image of the person. They also shape the image others have of the person holding the title.

When we speak of our self-image, we are not implying a single self-image but rather many, many images that form an overall composite self-image. For example, a man can have many titles, such as husband, father, brother, son, uncle, boss, colleague, partner, friend, or enemy, all of which form the basis of his self-image. In addition, we have self-images formulated by our characteristics and attributes (e.g., athletic, talented, clever, lousy driver, tech savvy, extroverted, introverted, etc.). All of these self-images form an environment in which you can operate comfortably (a.k.a., your comfort zone). As we grow and try new things, over time we expand our comfort zones.

A new self-image I had to grow into was that of being a commissioned officer in the military. I spent months in Officer Training School (OTS), as an Officer Trainee (OT) to earn a commission in the United States Air Force. What kept me motivated to complete the training was my goal of becoming a second lieutenant, the first level in the officer ranks. The military has a tradition of showing respect for higher-ranking officers by calling the indoor area to attention upon their arrival.

Immediately following my commissioning ceremony to second lieutenant, I reentered my OT dormitory to quickly pick up my packed suitcase and head straight to the airport. In the middle of my hasty exit, I was stopped by the sound of an underclassman OT's shout of, "Area attention" (meaning there was an officer somewhere in the OT dormitory). Conditioned by my many weeks of training as an OT, I immediately responded by coming to a complete stop, dropping my suitcase, and assuming the position of attention.

Since I was in a hurry, I was slightly agitated and was becoming more aggravated at just how long it was taking the intruding officer to yell back, "At ease" (thus allowing everyone to go back to whatever they had been doing before that officer entered the dormitory). After a long pause, to my embarrassment, a lower-class OT whispered to me, "Sir, you are the officer we are at attention for." Cracking up, I shouted, "At ease men, and have a wonderful day!" while attempting to keep some sort of composure. Granted, that situation caught me off guard, but the point is that my self-image hadn't caught up to my reality of being a commissioned officer. My comfort zone was that of an OT who had to stand at attention, waiting for an "At ease" command. Changing your self-image is a process. It takes time.

Self-images have been formed throughout our lives with or without our awareness that they are forming. Think of your self-images as a large collage of photographs representing who you are. Some of the photos have very positive images, and others may not be so positive; the collage represents many images along with their associated feelings. If someone tells you that your drawing or coloring is sloppy at an early age, it can produce a self-image that you are not very artistic. Similarly, being told that you are a poor student can set up an image that can prevent (by protecting) you from even trying more challenging academic pursuits. We tend to believe what we are told, unless we intentionally challenge the information we hear. This is especially true for younger children who rarely challenge their authority figures' assessment of their actions or behaviors but rather unconsciously hold on to these beliefs into adulthood.

Impact of Self-Images

So, what do we need to consider and think about to accomplish our step-by-step career path? How do we move into these new areas, and how do we get from where we are to where we think we should be? Better said, "How do we successfully propel our career toward new, unexplored destinations while traveling with only a suitcase full of self-images to fuel our journey?" Let us first consider metaphorically whether that suitcase of past self-images helps us to have hotel bellhops jumping to open doors for us, or whether that suitcase has slowed us down as if we are waiting in line for some TSA agent to inspect and challenge each and every item we carry. In other words, do your self-images push you forward or hold you back?

A real-life example of being moved forward by a new positive self-image happened to me in the eighth grade. Mrs. Erdman, the teacher in charge of the school's mathematical curriculum, helped me create a new self-image. Every grading period, our report cards were returned to us in homeroom for hand delivery to each class. In each class, our teachers would collect, record, and return the cards with our grade for that class.

This time, before our homeroom teacher distributed the cards, Mrs. Erdman approached me in the hall and said she wanted to show me what she, as head of the math department, had entered for my pre-algebra grade. She explained that she had met with the principal to obtain special permission to give me a very high 98 percent versus the usual maximum 95 percent. Her reasoning was that I had actually earned a 98 percent for the reporting period and not just a 95 percent. A grade of 98 percent was quite unusual for any student in that school, and it looked even more ostentatious next to my other marginally passing grades.

Mrs. Erdman wrote the 98 percent in blue ink and as large as she could. The convention of that time was always to use black ink for passing grades and red ink for failing grades. By the way, I had a few subjects with red marks from previous reporting periods. She then admonished me that if I could get that high of a grade in pre-algebra, it was time for me to get another subject up to the 95 percent mark and to continue progressing until all my grades were 95 percent. She also said she had stood up for me to get the 98 percent mark (instead of the usual maximum of 95) because I deserved it, and she now expected me to improve my other grades, one subject at a time. What a difference a teacher can make!

When I was presenting my report card to my other teachers, that large blue 98 percent did not go unnoticed. My self-image changed. I acted differently, my other teachers treated me differently, and I began to study the other subjects with the 95 percent mark as a goal I could achieve. By the time I was in high school, I was on the dean's list. My self-image had changed, and my comfort zone became broader—all because of Mrs. Erdman's positive input.

Unfortunately, negative self-images have the same power for achieving negative results. Often we may not even be aware of the self-images we accept. Positive self-images may have some defining moment, like a commissioning in the military, a graduating ceremony from medical school, a big blue 98 percent in pre-algebra, or some other accolade—all of which are very important. But more often than not, our self-images are being formed more subtly from our past experiences and from what others have told us about ourselves. Even without a defining moment or some demarcation, we often simply form self-images by taking what we were told at face value. Unfortunately, untrue negative self-images can be formed by simply believing what we were told (or thought we were told) about our skills, abilities, or talents as young children.

If a child is told that his penmanship is poor, his natural inclination is to believe that assessment. By accepting that assessment, he now feels comfortable producing sloppy handwritten homework that reinforces his poor penmanship. In other words, he continues to reinforce his belief with self-talk like, "Why even try to do something that can't be done?" We simply don't challenge the self-image because it is uncomfortable to do so. The result is an untrue belief that can hinder our career progression. Suppose a person believes he can't consistently get to work on time because, "Well, I am just not a morning person." By the way, is there actually such a thing as a morning person, or do the so called *morning people* just go to bed earlier?

Consider the logic of people simply changing their behavior to *early to bed, early to rise*. Why wouldn't a person make a change to avoid the negative consequences of tardiness? The answer is that trying to consistently arrive at work early would put this person outside of his comfort zone. The brain quickly protects this person with some clever justification: "By arriving late, I can stay later at work and take care of any late-afternoon *emergencies* that might pop up." Or "Not much productive work is ever done before everyone gets their coffee and settles down, so I don't need to be there for all that." Or how about, "Even though I am a little late, I get ten hours of work done in seven-and-a-half hours." Well, there you go, safe again—no need to change. It appears this person's mind somehow naturally locks on to all sorts of reasons to justify his counterproductive behavior and locks out any number of reasonable solutions to improve this shortcoming. But we will talk more about that in later chapters.

Bear in mind that when our brains are operating in autopilot mode, they are usually very helpful and very efficient, but there are times when we need to assess our thought lives and intentionally override the automatic thinking of our mind. Just as an FAA directive was issued to warn and help pilots assess the aircraft's unwanted autopilot inputs, we may also be listening to inputs (self-talk) that counter our attempts to progress.

In summary, we have discussed the protection we receive by behaving in ways that keep us in our comfort zones. The boundaries of our comfort zones are determined by the composite (collage) of our many mental images. These self-images are very important for our successful day-to-day functioning. Some of our self-images were initiated from receiving formal training, accomplishing something, or just hard work, while other self-images were acquired throughout our lives, without our cognitively accepting or challenging the validity of the images. In the next section, we will explore biblical truths that apply to our self-images and how our resulting behavior can be changed.

Ref:

Federal Aviation Administrations, Flight Standards Information Bulletin (FSIB) for Air Transportation (FSAT) 95-13: *Autopilot Disconnect Differences. The autopilot disconnect systems in the Airbus A-300 and A-310 are significantly different from the disconnect systems provided in other large transport-category airplanes. The lack of a stabilizer-in-motion warning appears to be unique to the Airbus A-300 and A-310. Pilots may not be aware that under some circumstances the autopilot may create an out-of-trim condition if they try to manually control the airplane. The A-300 and A-310 do not have the autopilot disconnect safety features to alert pilots that the THS is moving to oppose their manual control inputs. The accident may have been prevented if the autopilot had disconnected as the pilot pushed forward on the control column or if an alert had been provided to the pilots that the THS was in motion.*

Chapter 17
Biblical Importance of Self-Images

The good news about our collage of self-images is that we can intentionally add new self-images to our existing collection. Ephesians 4:23–24 instructs us, "And that you be renewed in the spirit of your mind, and put on the new self, which in the likeness of God has been created in righteousness and holiness of the truth." We have been given the ability to be in control of our self-images, thus allowing us to comply with Paul's instructions to the Ephesians.

It is important to understand that adding a new self-image does not remove existing self-images or expunge a conflicting self-image. All self-images remain; the stronger images will have the greater influence on our thinking and behavior. Fortunately, we can intentionally override counterproductive self-images with a newer, stronger imprint. Picture a collage with a brightly colored high-definition photo among other grey-and-white, dull newspaper print photos. The newsprint shots still have a place in the collage, but the color print stands out and gets our attention, essentially masking the duller photos.

Second Peter 2:22—Old Self-Images

Since our old self-images never go away, 2 Peter 2:22 warns us, "A dog returns to its own vomit" and "A sow, after washing, returns to wallowing in the mire." This reality explains why a recovering alcoholic is always susceptible to falling back into his or her previous unhealthy habits, even if those habits have been under control for some time.

This principle also explains how a born-again Christian can fall back into sinful habits that had seemed to be long gone. This backsliding occurs because the weakened, over-ridden self-images do not in fact disappear. These images can reappear anytime the overriding self-image weakens below a critical threshold. For instance, if a recovering alcoholic stops strengthening his or her newly formed non-drinking self-image by skipping Alcoholics Anonymous meetings and instead starts hanging out at sports bars, over time the old drinking self-image can be strengthened and re-emerge. Subsequently, the recently acquired non-drinking self-image will be less dominant, resulting in behavior that reverts back to the previous state. Likewise, when a Christian replaces fellowship time participating in church events with time spent in secular events, a power shift begins to occur. That power shift between competing self-images will likewise drive changes in a person's behavior.

What actually takes place inside the brain to form our habits is the development of neural pathways. Neurons are electrically excitable cells that maintain voltage gradients across their cell membranes by means of metabolically driven ion pumps. Changes in the cross-membrane ion voltage from varying concentrations of sodium, potassium, chloride, and calcium create an *all or nothing* pulse that activates synaptic connections with other cells. Neuron pathways are physically formed within the brain.

The following illustration captures the fleeting moment deep inside the brain as a neuron prepares to transmit a signal to its target. The stronger and more frequent neuron pulses produce pathways that have precedence over the weaker pathways. Just as a building has efficient conductive copper wires for electrical current pathways, your brain establishes ion paths for transmitting chemically generated pulses.

Biblical Importance of Self-Images

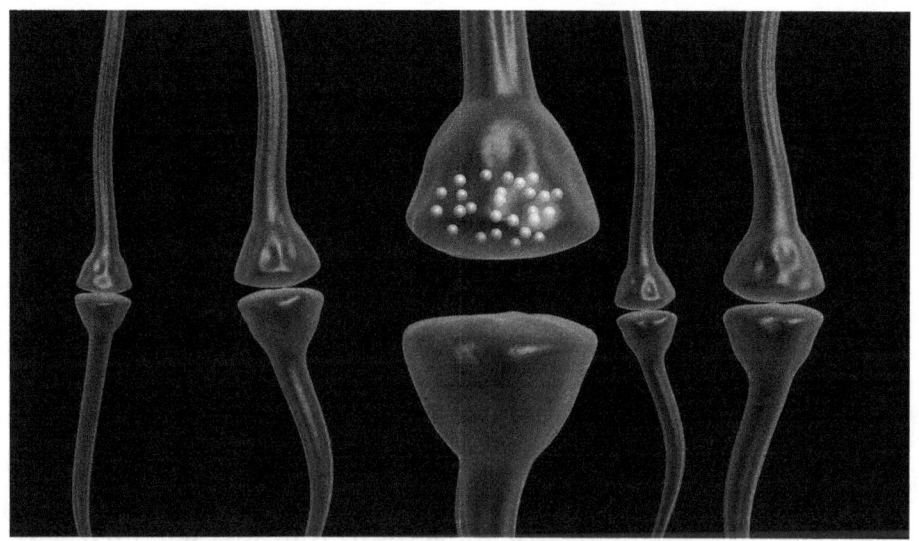

(*All or Nothing* Pulse Forming Between Neural Membranes)

While we're on the subject, this explains why trying hard to not think about something doesn't work. Trying not to think about something simple activates more ion pulses along the paths you are trying to not stimulate.

To change your thoughts or behavior, the old neural pathways need to be deactivated and abandoned by forming new ion pulse pathways that send a stronger signal along a different preferred pathway. Research has shown that it takes about three weeks to form a new habit for certain types of behaviors. Three weeks of intentional, disciplined behavior are needed to physically develop ion pulse pathways within your brain. Once the patterns are established, the behavior becomes routine, and a significant reduction in effort is needed to maintain that behavior. It is then a habit. Voila!

Note also that this newly formed habit pattern has actually expanded your comfort zone to accommodate this new habit. Now your brain is working *automatically* for you as it finds ways to keep you *secure* with this new behavior (habit). Likewise, establishing new self-images allows your brain to create a broader range of solutions and behaviors. The resultant behaviors operate within the protection of the expanded comfort zone that you helped establish.

Romans 7:19—Next Time

Expanding your comfort zone with new self-images takes time, and guess what? It may not be very comfortable. Expect a struggle as the power shift develops, and don't be discouraged when setbacks occur. The surest way to expand your comfort zone when introducing new self-images is to focus on the long-term behavior change and not be discouraged by an occasional setback. Simply say, "Okay, I learned from that. Next time I will do this …" And move on.

I remember changing to a low-carbohydrate diet years ago. The author of the diet explained how maintaining a balanced ratio of carbohydrates, protein, and fat beneficially increases metabolism and burns off excess weight. His encouragement to the readers, who from time to time would understandably drift from the ratio, was to not get discouraged; in six hours, those extra carbohydrates would be out of your bloodstream and you could *get right back on* maintaining the balanced ratio.

Similarly, expanding your comfort zone with new self-images to intentionally change behavior may require you to *get right back on* that behavior if you drift off. Simply use a "Next time I intend to …" statement and move on. Even the apostle Paul had his frustrations with change, as he tells us in Romans 7:19, "For the good that I want, I do not do, but I practice the very evil that I do not want." Nonetheless, Paul did not get discouraged; he continued on fighting the good fight to eventually author over two-thirds of the New Testament Scriptures.

Ephesians 4:23–24—Renew

As we discussed earlier, our brains can accept both external inputs from others and internal inputs from our own self-talk. By inten-

Biblical Importance of Self-Images

tionally establishing self-images that are outside our comfort zones, we force our brains to work to reconcile the differences. Our brains will either find a way to disregard the new self-image or include the new self-image by eventually broadening the comfort zone. The former will often prevail if the new self-image is not realistic; your brain will give you many reasons to disregard an unrealistic image and let it just disappear from your thoughts as effortlessly as forgetting last week's dinner vegetable. If the image is not realistic, it won't generate change. Just as the comedian joked about his doctor's unrealistic admonishment for him to stop smoking by quipping, "Absolutely, Doc. I quit smoking at least once a day," your brain can easily dismiss unrealistic self-images. It can also effectively disregard a new self-image that you are not intentional about. In other words, a momentary inspiration by itself isn't enough to generate lasting change. Change requires us to be intentional!

To better understand how your brain works to generate change, consider a very powerful phenomenon that occurs when your brain has to reconcile the difference between a realistic, strong self-image that differs from your current reality. Consider the following black background figures, the four circles each having a ninety-degree wedge cut from their inward facing quadrants.

MAKE YOUR WAY

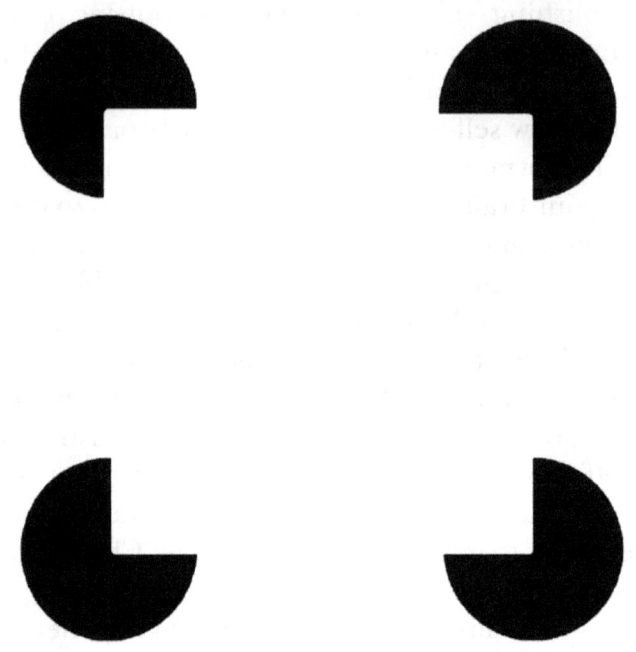

Making Sense of Our Surroundings

While looking at the four partial circles, our minds form a black square, filling in the blank spaces between the circles. The square doesn't actually exist except in our mind's eye. The black square is a visual representation of our mind *filling* in the missing pieces to help us make sense of our surroundings. Our mind found a way to make sense out of the missing quadrants of the four circles. How creative!

Apply this same working phenomenon to Ephesians 4:23–24: "And that you be renewed in the spirit of your mind, and put on the new self which in the likeness of God has been created in righteousness and holiness of the truth." Wow! By being renewed in the spirit of your mind, you are forming a new self-image—a likeness of God. When we are born again, we become righteous through what Christ has done for us and not by earning righteousness from our own efforts. God sent His Son to reconcile us to Himself even while we were still in our sin. We became righteous through Jesus' righteousness, not from our own works: "Not as a result of works, so that no one may boast. For we are His workmanship, created in Christ Jesus for good works" (Eph. 2:9–10).

Therefore, as Christians, when we are born again, we have an immediate new self-image of righteousness. This new image causes our brains to begin to fill in the disconnect between the new self-image and our current behavior that causes us to initiate new and different behaviors. We develop different friendships, go to different movies, tell different jokes, and stop doing the things that just don't fit with our new self-image. The important point is that we immediately become righteous and spend the rest of our lives sanctifying ourselves. As we begin acting on our self-image of righteousness, we progress toward the goal, not allowing momentary shortcomings to deter us. Our occasional setbacks are mere speed bumps as we learn to *Make Our Way* along the path of sanctification, empowered by our stronger new self-image.

Ephesians 1:14—Now Sealed

Because the genuine salvation experience is so emotionally powerful, the self-image created is very strong and overrides many of the behaviors conflicting with this new self-image—thereby creating real change. The Bible does not teach us to first clean up our act and change our behavior to earn His acceptance and righteousness. Not at all! No one would ever attain the righteousness of Christ in his or her own strength. But instead, the Scripture tells us that having believed, we have been sealed or given a secure promise. So we are able to start immediately, right now, acting with behaviors that support this new self-image. Ephesians 1:13–14 reminds us, "In Him, you also, after listening to the message of truth, the gospel of your salvation—having also believed, you were sealed in Him with the Holy Spirit of promise, who is given as a pledge of our inheritance ..." Thus, having believed, we now have an inheritance.

Similarly, any self-images that focus on our career goals must be reconciled with our immediate reality, and that in turn causes us to change our behavior. The change can be very positive, just as that of seeking righteousness, by stretching us to multiply our talents with the God-given abilities we have. Conversely, accepting a negative self-image activates the brain just as powerfully to protect the negative self-image formed, along with its corresponding limiting behaviors. Thus, if we happen to be out of work, the self-images of being laid off, fired, not needed, displaced, etc., can hinder our ability to find creative solutions for capturing that next job. This dynamic works both ways, so we need to take every thought captive so our creative minds will work for us. Being intentional with our thought lives allows us to be able to reconcile our current reality with what God has for our lives, our purpose, and our vocation.

With our minds working in the background (i.e., autopilot on fully engaged mode), creative solutions develop that begin the alignment of our behaviors with our new self-image. A common example of this background working of our mind is when, out of the blue, we remember the name of that song we were trying so hard to recall the day before. Or the name of that person we were trying to remember last night at the social event suddenly pops into our head. When it comes to aligning ourselves with a new self-image, we may not necessarily notice the creativity (because it is working in the background). However, we do notice those *coincidences* that just fall into place, confirming our new self-image.

Nonetheless, to ensure that our desired self-images dominate and generate the desired behavior changes, we have to be intentional about self-images and make the effort to take every thought captive. This requires an awareness of our supportive and non-supportive self-talk. In the next chapter, we will discuss and contrast the conqueror and captive languages.

CHAPTER 18

A New Language

When traveling abroad in a non-English-speaking country, I can easily pick up English conversations out of the *noise* of a crowded marketplace with many people speaking other languages. The English conversation is discernible above all the other languages I do not speak or understand. That is because my mind has the ability to processes the languages I know and allows me to ignore the others, basically filtering out the non-English languages as noise.

The so-called second-generation (2G) and third-generation (3G) wireless communications mobile phones and also Global Positioning System (GPS) receivers make use of an analogous capability referred to as Code-Division Multiple Access (CDMA). CDMA allows numerous signals to occupy a single transmission channel, effectively optimizing the use of available frequencies and bandwidth. The key to CDMA is to be able to extract the desired coded signals while rejecting everything else as random noise. This is done by computer chips with software algorithms that correlate the signals (decode) in the receiver units. Our brains automatically do the same by locking onto (decoding) a familiar language (code)—all without a calling plan or even the occasional dropped call!

As with CDMA receivers, our brains need to have the *code* to make sense out of the many noisy signals we are bombarded with. Our self-images serve as our decoders for the world around us and also determine our internal self-talk. If we have an established self-image of, "I am adaptive and resilient," our brains will provide self-talk to help us uncover ways to be adaptive and resilient. Likewise, if we have a self-image of being a poor student, our self-talk will *help* us maintain the level of a poor student (regardless of our true capability). Either of these responses has a way of keeping us comfortably aligned with that self-image. The act of being intentional with our self-images and our corresponding self-talk will allow our brains to consider solutions that otherwise would be disregarded and dismissed as nothing more than random noise.

Two Languages

Let's consider two philosophical states of mind and the corresponding languages of those states. The first state is that of a captive. Second Timothy 2:26 encourages us, "And they may come to their senses and escape from the snare of the devil, having been held captive by him to do his will." "Having been held captive" was not a willful choice on their part to do the devil's will. But rather "being held captive" implies being unknowingly snared by the subtle acceptance of secular cultural thinking as a result of living day to day in our fallen world. The sheer compilation of the hundreds of thousands of cultural messages we are exposed to every day influences our perspective.

The other state of mind is the conqueror frame of reference. Romans 8:37 tells us, "We are more than conquerors through Him who loved us." Ephesians 2:10 teaches us, "For we are His workmanship, created in Christ Jesus for good works, which God prepared beforehand so that we would walk in them." Walking in them requires a conqueror's mindset, not a captive's mindset.

As Christians living in a fallen world, we have a choice. Either we choose to passively remain captives, characterized by complaining, blaming, making excuses, and repeating ineffective behaviors, or we intentionally determine to be conquerors, characterized by pausing at decision points to consider options for desired outcomes, having the courage to take action or try something new, and using energy and resources to improve outcomes and experiences. It sounds like an easy choice, but it may require change in some areas. Let's look at a few examples of the self-talk exemplified by each state of mind.

- Captives focus on their weaknesses with statements like, "I don't have the skills to do anything else" (which may be true). The conqueror's focus, on the other hand, is on how to improve by using self-talk statements that are affirming, like, "I need to get some training to develop the skills I need to advance my career."
- The captive makes excuses and states, "I don't have the time to get the training." The conqueror seeks solutions and uses self-talk that encourages positive action: "I'm going to get up one hour earlier every day so I'll have uninterrupted time to study."
- Captives complain, "Why do I have to go for additional training? Why doesn't my boss recognize what I already have to offer?" Conquerors turn complaints into requests: "I'll see if my boss will allow me to flex my work schedule so I can go for the necessary training."
- Captives compare themselves unfavorably to others: "I'm too old to be taking classes, and it won't do any good." Conquerors seek help from those who are more skilled: "If I have trouble with learning the new material, I can ask my friend John, who's already gone through the training, to help me."
- Captives blame: "I didn't get selected for the open position because of all the emphasis on diversity hiring." Conquerors accept responsibility: "I didn't get selected for the promotion, but I'm going to work on broadening my experience so I'm ready for the next opportunity."

Unlike captives, conquerors accept responsibility for their situations. They plan and take action to improve their situations. They use their words and thoughts to improve an undesirable situation, while captives resort to choosing a "Yes, but ..." position while remaining captive to their circumstances, not seeking alternatives. The apostle Paul addresses captivity in his second epistle to Timothy. He discusses the need for such people to "come to their senses ... if perhaps God may grant them repentance leading to the knowledge of the truth, and they may come to their senses and escape from the snare of the devil, having been held captive by him to do his will" (2 Tim. 2:25–26).

Other contrasts between conquerors and captives are that captives wait passively for luck to go their way. They tend to make choices that increase immediate pleasures rather than staying the course to their ultimate goal. They consequently sacrifice dreams and goals by making choices that only reduce their immediate discomfort. On the other hand, conquerors design a plan for their lives as they want them to be, carry out that plan in the face of obstacles, take positive risks to advance their goals, and sacrifice immediate pleasure for the sake of their dreams.

Incidentally, studies have shown that recent college graduates often feel let down during their first year in the work force because they expected to be using so much more of their education on the job. Granted, that can be frustrating, but the real significance of a college degree for the hiring manager is that the employee has demonstrated the ability to stay the course and complete the *project* while learning to learn. An employee with a demonstrated conqueror mindset provides the hiring manager assurance that he or she will be able to successfully meet the challenges of the job over the long term. The completion of a college degree or vocational certification program is proof that the employee has self-discipline along with the ability to learn, both of which are very important for getting the manager's organizational goals met. The point is, don't shy away from whatever hard work is needed to prepare you for long-term success. Have a conqueror's mindset.

As you begin to analyze the captive and conqueror perspectives, you will realize the divergent nature of the two views. The self-talk that follows only gets more entrenched as the resulting outcomes reinforce one of the two states. This self-fulfilling effect is a real danger for the captive, as the mind only recognizes and decodes the language it knows, thus not considering many potential solutions and ideas shrouded within the noise of an unknown language.

As a visual to demonstrate this concept, picture a fighter pilot in an aerial dogfight. The pilot maneuvers his jet to a position that allows the missile's seeker to acquire a target Lock-On. With either a RADAR or Infra-red (IR) seeker-equipped missile, once the pilot receives confirmation of the seeker's Lock-On, the missile is fired and automatically narrows in on the target. With the *fire and forget* capability, the pilot *forgets* about the missile, thus freeing him to lock on to new targets and accomplish other tasks. This simple analogy highlights the fact that once a seeker has a Lock-On to a particular target, other targets (opportunities) are ignored by that missile's seeker. Once our captive or conqueror viewpoint gets a Lock-On, the other is ignored.

Lock-On or Lock-Out

Let's take a closer look at the well-established psychological principle called Lock-On or Lock-Out. If you Lock-On to "I can't do that," you naturally Lock-Out, "I can do that." And when you Lock-On to "I can do that," you Lock-Out, "I can't do that." This sounds simple enough, but it has huge consequences.

Observe the black vase in the middle of the following picture. As long as you concentrate and Lock-On to the vase in the center of the picture, your mind will Lock-Out the black silhouettes of the two men facing each other.

Lock-Out or Lock-On Principle

Conversely, when you Lock-On to the two silhouettes, your mind will Lock-Out the vase in the middle. In the same way, the captive mental state will Lock-Out solutions that the conqueror will naturally Lock-On to. The conqueror, conversely, will Lock-Out excuses and doubts that lead to nonaction.

Henry Ford said it very well, "If you think you can do a thing or think you can't do a thing, you're right." Therefore, even though you may have accurately assessed your strengths, know what your passions are, have realistic goals, and are inspired to make changes, your captive self-talk can work to hold you back. Under the same circumstances, however, conqueror self-talk will invigorate your mind to work at finding solutions (not stifling solutions) that will move you toward your desired goal. Either way, your mind is working to either Lock-On or Lock-Out solutions, thus keeping you safely in a familiar comfort zone.

Recall the parable of the sower in Matthew 13:18–23, where Jesus is teaching about receiving the kingdom. The seeds that were from the same bag fell on the side of the road, in rocky places, among the thorns, and finally on the good soil. The seeds that fell on the side of the road never took root (the mind was closed to the message). The seeds that fell on the rocky soil were received and initially took root, but they were not rooted deep enough to last through the heat of the day. The seeds that landed among the thorns took root but were choked out by the distractions of the world.

Only the seeds that fell on the good soil produced fruit. All the seeds were good, but not all the soil was prepared to receive them. As stated earlier, inspiration alone does not bring about change. Only the seeds that fell on the good soil yielded a crop—some a hundredfold, some sixty and some thirty. It takes being intentional by preparing one's thought life and language (self-talk) to subsequently receive and produce fruitful change. How to successfully accomplish this *intentionality* is the subject of the next chapter.

CHAPTER 19

Renew Statements

Recapping the last chapters:
- First, our mind works to keep us protected and safe within our comfort zones, oftentimes in the autopilot mode—without us being cognitively aware of our self-talk.
- Second, we form many, many self-images throughout our lifetimes. Some are intentional; some are not intentional.
- Third, we have a choice between a captive or conqueror perspective, and the choice drives the language of our self-talk.
- Fourth, whichever language we use, we will either Lock-On or Lock-Out certain courses of action.

Incorporating the above principles into an ordered (disciplined) practice will ensure the successful implementation of intentional change. That is change we can direct and control. The application of these principles will be focused toward career-development goals, but these same principles are effective for achieving change in any area of our lives.

To get started, we will develop "Renew Statements," which are statements structured in a format intended to stimulate the mind's natural creativity. This natural creative function of your brain will in turn provide *solution* pathways for accomplishing your career goals. Being intentional about change connotes taking control of your thought life to bring about a self-image change, just as we read in Paul's epistle to the Ephesians: "And that you be renewed in the spirit of your mind, and put on the new self which in the likeness of God has been created in righteousness and the holiness of truth" (Eph. 4:23–24).

In a nutshell, being renewed by putting on new self-images allows for the "receptiveness" of opportunities and preferences we may have previously overlooked (or never quite de-coded properly) in the past. As you put on the new self, the realization of formerly veiled solutions will open up avenues and reveal previously unforeseen possibilities. Additionally, by viewing your career goals as *preference paths* associated with positive consequences, the brain will be allowed to open up and Lock-On to more avenues that will guide you toward your goal; in other words, you will have a broader spectrum of feasible alternatives to consider. Conversely, setting overly restrictive goals will generate undue protection, which will merely amplify the "Lock-Out" function of the Lock-On/Lock-Out phenomenon.

You must also realize that the established self-images you want to eliminate do not just go away; their influence must be overridden by intentionally developing stronger new self-images. These stronger self-images will cause the needed changes for accomplishing your goals. Recall how we physically develop neural paths in our brains based on our new self-image(s). This process takes physical time. We may falter or have a setback during this process, but this is easily corrected by maintaining our conqueror self-talk with, "Next time I will …" statements.

Summing up, we arrive at six characteristics of Renew Statements that will collectively produce creative solutions for the accomplishment of our goals, i.e., intentional behavior change. We will be discussing each characteristic in detail and then presenting examples of Renew Statements. Renew Statements will be the enabling tool for accomplishing career goals by serving as the bridge for the hearer to become an effectual doer. Our career plan was based on our design and God's purpose for our vocation—the hearing. The doing is the execution of that plan. As the letter of James encourages us, "But one who looks intently at the perfect law, the law of liberty, and abides by it, not having become a forgetful hearer but an effectual doer, this man will be blessed in what he does" (James 1:25). Let's get started on the path of the doer.

The six characteristics of Renew Statements are:
1. Realistic, believable, and specific (aligned with our strengths and passions)
2. Supported by Scripture (So that God may be glorified ... and, It is written ...)
3. Framed in the *now* (not sometime later in my life), with action words that:
    a. Produce a *productive gap* between our new self-image and our current behavior
    b. Cause us to change our behavior to close the *productive gap*
4. Positive consequential end states—not restrictive (avoids the Lock-Out of plausible solutions)
5. Based on establishing a new self-image with the proper self-talk (conqueror not captive)
6. Written with emotion and visualization (producing an imprint) to be reviewed daily

Characteristic # 1

Realistic, believable, and specific (aligned with our strengths and passions)

In order to successfully establish a new self-image, it must be realistic, believable, and specific. If the self-image is not believable, our brains will work very hard to *protect* us by finding creative ways to keep us securely unchanged in our current comfort zones. As referenced earlier, all the *new-age* chanting and *positive thinking* have no power to change us. Ephesians 5:6 admonishes us, "Let no one deceive you with empty words ..." but we know that the truth will set us free. Simply chanting and repeating an unrealistic goal over and over has no power. Your brain will know your goals are outside its comfort zone and will automatically create self-talk to protect you from accepting this change—thus holding you back from achieving your goal.

Relative to career development planning, accurately assessing one's strengths and passions is critical (Servants by design inventory, EDD resources, community college counselors, etc.). By knowing your vocational design, you can intentionally set and accomplish goals that will advance your career and develop your skills for future growth and additional responsibility. Specific career goals could include any of the following: gain needed experience, complete additional training, earn a certification, or establish professional contacts that can help you.

Career goals need to be specific for two reasons: first, to know when the goal is accomplished so you can focus your attention toward other goals, and second, and most important, is because career goals have to be specific to allow your brain to develop a vivid and emotional new self-image. Such a self-image will compel your current behavior to be reconciled to it.

Characteristic # 2

Supported by Scripture (So that God may be glorified ... and, It is written ...)

In Matthew 5:16, Jesus teaches, "Let your light shine before men in such a way that they may see your good works, and glorify your Father who is in heaven." By establishing your goals with Matthew 5:16 as your motivation, you automatically avoid selfish, unrealistic, or ungodly goals. Thus your career goals become very believable because they fit your design and your purpose. Each Renew Statement is also backed up with supporting statements. Make use of the "It is written ..." formatted statements to support your Renew Statements with scriptural references. Encouraging words of support such as, "You are really good at ..." or "You have a gift for ..." from significant people in your life can be very powerful. Also, reference relevant accomplishments as support statements. All of these supporting statements help develop a strong self-image by validating your unique design and purpose.

Let me illustrate the above with an example of a worthy goal: Being a very good employee. Jesus' teaching in Matthew 5:16—"shining your light to glorify God"—validates the motivation of our goal. Through further study and meditation in the Scriptures, we can include Colossians 3:23, "Whatever you do, do your work heartily, as for the Lord rather than for men." Therefore, I want to be a contributing, good employee in a way that will glorify God. Next, we construct a realistic, believable, and specific Renew Statement:

At work I enjoy having a champion's state of mind and receive achievement awards routinely validating my accomplishments.

Follow this with an "It is written ..." supporting statement:

For we are his workmanship, created in Christ Jesus for good works which God prepared beforehand so that we would walk in them. (Eph. 2:10)

Recapping:

We have the reason for adding and believing a new self-image in the: "So that God will be glorified ..." We also have a Scripture providing the emotional impact to support the new image: "For it is written ..." This will firmly imprint our believable new self-image. The complete Renew Statement now reads:

So that God will be glorified, at work I enjoy having a champion's state of mind and receive achievement awards routinely validating my accomplishments. For it is written:
a. "We are his workmanship, created in Christ Jesus for good works which God prepared beforehand so that we would walk in them" (Eph. 2:10).

The new self-image is not only believable, but it also is formed with the strength to override any existing self-images that may have been hindering work performance in the past. Notice in this example the measurable and positive consequences of receiving awards. Receiving awards is specific, while at the same time not restrictive. Over time, the positive new self-image becomes the one we believe. It generates new behavior for us while the old self-image becomes a faded memory of who we used to be.

Notice the supporting Scripture is indented as a subparagraph. Feel free to list additional Scriptures or acknowledgment statements. Acknowledgment statements can come from your family, friends, peers, or personal devotional time. With your mind having an initial Lock-On, you will become aware of support from many sources. These additional supporting subparagraphs of your Renew Statements will strengthen your new self-images.

So that God will be glorified, at work I enjoy having a champion's state of mind and receive achievement awards routinely validating my accomplishments. For it is written:

> a. "We are his workmanship, created in Christ Jesus for good works which God prepared beforehand so that we would walk in them" (Eph. 2:10).

And confirmed by:

> b. Being recognized by the department manager during March's staff meeting, "Thank you, great job ..." (March 15, 2012).

Also be sure to include the date when each Renew Statement was created. This timestamp will allow you to easily track your progress and remind you of your successes.

Characteristic # 3

Framed in the *Now*

Frame the Renew Statement in the *Now*—not some time down the road in some distant land, far, far away—but in the *NOW*. And frame it with vibrant action words in the now as well. The *now* self-image will naturally produce a gap (or incongruity) between this self-image and our current behavior, which will set off a change in our behavior. The more vivid the image, the more urgent the gap and thus the more urgent the reconciliation will be. Recall the Renew Statement above, "At work I enjoy having ..." This is *NOW*, not some time in the future, not when I get my act together, not when I get the next promotion or when a new management team arrives. The statement is in the present. It is a present self-image that perhaps is not yet reconciled with my current work performance.

The Lord admonishes us in Leviticus 11:44, "Be holy, for I am holy"; that is now. How do we "be holy" except that we start now? The Scripture doesn't say to go get cleaned up first, study more biblical commentaries, or marry into a noble family; it simply says to change now and be holy. The context of this Scripture is for a new Israel with a new self-image, starting now.

Consider further the *now* aspect of being a born-again Christian. Scripture tells us, "And that you be renewed in the spirit of your mind, and put on the new self which in the likeness of God has been created in righteousness and holiness of the truth" (Eph. 4:23–24). Yet Paul writes to his beloved Philippians, "Work out your salvation with ..." We can see the *now* in the "created in righteousness," but we are still working out our salvation. In the same manner, our mind is reconciling the gap between our Renew Statement's self-image and our behavior, by gradually changing our behavior! Therefore, just as we are not being disingenuous by assuming righteousness as part of our Christian self-talk, we also can honestly assume the Renew Statement as something that is true in the present. The Renew Statement is correct in the *now*, even though the process is not finished. It is who we are, and we are in the process of reconciling our behavior to match that image. As a Christian, I know I am saved, but I continue to work toward being more Christ-like every day. The acknowledgment of who we are allows us to keep pressing toward the goal and not losing our hope along the way.

Characteristic # 4

Positive Consequential—not Restrictive

Having the positive consequential outcome, " …validating my achievements," will open your mind to the conqueror's solution set, enabling you to multiply your talents rather than securely burying them within the confines of your comfort zone. Do you recall from the earlier example that there are many jet routes that are available to the East Coast? Likewise, on our career journey we don't want to hinder our creativity with overly restrictive goals such as: "Winning the *2012 employee of the year award*." First off, if your focus was only on the criteria for the *2012 employee of the year* award (whatever criteria that may be), you would Lock-Out the *manager of the quarter* award or any number of other possible awards.

As an aside, I've been a participant on boards responsible for selecting an awardee from a pool of candidates. Just let me say that the process is not like a structured political election where you have the luxury of listening to the candidates debate each other throughout the election process. Nor is it like the pairings for the NFL playoffs. Usually the nomination and selection process is not that well structured. More often than not, there is a very short time to select the candidates; the candidates have to be popular to be known well enough to be considered; a manager has to have the extra time to write up the nomination letter by the suspense date; and on it goes. Typically the awards don't really indicate the best overall employee of the year but rather a very good employee selected from among other very good employees.

The point is that you shouldn't be restrictive. Let your mind use your preferences to creatively make you a champion employee, and the recognition will follow. Maybe the recognition comes in the form of a promotion or pay rise, without a trophy or a ceremony. Keep the goals positive, and consider them as your preferences, knowing there are many jet routes across the United States; it is the destination that matters. The idea is to first get airborne, moving in the right direction, and then the destination will become clearer as you approach it.

To further illuminate the preference approach, consider this as being analogous to a pilot flying under FAA-defined Instrument Flight Conditions (or anytime flying over an altitude of eighteen thousand feet), where the pilot is required by the FAA to file a flight plan. The flight plan has a preferred route, altitude, Mach number, arrival procedure, etc. After takeoff, circumstances outside of the pilot's control can impact routing (e.g., weather changes, conflicting air traffic, runway closures, etc.). Even though a particular route was preferred, there are many jet routes that would suffice. There are times when a pilot gets re-routed and correspondingly re-programs the flight computers that generate the commands to the autopilot.

Such is life. We choose preference statements because they head us in the right direction, while we remain agile enough to accommodate change. Adapting to changing circumstances and moving toward the desired destination is a solution-oriented, conqueror mentality. Turning back, giving up, and not pressing on toward the goal because of a minor *hiccup* with the plan is a defeated captive mentality. There will always be obstacles and challenges in our careers; we have to view each goal as a preference allowing the flexibility to take alternate routes that will keep us going in the right direction.

Staying flexible and being able to Lock-On to viable alternatives (ideas) is exactly what we want our minds to be doing for us automatically in the background. This creative process will reconcile our behavior toward the self-image we intentionally established through Renew Statement for the purpose of accomplishing our goals. Fortuitously, this is what our minds do best; we just have to provide the *intentionality* to prepare the *soil for the good seeds* and proceed toward our desired destination one step at a time.

By the way, when you land at the destination airport, the passengers typically won't be aware which jet route you actually flew (the original flight plan route or the air traffic controller's re-route). The destination is what counts, and learning to have the flexibility to get there when external circumstances change is the key. With every flight, you gain more experience, such as, "Next time I will plan on carrying additional reserve fuel to have more options for circumventing those thunderstorms over Milwaukee …" or "Next time I will put my clearance on request earlier so I have a better chance of being assigned my preferred route …"

Our Renew Statements are analogous to a flight plan in that we want to have positive alternatives to consider. Overly restrictive statements cause our minds to Lock-Out and not seek viable alternatives. And finally, know that there is always a next time—a next time to try again, a next time to improve, a next time to get closer to your goal.

Characteristic # 5

Based on establishing new self-image with the proper self-talk

Behavioral change will come as you embrace and strengthen your desired self-image through self-talk. Your self-talk will have to be that of a conqueror, "five talent" mindset (Matt. 25:14–30) and not that of a captive, one-talent mindset. Intentionally taking every thought captive is freeing and brings change. Conversely, passively allowing every thought to take you captive is as scary as sailing in a storm without a rudder. The conqueror language is also enforced by your network of supporters who believe in you. Intentional self-talk creates a problem for your brain to solve; your brain has to make sense out of this new self-image and the contrast with any past captive self-image that could be holding you back.

Considering the example of becoming a better employee, the old self-talk may have sounded something similar to: "I work in a dysfunctional organization, and that is why I can't …" or "I'm too old to get the training I need, and that is why I can't …" or "I am no good with computers so I can't use the new system"—thus no change. However, a Renew Statement in the <u>NOW</u> supported by your conqueror's language, generating the five-talent (Matt. 25) mindset, will form a gap your brain needs to close. As the new self-image forms, your brain has to deal with the gap. Something is going to give, and it will be your behavior.

The legendary coach of the Green Bay Packers football team, Vince Lombardi, is quoted as saying, "Winning is a habit. Unfortunately, so is losing." Our self-talk forms the self-images that determine our behavior—whether we are winners (conqueror self-talk) or losers (captive self-talk). Either way, one of those behaviors will establish our habits.

Paul writes to the Galatians, "I have been crucified with Christ, and it is no longer I who live, but Christ lives in me; and the life I live in the flesh I live by faith …" (Gal. 2:20). Paul considers himself as having been crucified and therefore dead to the old self, with his new self-image changing the way he lives now—by faith. Paul, writing to the Philippians, encourages them, "Not that I have already obtained it or have already become perfect, but I press on so that I may lay hold of …" (Phil. 3:12). Paul's self-image is established, and he is pressing toward the goal. Paul's self-talk was that of a conqueror.

Characteristic # 6

Written with emotion and visualization (produce an imprint) to be reviewed daily

Putting your carefully constructed Renew Statements in writing is critical. No matter how inspirational a message may have been on Sunday morning, by the next week we are often hard pressed to remember much of it (unless of course we took notes and periodically reviewed the material during the week). Simply listening to a single inspirational message usually isn't sufficient to produce behavioral change; that is not to say we are unintelligent, deaf, or incapable of change. We just naturally remain in our comfort zones by passively letting the moment of inspiration quietly drift away without changing us.

Again as James 1:22 tells us, "But prove yourselves doers of the word, and not merely hearers who delude themselves." Did you ever consider that your subconscious mind, by keeping you protected in your comfort zone, is actually deluding you? The idea of being self-deluded isn't very flattering, and neither is the notion of insanity, which is defined as "doing the same thing over and over again and expecting different results" (quote generally attributed to Albert Einstein). Let us move on and embrace change with intentionality, establishing new self-images to escape the *delusional and insane* protection of passively remaining in our comfort zones.

By writing our Renew Statements on paper, we can review them frequently to firmly establish our new self-images in our brains. This in turn develops the neural pathways necessary for invigorating behavioral change. Just how long will this take? Research has shown it doesn't take very long. A Google search of "how long does it take to change a habit?" resulted in over twelve thousand articles. What I discovered, as would be expected, is that the length of time depends on the urgency and difficulty of the change (habit was defined as doing without thinking).

In one recent study published in the *European Journal of Social Psychology*, Phillippa Lally and colleagues from University College London developed a graph depicting "automaticity" on the vertical axis versus the number of "days" on the horizontal axis. Using ninety-six volunteers, Lally was able to measure the variability between establishing an easy change (adding a glass of water daily to our diet) versus a difficult change (doing fifty sit-ups before breakfast). Her results showed a marked variation based on the difficulty of the change and also among volunteers for the same change, thus providing a refinement of the "twenty-one days to form a habit" measure that is commonly cited (Lally et al., 2009).

Renew Statements

The vast amount of research on habits and how to change them is helpful in understanding how our self-images change as well. However, the focus for habit research is mainly toward repeatedly doing something to form a new behavior or habit. The Renew Statement's focus is more intentional: managing our self-talk, creating a self-image, forming a gap, and causing our mind to actively seek to reconcile the gap. All of this will result in behavioral changes. Therefore, applying Renew Statements will accelerate behavior change more quickly and definitely more creatively than mere repetition of a behavior.

Knowing what we know about how the brain physically forms neural pathways suggests that both the frequency and intensity of our self-talk will determine the length of time needed to form a stronger self-image. We've discussed having the Renew Statement written down and readily available for daily reviewing to fulfill the frequency aspect of forming a self-image. We also need to address the intensity aspect.

Imprinting with emotion and visualization is very powerful for helping you to know who you are. In our example of receiving achievement awards, imagine yourself at the awards presentation event. Feel the emotion of the setting as you receive recognition for your work from a significant person at your company. The visualization and emotion add intensity to your Renew Statement. Also try including relevant photos or keepsakes to stimulate the intensity of Renew Statements.

Consider the apostle Paul's writings of encouragement to the Ephesians in Chapter 6, "Finally, be strong in the Lord ... (verse 10). Therefore, take up the full armor of God ... (verse 13), ... put on the breastplate of righteousness ... (verse 14), ... having shod your feet ... (verse 15), take up the shield of faith ... (verse 16), ... take the helmet of salvation, and the sword of the Spirit ... (verse 17), ... and with this in view" (verse 18). Putting on the heavy soldier's gear that Paul describes is less intense for us today than it was in the Roman era, so let's put this in the context of American football.

MAKE YOUR WAY

Visualize for a moment a slow-motion replay of an NFL game with two powerful players hitting head-on at full speed. Imagine watching the brutal physical force of that impact in slow motion replay: beads of sweat flinging, crunching shoulder pads, clashing helmets, a mouthpiece flying as the runner is thrown down onto the ball with a 250-pound lineman pouncing on his back. Now step it up a level to visualize Paul's image, circa AD 30, of hand-to-hand combat with Roman swords clashing, metal against metal, wounded men's blood smeared on shields, screams of agony, dead bodies, etc. What an emotional and visual image! This is what Paul wanted imprinted on the minds of the Ephesians. Is there any doubt that he wanted them to "be strong" spiritually and able to resist? There is no place for passivity in Paul's analogy, no hiding within comfort zones. It is simply raw intentionality for "having done everything, to stand firm."

Dominating self-images are imprinted through frequency and intensity. Therefore, daily reviewing your Renew Statements and crafting them with emotion will expedite the creation of new self-images. Each new self-image will in turn form a gap that your brain will creatively work to close. This "closing of the gap" will cause behavior change that in turn will accomplish your goals.

Tying It All Together

Let's review what we have learned in part V by using an example we can all relate to. This example is one of my own personal Renew Statements that I suspect many can relate to, since it exemplifies the creative power of the mind. The backdrop was my longtime desire to be physically fit as I got older. I noticed that I had gained ten pounds in the last ten years, which was one indicator that I wasn't as fit as I would have liked to be. (Projecting that weight gain rate into the future was a little alarming.) Therefore, at age fifty-eight, I wanted to make sure I would be physically fit for my sixtieth birthday.

Fortunately, I have been blessed with some very good physical fitness genes, easily accessible workout facilities, and a helpmate (my lovely Jeanie) who enjoys preparing healthy meals and isn't shy about managing portion control. Therefore, my goal of getting back to where I was ten years ago shouldn't have been too much of a challenge; except that it was. Granted, my weight goal wasn't anything like the contestants on the TV program, *The Biggest Loser*, but it was the last ten pounds—the tough last pounds to lose. The dilemma was that the techniques I had used to lose weight when I was younger just didn't work for me anymore. I was stuck at my heavier weight. The body just wasn't responding like it used to.

At fifty-eight-and-a-half, I accepted the fact that I would have to work a little harder to get the same results that I did when I was in my forties or thirties. Okay, no problem; it was doable—right? For those of you who may have been there, I decreased my caloric intake and exercised more to increase my caloric burn and ended up feeling sore and exhausted in the process. I achieved some limited success, but I did not reach my goal weight, nor did I sustain the loss over time. I realized that simply repeating the same behavior over and over wasn't going to get me any different results.

I decided to sit down and carefully craft my fitness Renew Statement to help accomplish this goal. The first step was to determine the desired outcome that would be realistic, believable, and specific. This was made fairly easy by researching fitness standards from various publications. Information is readily available for measuring body fat and muscle mass for an ideal weight based on your height, bone structure, and age. My metric for being physically fit was to be at my *ideal weight,* which was also easily measurable. So the specific (measureable) goal of ten pounds was realistic and believable since it was based on my design. I was able to determine my particular ideal weight as 142 pounds. (That may seem a bit low, but I am only 66 inches tall, and I did at one time wrestle at the 118-pound weight class in college.)

I began referring to 1 Corinthians 6:19–20, "Or do you not know that your body is a temple of the Holy Spirit who is in you, whom you have from God, and that you are not your own? For you have been bought with a price: therefore glorify God in your body." In the preceding verses, Paul is addressing immorality and what is lawful and profitable. Regarding lawful, he states in verses 12 and 13, "But I will not be mastered by anything. Food is for the stomach and the stomach for food …"

The parallel is that just as we control our stomachs, so we should control the rest of our bodies since they all belongs to God. Okay, with that Scripture in mind, I was more motivated than ever to control my body weight, and then I added the, "For it is written …" statement: "For God has not given us a spirit of timidity, but of power and love and discipline" (2 Tim. 1:7). Bearing in mind that discipline is a good thing—let's accomplish this goal!

My goal was realistic, believable, and specific while it also gave glory to God (Renew Statement Characteristics 1 and 2) (i.e., not letting my stomach control me, I glorify God by controlling my body, etc.). I didn't want to wait until I was within two weeks of reaching my sixtieth birthday to be who I was supposed to be, so I decided to start right now.

My Renew Statement follows: *I feel so confident, strong, and healthy now that I weigh 142 pounds, which is my ideal weight.* The new self-image I am imprinting is that of being my ideal weight—*NOW!* This is not to say I am there, but that is who I am—which forms a gap. Yikes, something is going to have to give (Renew Statement characteristic 3)!

Feeling confident, strong, and healthy is a very positive consequence of being fit and not at all restrictive. A restrictive statement such as, "I will lose the weight even if I have to starve myself," doesn't help to generate solutions. Also the specific weight of 142 pounds is my preference as an ideal weight (Renew Statement characteristic 4). The fitness metric of "ideal weight" can change with my workouts. If I lean toward more cardio training, I will burn more calories and lose some muscle mass (heavy mass) along the way, thus having a lower ideal weight. If I lean toward more weight resistance training, I will develop more muscle mass, thus increasing my ideal weight.

Referring back to the trip's flight plan, there is more than one path to get to your ideal fitness destination. I may have to return to the fitness information I initially used to revalidate my ideal weight along the way based on changes in my Body Mass Index (BMI); no problem. Getting a heading check is fine, remembering that my goal is fitness, with my weight being the metric to measure my progress toward accomplishing that goal.

As with any goal, we have to be realistic about the amount of time it will take until we begin to see the results. This is particularly true for a successful diet that is nothing more than changing our eating habits for the long term. Healthy weight loss should be gradual and will take time, even after an ideal weight self-image is firmly imprinted. We can't be discouraged when we happen to get off our workout routine or occasionally celebrate a holiday by consuming way more calories than we ever needed to sustain us to the next meal. Just remember to use the phrase, "The next time I plan to …" "The next time I have to travel to Peoria, I will bring my workout clothes and use the hotel fitness center." Or "*The next time I attend a holiday get together, I am going to eat a snack (Fullbar, salad, etc.) thirty minutes before I arrive so I won't be inclined to overeat.*"

The next step in our Renew Statement process is being intentional about our self-talk to reinforce our new self-image. I will tell you that very loving, well-intentioned friends can unintentionally distract you from your conqueror's self-talk with suggestions that you have a dessert or some sweets, even admonishing you with, "Oh, you don't have to worry about your weight." But don't believe it; listen to your self-talk and avoid those sweets. The reality is that we can't rely on others to establish a new self-image for us; they are far too nice to make us uncomfortable! We have to take control and make ourselves intentionally uncomfortable by mentally stepping outside our comfort zones. Did you ever happen to notice how many buffets and sweets are suddenly available to you as soon as you begin a diet? That is just our brain working overtime. It is the Lock-On principle at work, trying to protect our waistline from change.

The conqueror self-talk says, "I have not been given a spirit of timidity, but of power and love and discipline" (2 Tim. 1:7); therefore I can discipline myself and order a salad off the menu and not passively enter the extravagant buffet line. But suddenly, the battle for your thoughts begins with the captive self-talk quickly piping in, "Oh, but you may never again have an opportunity to enjoy such delicious food …" Break! Break! (That is airplane radio talk for transitioning to a new message.) I'm a conqueror; I have no time for foolish captive self-talk, because: "I feel so confident, strong, and healthy now that I weigh 142 pounds, which is my ideal weight." The battle of words for your thoughts is on. But you are a conqueror, so use your conqueror's self-talk and your behavior will follow your Renew Statement. (Renew Statement characteristic 5).

Finally, my self-image is being strengthened with each day as I recite my Renew Statement. In fact, I even have them memorized, along with the supporting Scriptures. They come to mind as I walk past the tempting pastries so prominently displayed at the coffee counter. Therefore, I Lock-Out what doesn't fit my self-image, and I Lock-On to what does fit it. Through my self-talk, my mind will naturally Lock-On to things that reconcile the gap resulting in plans to go to the gym, finding new opportunities to exercise, enjoying time playing racquetball with my sons, etc. As for me, I am developing a wonderful self-image with emotional feelings: feeling confident, feeling strong, and feeling healthy. That self-image becomes imprinted on my brain, thus transforming my behavior (Renew Statement characteristic 6).

Accomplishing My Renew Statement Goal—How Did It Work?

Did I lose those last stubborn ten pounds? Well, just how it worked was interesting because I eventually did lose the pounds. However, let me iterate it didn't work by positive thinking, chanting, or some metaphysical mental weight loss program. No, it took physically hard work and discipline to transform me. The transformation was brought about by my mind closing the gap between my Renew Statement and my weight, transforming me by the Lock-On of conqueror-type solutions and the Lock-out of captive behavior that would have held me back.

Here is the story. With my Renew Statement prepared, I began again with a regimen of less food and more exercise, but this time I discovered (Lock-On) a new fitness instructor (she was actually there long before I ever noticed her) who taught me a more effective cardio technique that burned more calories in a shorter workout period.

However, that wasn't enough by itself. I started really watching everything I ate and came across a calorie counter app (Lock-On) for my iPhone that was very helpful. But even that gadget wasn't enough. So I found some additional exercise classes and creatively discovered a way to fit five workouts a week into my schedule for a few weeks. But to my surprise, that surge still wasn't enough. I found that over the holidays, I had time to exercise even more, but I couldn't physically do any more exercising. I wasn't able to; my muscles didn't recover between the more frequent workouts, and I felt terribly sore and tired (not good). Nor could I sustain the time commitment. Although closer to my goal, I was now stalled and not losing any more weight.

No worries—I was not going to be discouraged, and my mind hadn't given up on reconciling the gap. I happened to enter a nutrition store for vitamins, and coincidentally (Lock-On), I got into a conversation with one of the salespeople who just happened to also be working out and training to lose weight. He directed me to some fat-burner pills that are the latest formula and the *best ever* scientifically developed for trimming you down.

Once again I was very hopeful that this just might be the silver bullet for achieving the old guy's weight goal, but no, those pills didn't work for me at all. I took half the prescribed amount the first day to get started and didn't sleep for two days. I was wired and totally irritable. Astutely, I decided to stay away from people until this stuff wore off and I could get a good night's sleep. Next, I realized (Lock-On) that drinking a glass of wine with dinner over the course of a year accumulated a lot of extra empty calories, so I decided to eliminate that routine. But again, even this wasn't enough to achieve my weight goal. And to make things worse, I was not feeling very energetic. What next?

Finally the solution, the Lock-On, was a book entitled *Master Your Metabolism* by Jillian Michaels (from *The Biggest Loser* TV program). The book explains the role your hormones have in regulating your metabolism and how you can improve your hormonal balance by eating the right foods. Once the hormones are in sync, not only will you burn fat more efficiently, but you will also have more energy (which I was now lacking).

Notice how the brain never gave up trying to reconcile my fitness self-image to my actual fitness? Also notice how things just kept coming into play that I hadn't considered or even noticed before. This was the Locking-On to possible solutions. If I hadn't been intentional about those last stubborn pounds, I would never have come to find the final mix of solutions that made it possible. My solution was the right mix of a sustainable exercise routine and a healthy balanced diet; a combination of all the things I was discovering blended together for my goal accomplishment. The solution sounds simple enough in the end, but *Making My Way* was a journey, with some deviations along the way, toward the successful accomplishment of the goal—in the end a very creative adventure.

What is really special is that someone else may have a very similar Renew Statement but will successfully reconcile the gap in a very different way. How creative is that? We are each uniquely made, and our goals will be achieved in uniquely creative ways as well. It is your Renew Statement, for your design. Of course, we can learn from each other, and I do recommend Jillian's book. However, always expect that you will find all kinds of new Lock-On options that meet your individual needs. So enjoy—this is what your brain does very well for you!

I included this Renew Statement example to demonstrate the creativeness generated for achieving this very measurable goal. Achieving your career goals with Renew Statements will work as effectively. Your mind will find ways to reconcile believable self-images. Achieving career goals through Renew Statements will sometimes seems so simple and natural. You'll be asking yourself questions like, "Why didn't I think of this a long time ago?" Or better yet, you'll be able to say, "Everything just fell into place; all the doors opened up, and the timing was perfect." When we understand the Lock-On and Lock-Out principles and are intentional about our thoughts, we can expect to find opportunities for growth and *goal getting.* "And the one on whom seed was sown on the good soil, this is the man who hears the word and understands it; who indeed bears fruit and brings forth, some a hundredfold, some sixty, and some thirty" (Matt. 13:23).

Applying Renew Statements to Your Career Plan

Now that we have an understanding of how to develop and apply Renew Statements to intentionally change behavior for the achievement of goals, we'll take a look at a career example. We will develop a sample Renew Statement that could be applicable to many readers as they progress toward greater responsibilities in their career fields. Consider the scenario where you are feeling *under-employed* and to some extent have been bored at your current position, but you feel *comfortable* with a steady paycheck and medical benefits. Knowing that your vocation is much more than a job, you have taken the information from the earlier sections on the "Network Advantage" and "Job-Capture Coaching" and performed the research to produce a career-development plan. The plan calls for accomplishing milestones as goals along the way. One of the skills you determined to be critical for long-term success in your career field is effective public speaking.

This speaking would include both informational technical briefings to colleagues and persuasive speaking for implementing new ideas to achieve departmental goals. The problem is that you have always been frightened at the thought of getting up in front of an audience and presenting anything. And even if the majority of the presentations were to be limited to an internal company audience, it would still be important do well. Therefore, you cannot allow a fear of public speaking to become a *fatal weakness* that could hold you back over the long term.

To get started, we should consider what the writer of Hebrews tells us: "And do not neglect doing good and sharing, for with such sacrifices God is pleased" (Heb. 13:16). Since sharing and helping others pleases God, and since public speaking is nothing more than sharing knowledge with others, we are ready to sacrifice our *comfort* and change. By helping others, we will glorify God. With that purpose in mind, we have determined that sharing ideas publicly is a reasonable goal, so we create a Renew Statement with:

> So that God may be glorified in me, I enjoy sharing my ideas and prepared remarks in front of audiences because I have something to say that will help them.

Follow this opening statement with a "For it is written ..." Scripture from Philippians 2:4, "Do not merely look out for your own personal interests, but also for the interests of others." This will further encourage the acceptance of this self-image as one that is very believable. Now our Renew Statement reads:

> So that God may be glorified in me, I enjoy sharing my ideas and prepared remarks in front of audiences because I have something to say that will help them. For it is written:
>
> a. "Do not merely look out for your own personal interests, but also for the interests of others" (Phil. 2:4).

As part of your career-development plan, public speaking is an area that can be developed through several milestones such as: 1) reading how-to books on speaking; 2) joining the local Toastmasters group; and 3) looking for opportunities at work to gain experience making presentations. When you follow through with training through self-help books on public speaking and participating with Toastmasters (a mentoring group with many local meetings), this Renew Statement is realistic, believable, and specific. With a little training and coaching, there is no reason why sharing helpful ideas cannot be enjoyable.

This Renew Statement is crafted in the *NOW*. Experiencing the enjoyment of sharing and helping is familiar to you, and it is a very good thing to do. This is nothing new; you already have experienced this emotion in other areas of your life. Therefore we accept that positive experience now, with a public speaking Renew Statement to create a *Gap* for your brain to resolve.

The positive consequences and nonrestrictive demands allow the brain to Lock-On to new opportunities to practice, new techniques to employ, and new ideas to present in interesting and helpful ways. If a particular technique doesn't work out very well, simply remember the "Next time I plan to ..." approach and learn from it without dwelling on the past. I personally have found that some hotels have the absolute worst microphones and sound systems you can imagine, so I have learned to ask questions about the room before I arrive, perform a sound check, get feedback from a trusted friend (someone who will be brutally honest) in the audience, and learn from each experience.

This Renew Statement is not restrictive and thus does not cause a Lock-Out in the way a demand would, such as, "I will not be nervous." Demands cause the brain to focus on what you *don't want* it to—in this example, nervousness. In fact being a little nervous can be used to your advantage, if you are not restrictive. The adrenaline rush can be used to make you more animated and help you to deliver a more energetic message. Incidentally, when I get nervous, I remind myself that the audience has shown up, and they desire for me to succeed. And by the way, it is all about them and how I can help them through my remarks. Now I have harnessed that nervousness to motivate me to help my listeners. How wonderful!

Your brain will Lock-On to creative ways to help you and to find solutions—as long as you don't constrict its creativity with excessive restrictions. You'll find yourself Locking-On to other supporting Scriptures and feedback from friends to add to you Renew Statement such as:

> So that God may be glorified in me, I enjoy sharing my ideas and prepared remarks in front of audiences because I have something to say that will help them. For it is written:
>
> a. "Do not merely look out for your own personal interest, but also for the interests of others" (Phil. 2:4).
> b. "A wise tongue makes knowledge acceptable" (Prov. 25:2).
>
> And confirmed by:
>
> c. "Thank you so much for sharing with us, I really appreciate getting that helpful information." — Coworker, Ms. Smith

Use the self-talk of a conqueror. It is perfectly fine to say to yourself, "Yes, I feel nervous just like all great speakers do. I will use this energy to reach the audience and share my ideas with them."

Finally, as with any Renew Statement, I have written it down and will review it daily, letting the enjoyment (emotion) of sharing and helping others imprint a new self-image of me as an effective public speaker. I can visualize the speaking engagement in my head and review my Renew Statement as I practice my presentation in front of the mirror. As the new self-image is being imprinted on my mind, I am memorizing the Renew Statement and supporting Scriptures verbatim, arming my mind with the conqueror's self-talk and thus changing my behavior to accomplish my goal. Finally my mind is fully engaged, helping me to *Make My Way*!

Supporting Statements

Often the best supporting statements are derived from something that just *jumps out* at you as truth, something that you Locked-On to, such as affirming feedback, scriptural reference, sermon messages, or recent experiences. It is important to record these to reinforce and strengthen your Renew Statements. I once had a revelation of what was possible as I watched the sunset over the ocean from my 20th floor office window. In addition to adding this in written form to my Renew Statement, I took a photo and used it for the *wallpaper* backdrop on my phone. This photo image constantly provided a visual reminder to me reinforcing what was possible if I was intentional.

Following are some scriptural references that I have used for my Renew Statements that you may find helpful:

- "…and what is the surpassing greatness of His power toward us who believe. These are in accordance with the working of the strength of His might." Eph. 1:19
- "For we are his workmanship, created in Christ Jesus for good works which God prepared beforehand so that we would walk in them." Eph. 2:10
- "Only be strong and very courageous; be careful to do according to all the law which Moses My servant commanded you; … have success wherever you go." Joshua 1:7-10
- "And do not neglect doing good and sharing, for with such sacrifices God is pleased." Heb. 13:16
- "For You formed my inward parts; You wove me in my mother's womb. I will give thanks to You, for I am fearfully and wonderfully made: Wonderful are Your works, And my soul knows it very well." Ps. 139-13-14
- "A wise tongue makes knowledge acceptable." Prov. 25:2

- "…and my message and my preaching were not in persuasive works of wisdom, but in demonstration of the Spirit and of power," 1 Corth. 2:4
- "Let your gentle spirit be known to all men, The Lord is near." Phil. 4:5
- "For God has not given us a spirit of timidity, but of power and love and discipline." 2 Tim. 1:7
- "His master said to him, Well done, good and faithful slave. You were faithful with a few things, I will put you in charge of many things; enter into the joy of your master." Matt. 25:21; 25:22 (2 or 5 talents)
- "But prove yourselves doers of the word, and not merely hearers who delude themselves. For if anyone is a hearer of the word and not a doer, he is like a man who looks at his natural face in a mirror; for *once* he has looked at himself and gone away, he has immediately forgotten what kind of person he was. But one who looks intently at the perfect law, the *law* of liberty, and abides by it, not having become a forgetful hearer but an effectual doer, this man will be blessed in what he does." James 1;22-25

There are also excellent free online Bible resources to help you find those supporting scriptures. I recommend both www.BibleStudyTools.com and www.BibleGateway.com to get you started.

Closing Encouragement

As you are getting started with Renew Statements, it is best to develop an initial list and work on all of them concurrently. Your brain will concurrently perform the creative work and Lock-On to solutions for goals. You may even find the new behaviors from your Renew Statements benefiting multiple goals at the same time. Feel free to refine your Renew Statements to make them even stronger as you learn more along the way. As you accomplish your goals, continue to add the next wave of goals to your career plan.

Harnessing the creative power of our brains to accomplish our God-given purpose is very exciting. Always keep the end in mind: "Well done good and faithful servant. You were faithful with a few things, I will put you in charge of many things; enter into the joy of your master" (Matt. 25:23). And we must not forget, "For to everyone who has, more shall be given, and he will have an abundance; but from the one who does not have, even what he does have shall be taken away" (Matt. 25:29). This last passage is a strong admonishment to not be passive about our vocation, our calling, that for which we were designed.

Afterword

As we conclude our time together, I am brought back to the men's prayer meeting where I first felt the strong pull to help others successfully pursue a vocational journey. I could sense that some of these men did not have an understanding of the possibilities or the means to achieve their potential without an encouraging mentor to help show them the way. I sought God on how to move forward with my calling. At that time, I didn't have any of the particulars of what I could do or what I needed to do. I just knew it was more than editing resumes and helping them land a weekly paycheck.

Developing the lecture series was the vehicle to organizing the materials and incorporating the available research into a cohesive outline for developing a repeatable result. The lecture series also allowed us to expand our audience beyond the men's prayer meeting. The purpose of this book is to further expand the number of people reached to help beyond what would be physically possible through our oral presentations alone. Being perfectly transparent, this book was a struggle and also a joy. I was definitely out of my comfort zone; authoring a book seemed impossible. I struggled. I resisted making the writing of this book the priority that it needed to be in my life. I didn't consider myself a serious author, and that was robbing me of the joy, I later discovered. I wrestled with changing my lifetime collage of self-images. As you can deduce, I too was *Making My Way*.

> Change does not roll in on the wheels of inevitability, but comes through continuous struggle.
>
> —*Martin Luther King, Jr.*

Work Environment—the Need

Part I revealed that whether the employment environment is up or down, in any given four-month period, approximately 3 percent of the jobs are in flux, with 3 percent job creation and 3 percent job loss. This 3 percent flux over four months equates to a 9 percent annual flux. Despite the total employment downturn starting in the fourth quarter of 2009, the job *flux* continued around 9 percent annually. Therefore, we should be pursuing the new jobs available in the flux upside. Furthermore, because jobs are always being lost, we need to be ever-more vigilant and prepared for our next job opportunity. Career planning is for everyone, whether you are just entering the work force or are already a seasoned professional. Things are always changing, and the flux goes on.

More importantly, we also reviewed the significance of our vocation in God's overall plan for us. Receiving a divine *high five* with the words, "Well done good and faithful servant. You were faithful with a few things, I will put you in charge of many things, enter into the joy of your master" (Matt. 25:21), is our vocational accolade worthy of pursuing for a lifetime.

I understood the employment environment, and I felt my calling. I knew I could use my talents to help others achieve their own vocational design.

Meeting the Need

Developing the *Make Your Way* lecture series was exciting for Jeanie and me. I was pretty much in my comfort zone doing research, making Microsoft PowerPoint slides, and presenting the materials to a very accepting audience of church members. I had amazing supporters. Jeanie and I would spend time discussing the themes and developing the talking points whenever we were together. It was wonderful to work with her and to get her ideas and feedback on my ideas. A deeper intellectual intimacy developed, and my work and romance met together to create something new, something bigger than us! Presenting the lecture series was also exciting. I had my pastors review our drafts and got superb insights, comments, and encouragement from them. All was going well until the *book* idea started becoming inevitable. This concept made me very uncomfortable.

We all agreed in principle that a book was the next step, and that is exactly what I considered it—the next step, sometime in the future, certainly not now. I was very satisfied to continue to consider the book as appropriate for some future time, comparable to how some international organizations convene on a global issue, only to agree to meet next year to discuss it further. I too was content to simply kick the can down the road for some other time. What was very uncomfortable for me was the idea of dedicating my time and energy to writing a book *now*. After all, I wasn't an author, and I was very busy with other things like working as a consultant, volunteering in professional organizations to further my career, and looking for a full-time aerospace job. So for a while I was quite successful at distracting myself from ever getting started with the book; I was just too busy with my comfortable roles.

The Next Step—Writing a Book

You miss 100 percent of the shots you never take.

—Wayne Gretzky

One day my senior pastor just happened to mention again, "You need to write the book." I felt the conviction again and decided that it was indeed time for me to write the book. I prayed and sought God's direction, and then I got started. I found that, after a few days, I would easily get distracted and wasn't making the progress I had expected. I wrestled with disciplining myself to set aside the time and not let work, family, or friends distract me. It was my brute force discipline pushing forward with the book that at times made it difficult to focus on the flow of the content or write with any creativity. I made some progress and even felt a sense of purpose and joy when I had a good day at it. But after a while, I got tired and slipped back into my familiar mode of not writing and being enticed by many convenient distractions. So I took what I knew and decided to establish a new self-image—that of a writer. Now my brain would help me change my behavior so I could get on with writing a book. (You know you've got to walk the talk.)

Accordingly, I knew that I knew that I was supposed to write this book. It was realistic, it was believable, and it was a specific goal assigned to me. My only problem was that I didn't consider myself a writer. I wasn't sure this book would ever get published, and if it did get published, I wasn't sure that anyone would ever read it. It was captive thinking that kept me Locked On to my current professional managerial perspective and not onto that of a writer. I ruminated over what would be the Return On Investment (ROI) for writing this book, how many hours of investment would it take, what would be the return for my effort, would it support my family, etc.? I was not engaged in conqueror thinking like a successful author who was called to write on this very subject would have been. To be successful, I needed to form a new *writer* self-image.

I knew that a book promoting a biblical basis to help members of the body of Christ achieve their God-given vocational design would give glory to God in many ways. And since I felt pulled so strongly to help others more with what I knew, the *It is written* was evident: "His master said to him, Well done, good and faithful servant. You were faithful with a few things, I will put you in charge of many things, enter into the joy of your master" (Matt. 25:21). I also gained additional support from, "And do not neglect doing good and sharing, for with such sacrifices God is pleased" (Heb. 13:16). I had full authority to be a writer, whether the ROI made financial sense or not. I was set aside to bring joy to my Master simply by being obedient.

My Renew Statement read:

> So that God may be glorified through me, putting *Make Your Way Career Series* into a book drives creativity, godly insight, and purpose for the next generation.

a. His master said to him, "Well done, good and faithful servant. You were faithful with a few things, I will put you in charge of many things, enter into the joy of your master" (Matt. 25:21).

b. "And do not neglect doing good and sharing, for with such sacrifices God is pleased" (Heb. 13:16).

The Renew Statement is written in the *now*. I recited this daily with emotion. As this became imprinted in my mind, my writing became more creative, I received more insight from my devotional time, and my pastors kept giving me Lock-On support teachings in their Sunday-morning sermons.

Now writing had very positive consequences and wasn't at all restrictive. A restrictive-type statement may have required me to write two thousand words every day or to spend so many hours per week on the book. My Renew Statement wasn't restrictive; therefore, I didn't push back because I wanted to write. I then noticed how I would Lock-On to those things that helped me write and naturally Lock-Out distractions that had previously prevented me from making good progress.

During one Sunday worship service, it came to me that holiness meant being separated and being separated for a purpose. Yep, you got it: being separated to write a book that I was called to write. This was my way, at least for this season, to be holy and set apart.

My set-apart time was good. I penned some creative stuff (thank You, Lord), and I felt a purpose for what I was doing. As author Walter Anderson says, "Nothing diminishes anxiety faster than action."

The impact of my conqueror's self-talk became evident, as close friends would talk to me as *the author* of this book even before it was published. I had branded myself as a writer, even though I am still in business development as a career field and may not write anything next month or even next year. But in any case, the self-image is there, and I can successfully reach my writing goals by behaving like a successful writer would behave. (What is writing behavior? It is a discipline of its own, which I discovered as I Locked-On to close the gap I had formed with my new writer self-image.) I devoted two hours to writing, took a two-hour break from writing, and then followed that with two more hours of writing. I didn't invent this tempo. I heard about it out of the blue as my mind instinctively searched for ways to close that uncomfortable gap formed from the new writer self-image.

That disciplined behavior became easy as Philippians 2:3–5 became very real to me. Paul writes to the Philippians, "Do nothing from selfishness or empty conceit, but with humility of mind regard one another as more important than yourselves, do not merely look out for your own personal interests, but also for the interests of others. Have this attitude in yourselves which was also in Christ Jesus." Notice how Paul refers to "with humility of mind" as an attitude of Christ. Setting our minds (controlling our thoughts) changes our behavior. I was no longer only looking out for my personal interests, but as a writer, I could also look out for the interests of others.

Forming that gap was intentional, and it was enhanced by daily reviewing my written Renew Statement. Those pleasant feelings that would come from hearing that wonderful "well done good and faithful servant" in my mind's ears strengthened my new image. I had formed a gap that needed urgent attention, and that is why I am now finishing the last planned section—the one that you happen to be reading. Thank you very much for journeying with me.

Blessings

Having a biblical perspective of the importance of work and truly understanding your unique design provides the career direction toward the fulfillment of a designed purpose that far exceeds a paycheck, union contract, retirement plan, or benefits package. *Making Your Way* along your career path entails building relationships and helping others, which fosters a real sense of belonging and being part of something bigger than you. I hope I was able to bring out that purpose through this book and to guide you to scriptural references to help you as you *Make Your Way* along your career journey.

However, there is even a higher purpose for *Making Your Way*. Paul tells us our citizenship is in heaven (Phil. 3:20), and he also writes, "Brethren, I do not regard myself as having laid hold of it yet; but one thing I do: forgetting what lies behind and reaching forward to what lies ahead, I press on toward the goal for the prize of the upward call of God in Christ Jesus" (Phil. 3:13–14). I was raised going to church and Sunday school, and yet when I was thirty-one years old, I struggled with what to do about this Jesus of the Bible. Even though I was drawn to read C. S. Lewis's *Mere Christianity*, I just wasn't able to accept what I was reading at the time. I put the book down for months because I couldn't accept the purity and goodness of the message, nor was I ready to give up what I was at the time to be transformed into something I didn't fully understand. I was comfortable where I was, even though I knew there was so much more for me.

My holding on to familiar comfort was akin to the childhood stubbornness that I exhibited at the age of ten. I had a pair of engineer boots that I had worn until there were holes through the soles and in the leather on the top of the toes. My mother had bought me new shoes, but I wouldn't give up the boots I had grown comfortable with, even though they were not functional or physically comfortable anymore (the winters got cold where I grew up).

I knew that the truths C. S. Lewis wrote about were indeed true. Months later, I gave up my stubbornness by picking up the book again. This eventually helped lead me to accepting Jesus as my Savior. It was a long time coming, and it was a huge self-image change. It was difficult for me to understand the depth and breadth and width of such good news as the gospel. As a new Christian, I dived into the Bible and read supporting commentaries. I was experiencing the Lock-On phenomenon as I was being transformed; I was only faintly aware of the increasing Lock-Out of the old behaviors. I had a new citizenship with a new language, and I was enjoying it immensely.

With a heavenly citizenship, we now can understand Jesus's words, "Take my yoke upon you and learn from Me, for I am gentle and humble in heart, *and you will find rest for your souls*. For My yoke is easy and My burden is light" (Matt. 11:29–30). Whether you are just now just being drawn to accept Jesus as your Savior or you already have had a born-again experience, knowing who you are in Christ is transforming. Know your citizenship, and the transformation of your behavior will follow. You can understand the urgency Paul must have felt for the Ephesians as he wrote, "That the God of our Jesus Christ, the Father of glory, may give to you a spirit of wisdom and of revelation in the knowledge of Him"—praying for the revelation, the Lock-On to the things of God. Paul goes on, "I pray that the eyes of your heart may be enlightened, so that you will know what is the hope of His calling, what are the riches of the glory of His inheritance in the saints, and what is the surpassing greatness of His power toward us who believe …" (Eph. 1:17–18).

Dear beloved, we have been given a mind to use to Lock-On to the fullness God has for each one of us and to Lock-Out the worldly distractions that could keep us from understanding His loving-kindness. This book provides coaching on how to discipline your thoughts for successful career development, and our sincere hope is that you are now also well-equipped to reach your calling—in all areas of your life. Bring glory to God by using the full citizenship you have in heaven.

God Bless,
Spence and Jeanie

Acknowledgments

Not being a writer by trade or ever having had a thought of writing a book previously, I am totally appreciative for the encouragement and support I received from my wife, Jeanie. While she understood the brutal facts regarding the likelihood of successfully publishing and selling a book, she nonetheless encouraged me—simply because writing this book was what we were called to do. She identified the underlying physiological and behavioral theory principles and their applicability to the work we were developing. She is also responsible for bringing life to the pages through the use of personal experiences and anecdotes, thus sparing the readers from my propensity toward a *Flight Manual*, technical style of writing. This would surely have put you all to sleep.

I owe a great deal to my pastors, Rob McKenna and Wes Harding at The Bridge in El Segundo, California. Without their vision for how best to meet the needs of our community, I would have never gone down the path of developing a lecture series or writing this book. Not surprisingly, both pastors kept feeding me timely messages with each passing Sunday sermon.

I am thankful for Pastor Randolph Michaelsen from Kings Harbor Church, who took the time to meet with me. As an expert outsider, he gave me the conformation that there was something here worth pursuing—something that was very much needed and something very practical that the church could offer as an outreach to the community.

Mr. Bruce Garrison was my editor; it was truly a blessing to have had the opportunity to work with such a professional. I highly recommend Bruce for all your writing and editing needs. Bruce can be reached at www.brucegarrison360.com.

MAKE YOUR WAY

Mr. Bill Tilney of The Tilney Design Group was the inspiration for the *myPlanner* website. We met several times to explore ideas for how best to follow-up and help the *Make Your Way* readers and seminar attendees pursue their long-term career planning. In essence, how do we effectively mentor and coach people through the many challenges of a long-term vocational journey? We decided the *Make Your Way—myPlanner* would be the most efficient way to reach out and help the greatest number of people within our limited resources. Bill can be reached for website design solutions at: www.linkedin.com/pub/bill-tilney/36/53b/2a1

Special thanks for the work of Dr. Randall S. Hansen, CEO and Founder of Quintessential Careers. Please visit: www.QuintCareers.com. It is an honor to include a small segment of Dr. Hansen's plethora of career materials in this book. Granting permission to use excerpts from Quintessential Careers' "Interview Question Bank" is in keeping with Dr. Hansen's overall mission of *empowering as many people as possible to have better jobs, satisfying careers, and fulfilling lives.* A mission statement I could not agree with more, thank you.

And lastly, I thank my children for their understanding. This book, along with my consulting practice, had me intently working long hours at home. This was definitely an adjustment for them. I was at home but not available, working but on a tighter budget. Change had come, and more was expected of them. They helped out and stepped up to a greater responsibility—a greater responsibility toward meeting each other's needs.

APPENDIX A

Sample Career Plan

In this example our twenty-six-year-old software (S/W) developer begin the career planning process.

Step 1: To get started, our S/W developer determines where he/she would like to finish. This may very well change over time; the idea now is to establish an initial direction for your career plan.

Step 2: Begin working backward from the *finish* by asking what earlier position would be needed to be qualified to obtain that desired position or end state. Then continue with that line of questioning to the next preceding position and the next until the current employment position. Keep in mind the *employment energy* associated with each age group.

Step 3: Consider what it will take to be competitive for each desired position (what would the hiring manager expect); these are the career *milestones.* Some of the many considerations are listed in the *career plan filter* box. There can be one to many milestones for each desired position depending on the circumstances. Our S/W developer's career path starts with the current position and determines the need for being assigned to a major project (this provides security and experience for advancing within the industry). This milestone will accomplish the necessity of being recognized as an expert on the job.

Since achieving success will be a driver in the near future, our S/W developer will need to obtain S/W certifications and become proficient in additional S/W languages through training and broader assignments. Further down the line a master's degree in computer science will be required for advancement, along with a level of proficiency in public speaking. The public speaking will be needed for presentations to senior management and internal staff communications.

Our astute S/W developer also sees the need for an MBA and significant funds for investing as a partner during that career season. In addition to these initial planning milestones, more milestones will be included as more clarity and advice is obtained from work experience and network contacts. As for now, this is a good first cut at the plan. Completion dates (mm/yy) are then assigned to each milestone.

Step 4: Inch-stones are then established to accomplish the step-by-step details of each milestone. In our S/W developer's first milestone of being assigned to a major S/W program we see eight initial inch-stones that were easily determined. The more-distant future milestones will naturally have less granularity and most likely fewer specific milestones for now.

Sample Career Plan

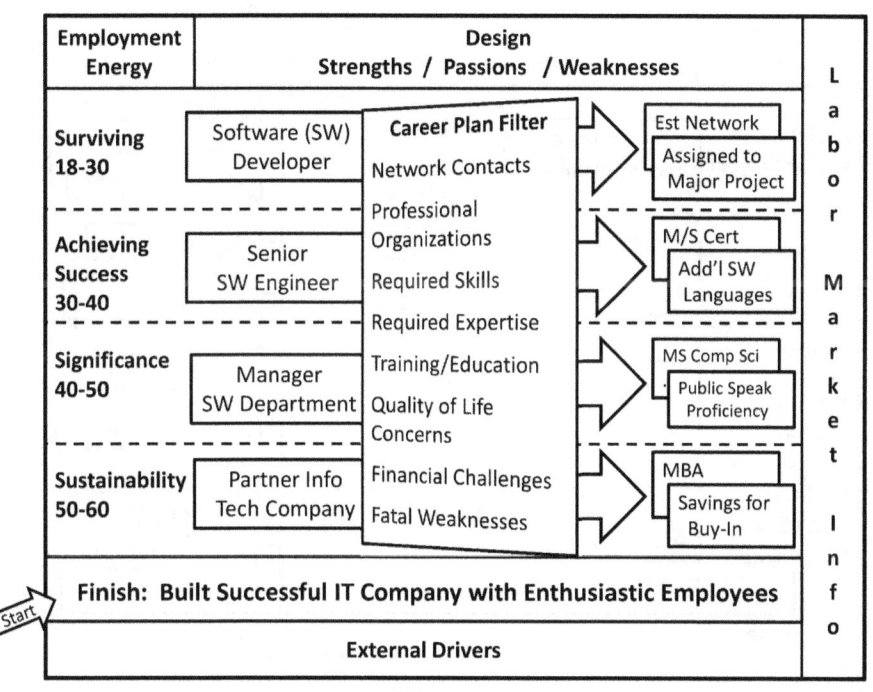

Process for Establishing Career Milestones

MAKE YOUR WAY

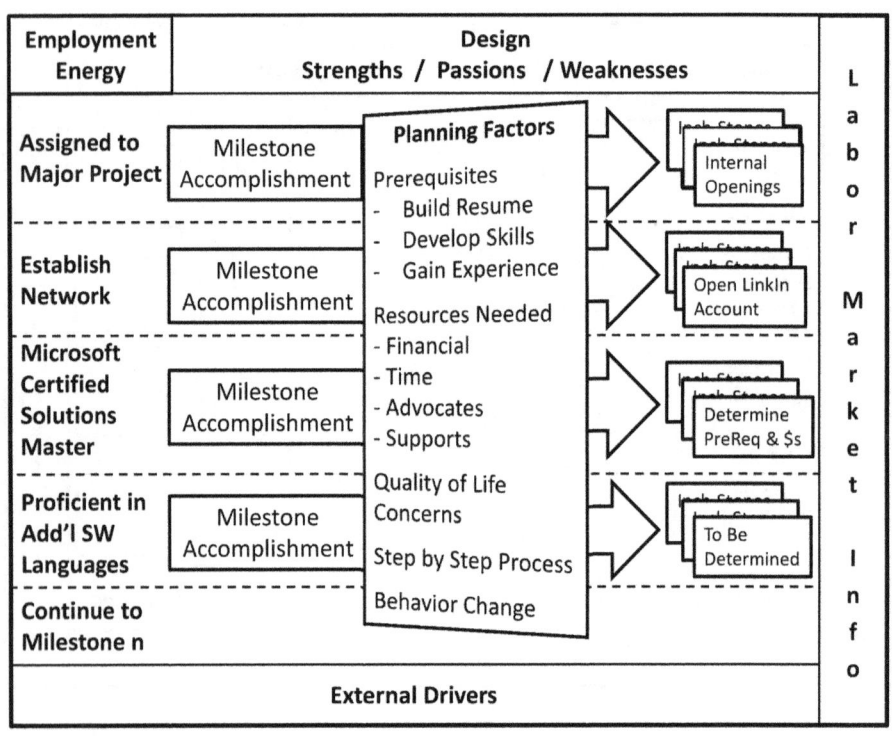

From Career Milestones to Inch-stones

Sample Career Plan

Career Position	Milestone	Inch-Stones	Start Date	End Date	Open Closed	Notes
S/W Developer	Major Proj Assignment	Summary	1/13	12/13		
S/W Developer	Major Proj Assignment	Research Open Internal Positions	1/13	1/13	Closed	What positions are currently eligible for
S/W Developer	Major Proj Assignment	Research Open External Positions	2/13	2/13	Closed	What external opportunities are available
S/W Developer	Major Proj Assignment	Discuss with your Management	2/13	2/13	Closed	Have your management help you
S/W Developer	Major Proj Assignment	Speak with HR Representative	2/13	2/13	Closed	Seek advice from HR for career progression
S/W Developer	Major Proj Assignment	Learn about Company Projects	2/13	8/13		Google and Network to get info
S/W Developer	Major Proj Assignment	External Informational Interviews	2/13	6/13		Request 20 min informational meetings
S/W Developer	Major Proj Assignment	Build Resume for Desired Projects	2/13	8/13		Accept new tasks to *build* resume
S/W Developer	Major Proj Assignment	Interview for Projects	3/13	12/13		Submit compelling resume
S/W Developer	Establish Network	Summary	1/13	8/13		
S/W Developer	Establish Network	Establish LinkedIn Account	1/13	1/13		
S/W Developer	Establish Network	Determine top 5 Companies to work for	1/13	1/13		Consider whether relocation is an option
S/W Developer	Establish Network	Establish 3 contacts in each Company	2/13	8/13		new employee, a peer, and one level up
S/W Developer	Establish Network	Research top 5 Companies	2/13	7/13		Learn everything you can about their products
S/W Developer	Establish Network	Register on Top 5 Companies Career Sites	3/13	3/13		Set up an auto notification search criteria
S/W Developer	Establish Network	Attend Professional Org Events Monthly	2/13	2/15		Thee were several locally listed on the LMI
S/W Developer	Establish Network	Connect with Industry Mentor	2/13	8/13		Most likely thru attending events
Sr S/W Engineer	MS Cert Sol Master	Summary	4/13	10/16		
Sr S/W Engineer	MS Cert Sol Master	Determine Prerequisites and cost	4/13	5/13		Company tuition assistance, savings, or loan
Sr S/W Engineer	MS Cert Sol Master	Complete Prerequisites - MCSE	6/13	12/15		
Sr S/W Engineer	MS Cert Sol Master	Submit Application	1/16	1/16		
Sr S/W Engineer	MS Cert Sol Master	Attend Classes	2/16	8/16		Form habits to make time for classes
Sr S/W Engineer	MS Cert Sol Master	Complete Testing	10/16	10/16		
Sr S/W Engineer	Add'l S/W Languages	Summary	1/18	1/20		Inch Stones To Be Determined
Manager S/W Dept	MS in Comp Sci		1/20	1/22		Inch Stones To Be Determined
Manager S/W Dept	Public Speaking Profeciency	Summary	1/22	1/24		Inch Stones To Be Determined
Partner in Tech Firm	MBA		1/25	1/27		Inch Stones To Be Determined
Partner in Tech Firm	Funds for Buy-IN	Summary	1/18	1/31		Additional Inch Stones To Be Determined
Partner in Tech Firm	Funds for Buy-IN	Start initial savings @ $100 per week	1/18	1/31		$5200/yr compounded annually

Putting it all Together with a Tracking Sheet of Career Milestones and Inch-stones

www.MakeYourWayResources.com 297

Appendix B

Sample Job Requisition

Marketing Manager—Job Requisition #98765

Job Objective: Responsible for developing and maintaining marketing strategies to meet organizational objectives. Evaluates customer research, market conditions, and competitor data, and implements marketing plan changes as needed. Oversees all marketing, advertising, and promotional staff and activities.

Responsibilities: Responsible for the marketing of medical equipment and services tailored exclusively to the needs of the geriatrics market.

- Demonstrating technical marketing skills and product knowledge of medical type products.
- Developing annual marketing plan in conjunction with sales department, and detailing activities to follow during the fiscal year, which will focus on meeting organizational objectives.
- Managing the Marketing Department budget. Delivery of all marketing activity within agreed budget. Direction of marketing staff where budgets are devolved.
- Managing all aspects of print production, receipt, and distribution.
- Achieving frequent, timely, and positive media coverage for products across all available media.
- Managing the entire product line life cycle from strategic planning to tactical activities.
- Specifying market requirements for current and future products by conducting market research, supported by ongoing visits to customers and non-customers.

- Driving a solution set across development teams (primarily Development/Engineering and Marketing Communications) through market requirements, product contract, and positioning.
- Developing and implementing a company-wide go-to-market plan, working with all departments to execute.
- Analyzing potential partner relationships for product lines.

Relationships and Roles:

Internal/External Cooperation

- Demonstrate ability to interact and cooperate with all company employees.
- Build trust, value others, communicate effectively, drive execution, foster innovation, focus on the customer, collaborate with others, solve problems creatively, and demonstrate high integrity.
- Maintain professional internal and external relationships that meet company core values.
- Proactively establish and maintain effective working team relationships with all support departments.

Job Specifications:

- Four to six years of sales experience in the marketing industry.
- Extensive experience in all aspects of developing and maintaining marketing strategies to meet organizational objectives.
- Strong understanding of customer and market dynamics and requirements.
- Willingness to travel and work in a global team of professionals.

Proven ability to oversee all marketing, advertising, and promotional staff and activities.

APPENDIX C

Sample Cover Memo

(responding to posted job requisition)

Sandra Beck
123 Main Street
Phoenix AZ 85037

Ms. Hiring Manager
VP, Marketing
Smith Medical Supply Inc.
1000 Wilshire Blvd
Los Angeles, CA 90000

Dear Ms. Hiring Manager,

Subject: Marketing Manager—Job Requisition #98765

I have over seven years' experience in marketing and sales of medical equipment and supplies. In pursuing my passion for marketing products that will help others, I recently completed my associate of arts degree in marketing. I also stay active in several marketing professional organizations. *(Include any contacts or referrals as appropriate.)*

I would bring to your company a broad range of skills, including:

- Developing and maintain marketing strategies
- Analytical competitive assessments
- Management experience
- Exhibit and trade show expertise and brand management

I would welcome the opportunity to further discuss this position with you. Smith Medical Supply has an excellent product line with great potential for expansion into new market areas. I will follow up with a phone call next week. You can also reach me directly at (408) 555-7777 or by e-mail: Sandra.Beck@yahoo.com.

I have enclosed my resume for your review, and I look forward to speaking with you soon.

Thank you for your consideration.

Sincerely,

Sandra Beck
Sandra Beck

Enclosure

APPENDIX D

Resume Format Samples

Chronological Resume

Functional Resume

Hybrid Resume

MAKE YOUR WAY

Sandra Beck *(Chronological Format)*   Sandra.Beck@yahoo.com
123 Main Street   (408) 555-7777 Mobile
Phoenix AZ 85037   www.linkedin.com/in/SandraBeck

Marketing and Sales Manager

Experience Summary:

Over seven years' experience developing and maintaining marketing strategies to meet the objectives of the medical product and services unit. Evaluated market conditions and competitor data, and implemented marketing plans as required. Oversaw all marketing and advertising activities for a medical products division.

2010–Present, Seaside Realty, Manager Wells Fargo Account

- Successfully closed escrow on 75% of properties prior to foreclosure auction, reducing losses to client by over $3,000,000
- Established a program to fast tract VA and FHA qualification, resulting in eight homeowners qualifying without having a down payment

2006–2010, Johnson's Medical, Inc., Manager Trade Show

- Oversaw the development of marketing media for use on ultra-definition video wall display technology that eliminated the need for expensive product mock-ups, resulting in an annual savings of $74,000
- Effectively managed a department of twelve customer representatives responsible for increasing annual follow-on sales from 75% to 93% over a three-year period
- Initiated medical equipment market research, which led to implementing new pricing options for a more competitive approach in a changing market
- Established marketing policy that leveraged quantity buys of corporate and division exhibit materials, reducing annual expenditures by 22%
- Managed multiple advertising agencies' contracts within budget and on schedule, while ensuring a consistent corporate brand across all product lines

2002–2006, Johnson Medical, Inc., Customer Service Representative

- Received the 2007 Outstanding Customer Service Representative of the Year award from among 165 nominees nationwide
- Established an intra-company tracking tool to leverage exhibit contact information between divisions, resulting in over $2.4M additional cross-division sales for 2006
- Developed online customer feedback survey, which resulted in seven product improvements
- Effectively researched growth areas and developed a marketing plan, leading to successful exhibits at three new trade shows reaching hundreds of new customers
- Established trusted relationships within industry; elected to serve on the Board of Directors for the local chapter of the National Marketing Representative (NMR)

Resume Format Samples

Sandra Beck *(Chronological Format)*   (408) 555-7777 **Mobile**

2000–2002, Johnson Medical, Inc., Administrative Assistant to VP Marketing
- Developed and maintained a calendar of industry marketing and business development events to effectively plan activities and eliminate redundant expenses
- Designed three invoicing training classes presented to over fifty students annually, significantly reducing the "unbillable" expenditures.
- Prepared agenda and coordinated executive-level meetings between company vice presidents and civic leaders, facilitating better coordination and processes
- Effectively maintained marketing expenses summaries for presentation at corporate a budget reviews, ensuring the efficient use of funds

1997–2000, Johnson Medical, Inc., Receptionist
- Developed an electronic spreadsheet that organizes customer product preferences, producing customized address lists for future mailings
- Earned exemplary ratings for three of the last four company procedure compliance audits
- Effectively planned and coordinated a successful company off-site strategy session at nearby facility for over seventy-five attendees
- Received outstanding annual performance ratings for initiating corrective actions and ability to handle customer complaints

1996-1997 Advantage Temps, On-Call Receptionist
- Effectively implemented standard operating procedure changes, leading to the reinstatement of a satisfactory audit rating after having had two major findings the previous year

Education:

Associate of Arts in Marketing, Strayer University
Marketing Certification, Redlands University
Advanced Course in Strategic Marketing, American Marketing Association
Measuring and Maximizing Marketing ROE, American Marketing Association seminar

Professional Organizations:

Secretary, National Marketing Representatives, Los Angeles Chapter
VP Membership, Marketing and Sales Research Association Southern California Chapter

Sandra Beck *(Functional Format)*
123 Main Street
Phoenix AZ 85037

Sandra.Beck@yahoo.com
(408) 555-7777 Mobile
www.linkedin.com/in/SandraBeck

Marketing and Sales Manager

Experience Summary:

Over seven years' experience developing and maintaining marketing strategies to meet the objectives of the medical product and services unit. Evaluated market conditions and competitor data, and implemented marketing plans as required. Oversaw all marketing and advertising activities for a medical products division.

Marketing Management

- Effectively managed a department of twelve customer representatives responsible for increasing annual follow-on sales from 75% to 93% over a three-year period
- Managed multiple advertising agencies' contracts within budget and on schedule, while ensuring a consistent corporate brand across all product lines
- Established an intra-company tracking tool to leverage exhibit contact information between divisions, resulting in over $2.4M additional cross-division sales for 2010
- Initiated and maintained a tracking system, which prioritized all staff meeting action items and highlighted resultant progress
- Effectively maintained marketing expenses summaries for presentation at corporate budget reviews, ensuring the efficient use of funds

Marketing Medical Products

- Oversaw the development of marketing media for use on ultra-definition video wall display technology that eliminated the need for expensive product mock-ups, resulting in an annual savings of $74,000
- Initiated medical equipment market research, which led to implementing new pricing options for a more competitive approach in a changing market
- Established marketing policy that leveraged quantity buys of corporate and division exhibit materials, reducing annual expenditures by 22%
- Effectively researched unknown growth areas and developed a marketing plan, leading to successful exhibits at three new trade shows reaching hundreds of new customers
- Received the 2007 Outstanding Customer Service Representative of the Year award from among 165 nominees nationwide

Communications

- Developed online customer feedback survey, which resulted in seven product improvements
- Established trusted relationships within industry; elected to serve on the board of directors for the local chapter of the National Marketing Representative (NMR)

Sandra Beck *(Functional Format)*   **(408) 555-7777 Mobile**

Communications (Continued)

- Developed and maintained a calendar of industry marketing and business development events to effectively plan activities and eliminate redundant expenses
- Hand-selected to mentor new administrative assistants, resulting in a 25% reduction in first-year turn over
- Designed three invoicing training classes presented to over fifty students annually, significantly reducing "unbillable" expenditures.

Work History:

2010–Present	Seaside Realty
1997–2010	Johnson's Medical, Inc.
1996–1997	Advantage Temps

Education:

Associate of Arts in Marketing, Strayer University
Marketing Certification, Redlands University
Advanced Course in Strategic Marketing, American Marketing Association
Measuring and Maximizing Marketing ROE, American Marketing Association seminar

Professional Organizations:

Secretary, National Marketing Representatives, Los Angeles Chapter
VP Membership, Marketing and Sales Research Association Southern California Chapter

MAKE YOUR WAY

Sandra Beck *(Hybrid Format)*   Sandra.Beck@yahoo.com
123 Main Street   (408) 555-7777 Mobile
Phoenix AZ 85037   www.linkedin.com/in/SandraBeck

Marketing and Sales Manager

Experience Summary:

Over seven years' experience developing and maintaining marketing strategies to meet the objectives of the medical product and services unit. Evaluated market conditions and competitor data and implemented marketing plans as required. Oversaw all marketing and advertising activities for a medical products division.

Marketing Management

- Effectively developed annual marketing plans and managed the detail sales activities to achieve an increase in annual follow-on sales from 75% to 93% over a three-year period
- Oversaw the development of marketing media for use on ultra-definition video wall display technology that eliminated the need for expensive product mock-ups, resulting in an annual savings of $74,000
- Managed multiple advertising agencies' contracts within budget and on schedule, while ensuring a consistent corporate brand across all product lines
- Effectively researched unknown growth areas and developed a marketing plan, leading to successful exhibits at three new trade shows reaching hundreds of new customers
- Established an intra-company tracking tool to leverage exhibit contact information between divisions, resulting in over $2.4M additional cross-division sales for 2006
- Established trusted relationships within the industry; was elected to serve on the board of directors for the local chapter of the National Marketing Representative (NMR)
- Developed online customer feedback survey, which resulted in seven product improvements
- Initiated medical equipment market research, which led to implementing new pricing options for a more competitive approach in a changing market
- Established marketing policy that leveraged quantity buys of corporate and division exhibit materials, reducing annual expenditures by 22%
- Effectively maintained marketing expenses summaries for presentation at corporate budget reviews, ensuring the efficient use of funds
- Designed three invoicing training classes presented to over fifty students annually, significantly reducing the "unbillable" expenditures.
- Received the 2007 Outstanding Customer Service Representative of the Year award from among 165 nominees nationwide

Sandra Beck *(Hybrid Format)*   **(408) 555-7777 Mobile**

Work History:

2010–Present	Seaside Realty
1997–2010	Johnson's Medical, Inc.
1996–1997	Advantage Temps

Education:

Associate of Arts in Marketing, Strayer University
Marketing Certification, Redlands University
Advanced Course in Strategic Marketing, American Marketing Association
Measuring and Maximizing Marketing ROE, American Marketing Association seminar

Professional Organizations:

Secretary, National Marketing Representatives, Los Angeles Chapter
VP Membership, Marketing and Sales Research Association Southern California Chapter

Works Cited

Unless otherwise noted all Scripture was taken from the NEW AMERICAN STANDARD BIBLE®, Copyright © 1960, 1962, 1963, 1968, 1971, 1972, 1973, 1975, 1977, 1995 by The Lockman Foundation. Used by permission.

Angus-reid.com. www.angus-reid.com/polls/view/35900/americans praise flight attendants for their courtesy and respect/. Retrieved 2010-08-25

Alba, Jason. 2007. *I'm on LinkedIn—Now what???*. Cupertino, CA: Happy About. www.imonlinkedinnowwhat.com

Alba, Jason, quoting from www.JibberJobber.com.

Bolles, Richard Nelson. 2010. *What Color is Your Parachute?* Berkeley, CA: Ten Speed Press.

Buckhout, Robert, Figueroa, Daryl, Hoff, Ethan. *Effects of suggestion and bias in identification from photographs.* Bulleting of the Psychonomic Society, Vol 6(1), Jul 1975, 71-74

Bureau of Labor Statistics. www.bls.gov, www.bls.gov/nls/nlsfaqs.htm

Business Networking International, http://www.bni.com/

Catelinet, Phil is quoted in the account published by the New York Daily News (3 Sep 2010) as stating, "I wish we could all quit our jobs like that."

Corcodilos, Nick. author and host of *Ask the Headhunter®*. www.corcodilos.com/blog/

DeCarlo, Laura and Guarneri, Susan. 2008. *Job Search Bloopers*. Pompton Plains, NJ: Career Press.

Goleman, Daniel. 2006. *Social Intelligence*. New York: Bantam Dell.

Gilbert, Daniel. 2006. *Stumbling on Happiness*. New York: Knopf, page 60

Federal Aviation Administration (FSAT) 95-13, *Autopilot Disconnect Differences*. www.faa.gov/other_visit/aviation_industry/airline_operators/airline_safety/info/all_infos/media/2008/FSAT9513.pdf

Fellowship of Companies for Christ International (FCCI), www.fcci-online.org

Ferrazzi, Keith. www.ferrazzigreenlight.com/Keith

Ferrazzi, Keith with Raz Tahl. 2005. *Never Eat Alone*. New York: Doubleday.

JibberJobber. www.jibberjobber.com

Job Hunt. www.Job-hunt.org

Job Hunter's Bible. www.jobhuntersbible.com

Kahler, Taibi, Ph.D. Process Communication Model www.youruniquedesign.com/about/history.htm

Lally, Philippa and colleagues from University College London. 2009. *European Journal of Social Psychology.* Volume 40, Issue 6, pages 998–1009, October 2010. (Article first published online: 16 July 2009.)

Lewis, Robert. 2005. *The Quest for Authentic Manhood.* Nashville, TN: LifeWay

Lowndes, Leil. 2003. *How to Talk to Anyone: 92 Tricks for Big Success in Relationships.* New York: McGraw-Hill.

Make Your Way Design Profile is a special application developed by Dr. Robert Maris and Dr. Jerry C. Richardson for *Make Your Way Resource* of the original Process Communication Model© developed by Dr. Taibi Kahler, along with additional materials. www.ServantsByDesign.com (login required).

Man in the Mirror, www.maninthemirror.org

Michaels, Jillian. 2009. *Master Your Metabolism.* New York: Crown Publishers.

Michaelsen, Johanna. 1982. *The Beautiful Side of Evil.* Eugene, OR: Harvest House Publishers.

Misner, PhD, co-founder of Business Networking International (BNI). 2008. *Masters of Networking.* TX: Bard Press

Nightingale, Earl. Author. *Brainy Quote.* www.brainyquote.com/quotes/quotes/e/earlnighti159037

Okun, Morris Professor, Arizona State University (Science Daily Nov 3, 2010)

Online Etymology Dictionary. www.etymonline.com/index.php?term=happy

Quintessential Careers. www.quintcareers.com/cover_letter_samples

Oxford English Dictionary Online. www.oed.com

Riley Guide. www.rileyguide.com

Sales Careers Online. www.salescareersonline.com

Servants By Design™ *Inventory.* www.YourUniqueDesign.com

South Bay Professional Association, http://www.torrance.com/sbpa/

U. S. Department of Labor. www.dol.gov

Warmcaller. www.warmcallcenter.com

About the Authors

Mr. Spencer Bauer and Dr. Jeanie Nishime attend church at The Bridge in El Segundo, California, where they were married in 2007. Spence has served as an elder since 2004 and led a weekly career development group. Their connections within industry and education organizations provide them with unique insights into how biblical principles can effectively be applied to meet today's employer needs.

Mr. Spencer Bauer has held senior management positions in the aerospace industry, responsible for profit and loss (P&L) of organizations while working directly with Human Resources departments for staffing needs. Currently he has his own consulting business. He has previously been a senior director, strategic and business development manager, program manager, and principal investigator for engineering projects. Spencer is a retired Air Force Reserve pilot, commanding numerous missions supporting Desert Storm and Iraqi Freedom. He also has two master of science degrees, is president of the Los Angeles Chapter of the Armed Forces Communications and Electronics Association and served as the president of the Greater Los Angeles Chapter of the National Defense Industrial Association.

Dr. Jeanie Nishime has over twenty years of experience as a community college counselor and dean of counseling. She is currently the vice president for student and community advancement at El Camino College. She also serves on the board of education for the El Segundo Unified School District. Jeanie has a masters in counseling, a career guidance certificate, and a doctorate in institutional management. She has been extensively involved in various professional organizations within the California community colleges and currently serves on the board of directors for the Association of California Community College Administrators (ACCCA). In 2009, she received the ACCCA Volunteer of the Year award.

Make Your Way—Resources

Make Your Way—myPlanner

We have developed another *Make Your Way* resource to help you bring all your career information into an organized working area appropriately called *myPlanner*. This online planner provides you your personal working environment for career planning complete with book summaries and step-by-step instructions for developing, assessing, editing, and storing your: design strengths and passions; career milestones and plans; PAR statements; interview responses; network contacts; and much, much more. It also includes up-to-date recommendations and direct links to our latest resources and tools to help you with your career planning and goal achievement.

The *Make Your Way—myPlanner* is the perfect complement to *Make Your Way—the Book*. Visit www.MakeYourWayResources.com for a free trial membership.

Make Your Way—in Person

Make Your Way speaking engagements, seminars, and workshops are available to address the specific needs of your group. Please contact us for upcoming presentations in your area.

Make Your Way—the Book

Additional copies of the book can be ordered from our website and sent directly to your friends, colleagues, and relatives. Group purchase discounts are also available.

To learn more visit: www.MakeYourWayResources.com or call (310) 607-9449

www.ingramcontent.com/pod-product-compliance
Lightning Source LLC
Chambersburg PA
CBHW070916180426
43192CB00037B/1254